HORACE

Satires

HORACE

Satires

Translated by
John Svarlien

Introduction and Notes by
David Mankin

Hackett Publishing Company, Inc.
Indianapolis/Cambridge

I dedicate this translation to Diane.

Copyright © 2012 by Hackett Publishing Company, Inc.

16 15 14 13 12   1 2 3 4 5 6 7

For further information, please address
    Hackett Publishing Company, Inc.
    P.O. Box 44937
    Indianapolis, Indiana 46244-0937

    www.hackettpublishing.com

Cover design by Brian Rak
Interior design and composition by Mary Vasquez
Printed at Data Reproductions Corporation

Library of Congress Cataloging-in-Publication Data

Horace.
    [Satirae. English]
    Satires / Horace ; translated by John Svarlien ; introduction and notes by
David Mankin.
        pages. cm.
    Includes bibliographical references.
    ISBN 978-1-60384-844-2 (pbk.)—ISBN 978-1-60384-845-9 (cloth)
    I. Svarlien, John. II. Mankin, David. III. Title.
    PA6396.S3S89 2012
    871'.01—dc23
                                            2012014016

CONTENTS

ABBREVIATIONS

A.P. = *Anthologia Palatina*
App. *B.C.* = Appian, *The Civil Wars*
Apul. *Met.* = Apuleius, *Metamorphoses*
BCE = Before the Common (Christian) Era
Bell. Afr. = anonymous, *The Civil War in Africa*
Bell. Hisp. = anonymous, *The Civil War in Spain*
C. = the first name Gaius
Call. = Callimachus
    Aet. = *Aetia LCL*
    epigr. = epigrams *LCL*
    fr., frr. = fragment(s) *LCL*
    H. = hymns *LCL*
Catul. = Catullus, *poems*
CE = The Common (Christian) Era
Cels. = Celsus, *On Medicine*
Cic. = Marcus Cicero
    Ac. = *On Academic Philosophy*
    Amic. = *On Friendship (De Amicitia)*
    Arch. = oration for Archias
    Att. = letters to Atticus
    Brut. = *Brutus*
    Cael. = oration for Caelius
    Catil. = orations against Catiline
    Clu. = oration for Cluentius
    De Or. = *On the Orator*
    Div. = *On Divination*
    Dom. = oration concerning his home
    Fam. = letters to his friends
    Fat. = *On Fate*
    Fin. = *On Ends*
    Flac. = oration for Flaccus
    Inv. = *On Invention*
    Leg. = *On Laws*

Man. = oration for the Manilian law
Mur. = oration for Murena
N.D. = *On the Nature of the Gods*
Off. = *On Duties*
Parad. = *Stoic Paradoxes*
Part. = *Elements of Oratory*
Phil. = *Philippic Orations*
Pis. = oration against Piso
Q. Fr. = letters to his brother Quintus
Quinct. = oration for Publius Quinctius
Rab. Post. = oration for Rabirius Posthumus
Red. Sen. = oration to the Senate on his return
Rep. = *On the Republic*
Sen. = *On Old Age*
Sest. = oration for Sestius
Sul. = oration for Sulla
Top. = *The Topics*
Tusc. = *Tusculan Disputations*
Verr. = orations against Verres
[Cic.] *Sal.* = oration against Sallust (false attribution)
CIL = *Corpus Inscriptionum Latinarum*
Cn. = the first name Gnaeus
Col. = Columella, *On Agriculture*
com. = fragments of Latin comedy
Dig. = *Digest of Roman Law*
Dio = Dio Cassius, *Roman History*
Diog. Laert. = Diogenes Laertius, *Lives of the Greek Philosophers*
Enn. = Ennius
    Ann. = *Annales*, in Skutsch, O., ed. *The Annales of Quintus Ennius.* Oxford: Clarendon Press, 1985.
    sc. = dramatic fragments, in *ROL* I
fl. = *floruit*, "was active"
FLP = Courtney, E., ed. *The Fragmentary Latin Poets.* Oxford: Clarendon Press, 1993.
fr., frr. = fragment(s)
Gel. = Aulus Gellius, *Attic Nights*
H. = Horace
    Ars = *Ars Poetica*
    Ep. = *Epistles*
    Epd. = *Epodes*
    Odes = *Odes*

Saec. = *Carmen Saeculare*
Sat. = *Satires*
Hom. = Homer
    Il. = *Iliad*
    Od. = *Odyssey*
HP = Long, A., and Sedley, D., eds. *The Hellenistic Philosophers.*
    Cambridge: Cambridge University Press, 1987.
HS = sesterces (Roman money)
ILS = *Inscriptiones Latinae Selectae*
Intro. = Introduction to this book
Juv. = Juvenal, *Satires*
km = kilometers
L. = the first name Lucius
LCL = Loeb Classical Library
Lex XII = The Twelve Tables in *ROL* III
Licin. = C. Licinius Calvus, fragments in *FLP*
Liv. = Livy, *History of Rome*
Liv. *Per.* = Livy, *Periochae* (abridgments of lost books)
Lucil. = Lucilius, fragments in *ROL* III
Lucr. = Lucretius, *On the Nature of Things*
M. = the first name Marcus
Macr. *Sat.* = Macrobius, *Saturnalia*
Mart. = Martial, *Epigrams*
MSS = medieval manuscripts
Ov. = Ovid
    Am. = *Love Elegies*
    Ars = *Art of Love*
    F. = *Calendar Poem*
    Met. = *Metamorphoses*
    Rem. = *Cure for Love*
    Tr. = *Sorrows*
Pers. = Persius, *Satires*
Petr. = Petronius, *Satyricon*
PGM = Betz, H., ed. *The Greek Magical Papyri in Translation*, vol. I.
    Chicago: University of Chicago Press, 1996.
Phaedr. = Phaedrus, *Aesopic Fables*
Pl. = Plautus
Plin. *Nat.* = Pliny the elder, *Natural History*
Plut. = Plutarch
Priap. = *Priapic Poems*
Prop. = Propertius, *Elegies*
Porph. = Porphyrio, *Commentary on Horace*

Pseudacro = notes in Horace MSS attributed to Acro
Publ. Syr. = Publilius Syrus, fragments of comic poetry and proverbs
Q. = the first name Quintus
Q. Cic. Pet. = Quintus Cicero, *Advice on Seeking Office*
Quint. = Quintilian, *The Education of the Orator*
Rhet. Her. = anonymous, *Rhetoric Instruction for Herennius*
ROL = Warmington, J., ed., trans. *Remains of Old Latin*, vols. I–IV.
    Cambridge, MA: Harvard University Press, 1967.
Sal. = Sallust
    Cat. = *The Conspiracy of Catiline*
    Jug. = *The War against Jugurtha*
Sen. = Seneca the younger
    Ep. = *Epistles to Lucilius*
Ser. = the first name Servius
Sex. = the first name Sextus
Sp. = the first name Spurius
Suet. = Suetonius
    Aug. = *Life of Augustus*
    Gramm. = *Lives of Grammarians and Rhetoricians*
    Jul. = *Life of Julius Caesar*
    Vita = *Life of Horace*
Tac. = Tacitus
    Ann. = *Annals of Imperial Rome*
    Dial. = *Dialogue about Orators*
    Hist. = *Histories*
Ter. = Terence
Tib. = Tibullus, *Elegies*
[Tib.] = works wrongly attributed to Tibullus
TRF = Ribbeck, O., ed. *Tragicorum Romanorum Fragmenta*. Leipzig:
    Teubner, 1897.
Val. Max. = Valerius Maximus, *Famous Deeds and Sayings*
Var. = Varro
    L.L. = *On the Latin Language*
    Men. Astbury = fragments of Menippean satire in Astbury, R.,
    ed. *M. Terentius Varro Saturarum Menippearum Fragmenta*. Leipzig:
    Teubner, 1985.
    R. = *Res Rusticae*
Virg. = Virgil
    A. = *Aeneid*
    Ecl. = *Eclogues*
    G. = *Georgics*

INTRODUCTION

Horace's Rome: From Republic to Principate

Quintus Horatius Flaccus (Horace)[1] lived and wrote, as the saying goes, "in interesting times." He was a witness to and played a part, if a small one, in an event of world historical significance: the ghastly death throes of an old order, the free Roman Republic, and frightening birth of a new one, the Principate or Empire. The Republic, which had survived external and internal threats for close to 400 years, at last "collapsed from its own might" (*Epd.* 16.2). Attempts at social reform led to mob violence in the city (133, 121, 120, and 100 BCE); the Italian allies, in what proved to be a kind of rehearsal for Roman armies fighting each other, revolted against Rome (91–88 BCE); following this, the ambitions of eminent generals and politicians culminated in a murderous, full-scale civil war, the first in Rome's long history (88–81 BCE; see 1.2.82n.). With the victory of L. Cornelius Sulla (*Sat.* 1.2.82n.), the Republic was to a certain extent restored, with free and meaningful elections and the rule of law, but its remaining days were disturbed by threats to the empire, slave revolts, mutinies, plots against the senate, power struggles between opposing factions, and, increasingly, civil disorder (58–52 BCE). All of this led to another round of civil war pitting Julius Caesar against a group led by Cn. Pompeius Magnus (Pompey) that claimed to be defending the traditional freedom

---

1. A Roman citizen would have at least two, but often three or even more names. The first name (*praenomen*), usually abbreviated, distinguished him from his brothers; the "gentile" name (*nomen*), usually a form ending in *–ius*, indicated the clan (*gens*) to which his ancestors, natural or acquired, belonged; the surname (*cognomen*) and any other added names (*adnomen*) were often originally nicknames that were passed on and came to designate a specific family within the clan. Horace gives the elements of his name in various works, but it is also attested in full on a famous inscription (*ILS* 5050) recording his writing of the *Carmen Saeculare* in 16 BCE (below).

(*libertas*; see *Sat.* 1.3.75n.) of the senate and Roman people. Caesar's victory (46 BCE) was followed by his assassination (March 15, 44 BCE) at the hands of former enemies, led by M. Junius Brutus and C. Cassius, whose lives he had spared but who were convinced he was aiming at the absolute power of a king (see *Sat.* 1.7.44n.).

The success of the liberators, as they called themselves, inspired many Romans, including the young Horace, with the hope that the Republic might yet survive. But it was not long before new factions arose to challenge the liberators, one led by M. Antonius (Mark Antony) and another by Julius Caesar's great nephew and heir, C. Octavius, now named C. Julius Caesar Octavianus. This new Caesar, as the Romans called him, or Octavian, as he is usually called in modern accounts, at first took the side of the senate against Antony, but then made common cause with him and with another powerful Roman, M. Aemilius Lepidus, to form (against law and custom) a triumvirate (three-man junta) whose ostensible purpose was to restore public order. With Julius Caesar's armies as their instruments, they turned on their enemies, proscribing (*Sat.* 1.7.2n.) and murdering hundreds, and defeating the armies of the liberators once and for all, at the battle of Philippi.

After Philippi, Octavian and Antony (Lepidus proved largely irrelevant) essentially ruled Rome and its empire, opposed only by some die-hard senators and Sextus Pompeius, the son of Pompey, whose fleet of Romans, pirates, and ex-slaves threatened the food supply of Italy. Octavian first fell out with Antony's brother L. Antonius, who holed up in Perusia and only surrendered after a brutal siege (41–40 BCE) that nearly erupted in another full-scale civil war (*Sat.* 1.3.147, 1.10.117nn.). This was avoided when the triumvirs renewed their coalition by the treaty of Brundisium (40 BCE) and also made temporary peace with Sextus Pompeius at Misenum (39 BCE). These agreements left Octavian in charge of the western empire and Antony in charge of the east, and were cemented by Antony's marriage to Octavian's sister Octavia. Antony went east to prepare for war against Parthia and ended up falling into an "entangling alliance" with Cleopatra, the ruler of Egypt, the last independent kingdom in the Mediterranean. In the west, Octavian, despite the agreement, turned against Sextus Pompeius (38 BCE) but suffered several reverses. In the meantime, there was renewed tension with Antony, temporarily resolved with another treaty struck at Tarentum (spring of 37 BCE; see *Sat.* 1.5). In the following year, largely through the strategy of his other principal advisor, M. Vipsanius Agrippa (*Sat.* 2.3.285n.),

Octavian was able to win decisive victories over Pompeius, the last at Nauplius (November of 36 BCE).

Even with a world to divide between them, Octavian and Antony were soon at odds again. After his return from Tarentum, Antony began living openly with Cleopatra, as if preferring her and their children to his Roman wife and offspring. It is not clear whether he meant to become some sort of Eastern king (see above) or whether Octavian, wishing to rule alone, convinced the Roman senate and people that this was Antony's plan. Relations deteriorated until 32 BCE (the likely date for Horace's completion of Book 1), when Antony divorced Octavia and Octavian declared war on Cleopatra, as if the coming struggle were to be a foreign, not a civil, war. But at Actium (September of 31 BCE), Romans once again fought Romans in a sea battle—at which Horace was probably present (*Epd.* 9)—that ended in a rout of Antony and Cleopatra. They fled back to Egypt, but Octavian, after taking care of various matters in the east, followed, finally defeating them at the battle of Alexandria (August of 30 BCE), after which both committed suicide.

The civil war between Octavian and Antony would be the last civil war among the Romans for nearly a century. Octavian, once he forced on the senate and people a settlement that made him, in essence, the sole ruler at Rome, would bring a fair measure of peace, security, and prosperity back to Italy and much of the empire. But for readers of these works, including Book 2, it is important to remember that nobody in the 30s and 20s BCE could have predicted the new era of peace and security with certainty. Indeed, if the works of Horace, Virgil, and their younger contemporaries are any indication, the generation that had lived through the fall of the Roman Republic found it difficult to shake the sense both of how fragile even mighty Rome had proven to be, and of how great a price Rome had paid in lost lives, in ravaged and confiscated property, in the shattering of traditional social mores, and above all in the loss of the freedom that had for centuries been the hallmark of the Republic.

The Life of Horace: From Conquered Republican to Principate Poet

The extant ancient sources for information on the life of Horace consist of his own works; a short biography transmitted with his text that was probably written by the famous biographer Suetonius in the early second century CE; and remarks in certain scholia—all commentaries on his poems—cited as the work of Porphyrio (third or fourth century CE) and Pseudacro (compiled in the fifth century CE). All of these sources have to be used with caution. Although Suetonius and the scholiasts probably had access to nonextant sources closer to Horace's own time, they write as citizens of the Roman Empire (Principate), at times unaware of how different things were in the Republic that preceded it. As for Horace's own works, the Horace we meet in them is, as John Svarlien reminds us in his Translator's Preface, a poetic persona subject to change—not only from work to work (e.g., the *Epodes* as opposed to the *Satires*), but also within a single genre (compare Horace's self-presentation as a satirist in *Sat.* 1.4 with that in *Sat.* 2.1) and even a single book (*Sat.* 2.6 versus *Sat.* 2.7).

But there are some facts, and these help situate Horace's works in their place(s) and times with greater certainty. Horace was born on December 8, 65 BCE (Julian calendar), the son of an ex-slave who had become an auction agent (*Sat.* 1.6) and who was wealthy enough to have Horace educated in Rome and then Athens in a manner fitting for an equestrian or even senator (*Sat.* 1.6, *Ep.* 2.1.69–71, *Ep.* 2.2.41–45). While in Athens, Horace joined the army of M. Junius Brutus—who, as we saw, had been a leading conspirator in the assassination of Julius Caesar—and rose to the high rank of tribune of the soldiers (*Sat.* 1.6.62n.). He fought in the battle of Philippi (October of 42 BCE), in which Brutus and his cause were crushed, and then returned to Italy, where he found that his father's estate had been confiscated. Later, he would claim that he was impoverished and took up writing to make a living (*Ep.* 2.2.51–54), but in fact he somehow obtained a lucrative and prestigious position as a government clerk (*scriba quaetorius*; see *Sat.* 2.6.47n.), and he remained an equestrian in rank,[2] technically the equal of many of the men with whom he would become associated.

---

2. By the mid-second century BCE, if not earlier, Roman citizens were thought of as divided into three classes (*ordines*). At the top was the senatorial, consisting of men, most of them with great wealth in landed property, who had been elected to one or more of the important magistracies (quaestor or tribune of the people, aedile, praetor, consul, and censor) and as members of the senate and continued their public service. Below that was the equestrian, originally associated with the Roman cavalry (*equites*), also wealthy, but more often involved in commercial activities such as trade and collection of taxes, and choosing to remain outside of formal public life. The lowest order, that of the people

These included the famous poet P. Vergilius Maro (Virgil), five years Horace's senior, who, along with another literary figure of the time, L. Varius Rufus, probably around June of 38 BCE, introduced him to Maecenas. A few months later, he became part of Maecenas' circle of friends (*Sat.* 1.6.73n.), and they remained close not only for the rest of their lives but also in death (1.8.11n.).

C. Maecenas was an equestrian originally from Etruria who was already one of Octavian's closest advisors at the time of the civil war that ended at Philippi and would continue in this capacity until the late 20s BCE. During the 30s BCE, when Octavian was absent from Rome for military campaigns, Maecenas would tend to Octavian's interests. And although Maecenas had a reputation for decadent living, he, like Horace, was present at Philippi, albeit on the opposing, victorious side. With Horace now in tow, he also participated in parts of the war against Sextus Pompeius, and at Actium. He was immensely wealthy, had pretensions as a literary figure, and was friendly with a number of the finest poets of his time. Beginning in the time of the Roman Empire, Maecenas has usually been seen as a formal "patron" of the writers, supporting them while they wrote but also encouraging if not ordering them to write material favorable to Octavian and the new order emerging at Rome. But there are problems with this picture, at least in regard to Horace, who probably did not need financial support (see *Sat.* 2.6.1–3n.) and who, perhaps disingenuously, emphasizes his independence in all his works and depicts Maecenas' friendship as based, above all, on mutual regard and genuine affection.

For the period of Horace's life after the beginning of Octavian's principate there is little external information. At some point Octavian, now the Emperor Augustus, asked him to become his secretary, but Horace politely refused, and this fits with the image he presents of himself in his later works as still concerned with politics and war but more deeply involved in the pleasures of friendship and philosophical contemplation, not to mention wine, women, and song. In 16 BCE, when Augustus decided to celebrate an important festival called the Secular Games (*Ludi Saeculares*), Horace was chosen to compose the song performed by a chorus of young girls and boys (*Carmen Saeculare*). He died, according to Suetonius, on November

---

(*populus*), was the most various, since it included everyone in the citizen body who was not a senator or an equestrian.

27, 8 BCE, shortly after Maecenas, something he had predicted (*Odes* 2.17.10–12).

As we have seen, Horace claims that he began writing after he lost his inheritance. It is not clear when he began to work on what would become the first book of *Satires*, but it must have been completed, if not published, by early 32 BCE (*Sat.* 1.10.117n.). His next work, the *Epodes*, or, as he called them, the *Iambi*, are set in and were probably published shortly after the period from the spring of 31 BCE to no later than midsummer of 30 BCE. It is possible that he was working on the second book of *Satires* at this time; there are indications that it was published in early 29 BCE (*Sat.* 2.1.14n.). His most famous works, the first three books of *Odes*, seem to have been published together in 23 BCE, but Book 1 may first have appeared separately in late 29 BCE and Book 2 in 25 BCE. The date of the *Ars Poetica*, also known as *Ep.* 2.3, is unknown, but it may be closer in time to the *Satires* than to *Ep.* 1 (20 or 19 BCE), *Ep.* 2.2 (late in 19 BCE), the *Carmen Saeculare* (16 BCE), the fourth book of *Odes* (15 or 14 BCE), and Horace's final extant poem, *Ep.* 2.1, the *Epistle to Augustus* (13 BCE?).[3]

Horatian Satire

Ancient students of satire connected the Latin word for the genre, *satira* (also spelled *satura*) with the adjective *satur* (meaning "full" or "filled-up") and traced its origins to three traditions from deep in the Roman and Latin past. The first was the *lanx satura*, a plate filled with a farrago of food offerings to the gods; the second the *lex satura*, a law covering a range of unrelated matters (omnibus bill); and the third a sort of preliterate, improvised dramatic performance known as *saturae*. The first two point to the importance of a variety of topics, the third to entertainment value. A non-Roman and non-Latin element is also mentioned: some connection with *satyrs*, minor Greek gods combining human and horse or goat features, who formed the choruses in a type of Greek drama called Satyr Plays (*Satyroi*; see *Ars* 220–50). Although this last is almost certainly based on a false etymology, it suggests that Romans, however much they would claim

---

3. Readers should be advised that the dates offered here are conjectural and that those for the *Epodes* and *Odes*, based on the author's own researches, are controversial.

satire as their own special genre (cf. Quint. 10.1.93, "Satire is entirely ours"), sensed that there was Greek influence from the beginning. The first literary satire was generally thought to be the work of Rome's first great poet, Q. Ennius (1.4.70, 1.10.90–91n.), who wrote either "satires" (*satirae*) or, more likely, a single work called *Satura*; either way, the surviving fragments (in *ROL* I and *FLP*) indicate a wide range of subject matter, including food, sex, humorous details of daily life in the city, ethical philosophy (possibly based on the prevalent doctrines of Ennius' time, Stoicism and Epicureanism), and a strong element of autobiography or at least self-presentation. It is possible that, in his choice of meters and his rambling approach, Ennius was influenced by a Greek poetry that was known as Menippean satire (the Greeks called it simply *Menippea; satira* is not a Greek word), which also included passages in prose. Closer to Horace's time, the great Roman scholar (and investigator of satire's origins) M. Terentius Varro (116–27 BCE) would write his own *Menippea*, and later the form would be taken up by Seneca, in his *Apocolocyntosis* and Petronius in his *Satyricon*.

But it was C. Lucilius (167?–102 BCE), a wealthy and eminent equestrian (*Sat.* 1.6.78n.) from the Latin town of Suessa Arunca, who added to the original farrago two additional ingredients that, as much as any, would define Roman verse satire as a genre for the rest of the ancient world and beyond. His *satirae* survive only in fragments (about 1280 lines), many lacking context; even when they are attributed to specific books, they are difficult to assign to individual poems. But these and many testimonies, including those in Horace's *Satires*, provide enough evidence for us to recognize his innovations. After writing his earliest pieces in Greek dramatic meters or in other Greek meters suited for short poems, he switched to the Greek dactylic hexameter, the measure of Homeric and Ennian epic; Hesiodic and, later, Latin didactic poetry; and Hellenistic pastoral, famously imitated by Virgil (*Eclogues*). This created a paradoxical but inescapable connection between the loftiest of ancient poetic genres and one that often dealt with low matters and even pretended not to be poetry at all (see *Sat.* 1.4.42–45). Even more significantly, he added a strong and at times seemingly partisan focus on the social and political scene of his time, and followed the earlier Greek comic poets (see *Sat.* 1.4) with scathing personal attacks on his contemporaries (see *Sat.* 1.6 and 2.1).

In both books of Horace's *Satires*, Lucilius is a frequent presence, even when not named, with Horace adapting some of his subject matter, echoing his verses, and mentioning characters that appeared in his satires. But in Book 1, Horace for the most part seeks to distance and differentiate himself and his brand of satire from that of his precursor. It is significant that, although he puns on it (*Sat.* 1.1.128 and possibly 1.6.80), he nowhere in the book uses the word *satira*, instead referring to his verse as *sermo*, "conversation," and the first three poems suit this term. They seem to show Horace as a yet not clearly identified figure, strolling about the city (the de rigueur setting of all Roman satire) in a leisurely way, discussing rather than attacking various faults of character and conduct. In the fourth poem, Horace begins to reveal more about himself, claiming that his departure from Lucilius, whom he criticizes not only for the content of his satires but also for their turgidity and lack of polish, is due to the influence of his father. The next three poems are in a sense less alien to Lucilius, as they involve the political sphere, but even here Horace distances himself, affecting disinterest in the serious implications of the journey that led to the Treaty of Tarentum (*Sat.* 1.5), insisting on his lack of ambition (*Sat.* 1.6), and depicting his one-time hero Brutus in a somewhat discreditable light (*Sat.* 1.7). The superiority of present to past and, by implication, new satire to old, is a theme in the ludicrous Priapus poem (*Sat.* 1.8), even if, in the next poem, Horace has to rely on divine intervention to escape from a boor suspiciously like a modern avatar of Lucilius (*Sat.* 1.9). Lucilius, as well as his present-day imitators and admirers, are mocked again in the final poem (*Sat.* 1.10), and, while Horace also finds room for praise of the inventor of the genre, the book ends with him situating himself among the most respected poets and critics of his own time.

Horace's attitude toward Lucilius in Book 1 is related to a number of other themes, and especially to a kind of cautious optimism that pervades much of it. If satire can now be tamed and polished, the same may be true of human faults and, even more importantly, the forces that had so far led Rome into three civil wars. There is no hint in the book that the Treaty of Tarentum failed, that another civil war ensued, or, on a symbolic level, that Canidia, the witch driven off by the scarecrow in *Sat.* 1.8, had not been exorcized from Rome once and for all. But in Book 2, things have changed. In the opening poem, it is clear that Octavian has won that fourth civil war (*Sat.* 2.1.14n.), that the bipartisan friendships of *Sat.* 1.5 and 1.10 are likely to be a thing of the past, and that, for the present if not the long term, one man would be the sole ruler of Rome. In these circumstances,

Lucilius seems to return with a vengeance, with Horace claiming, against everything he had said in Book 1, to be a poet very much like the "old man," especially if he is provoked; and in most of the other poems, Horace more or less disappears except as a listener to the rants of a series of figures who often resemble Lucilius rather than Horace in their mode of criticism, except that their main topics of discussion are rarely philosophical and never directly political. The main obsession of the book is with food, as if in a time of uncertainty about what and how to speak or write this was the only safe topic. In the second satire, the Epicurean philosophy of Ofellus seems to be approved by Horace, but his explanation of it is tied to eating rather than any serious moral issues. So, too, with Catius' pseudo-Platonism (*Sat.* 2.4), while the ridicule his guests direct at Nasidienus (*Sat.* 2.8) has to do with his ineptitude as a banquet host, not any moral failing. Even when philosophy is more at issue, the speakers are ignorant, small-minded, and bombastic (Damasippus in *Sat.* 2.3) or ludicrously materialistic (Tiresias in *Sat.* 2.5). Only in the sixth satire do we meet a Horace reminiscent of the one we got to know, or thought we got to know, in Book 1, yet here too there is a difference: he is no longer so independent, and he seems confused (this is the case also in *Sat.* 2.1 and 2.3) about the very nature of his satire—which now, tellingly, he calls by its proper name (2.6.22; cf. 2.1.1). Furthermore, the truth of what he says about himself in this poem is immediately called into question in the next (*Sat.* 2.7), where his slave Davus indulges in Saturnalian license to attack his master with as much gusto as Lucilius attacked any of his antagonists.

It is perhaps no surprise that Horace would not write satire again. His *Epistles* are not unrelated to satire, but their content is far less various. They focus more deeply on philosophical issues, and, except here and there, they lack both the cheerful fun of Book 1 and the antic sense of a world gone haywire of Book 2. But the Romans were not done with verse satire; Horace's satires became school texts, annotated by critics and teachers (now represented by the fourth- and fifth-century CE scholia of Porphyrio and Pseudacro); Persius and especially Juvenal put their own stamps on the genre; and it had a marked influence on works in other genres, such as Lucan's *Civil War*. Even with the fall of the ancient world, it continued to be read (there are hundreds of manuscripts of Horace and Juvenal), and since the Renaissance it has flourished in editions, imitations, and translations such as this.

NOTE ON THE NOTES

In the Notes following the text of the poems and in the Introduction, the individual satires are cited by book number, satire number, and line number (e.g., 2.5.5 = Book 2, satire 5, line 5). For Horace's works, *Sat.* = *Satires*, *Epd.* = *Epodes*, *Odes* = *Odes*, *Ep.* = *Epistles*, *Ars* = *Ars Poetica*, and *Saec.* = *Carmen Saeculare*, while for the scholia (ancient commentaries on Horace), Porph. = Porphyrio (third or fourth century CE) and Pseudacro = the miscellaneous material transmitted under the name of the third-century CE critic Acro. For a complete key to abbreviations, see Abbreviations.

Translations of almost all texts cited in the Notes can be found in the Loeb Classical Library (abbreviated in the notes as *LCL*), with the fragments of Lucilius and Republican dramatic poems collected in Warmington, J., ed. *Remains of Old Latin,* vols. I–IV. Cambridge MA: Harvard University Press, 1967 (herein *ROL*). Texts pertaining to Hellenistic philosophy (Epicureanism and Stoicism) are cited from Long, A., and Sedley, D., eds. *The Hellenistic Philosophers.* Cambridge: Cambridge University Press, 1987 (herein *HP*).

The Notes are meant to provide nonspecialist readers with information that might contribute to their understanding of the *Satires.* Much of this material has been collected in more scholarly commentaries and studies that, for reasons of space, it has not been possible to acknowledge properly, but they can be found among the Suggestions for Further Reading. So, too, with the interpretations offered in both the Notes and the Introduction; if any of these are the editor's own, he accepts full blame for them.

TRANSLATOR'S PREFACE

The brilliance of Horace's *Odes* has tended to eclipse his other work and, not surprisingly, there are far fewer translations of the *Satires*. Yet the *Satires*, published in one of the most uncertain and critical decades in Rome's long history, are remarkable poems. It was with this work that Horace made his name at Rome as a poet and created that thoroughly engaging literary phenomenon, the Horatian persona. And, with all due respect to his literary forebear Lucilius (whose verse survives only in fragments), Horace fashioned in these eighteen poems a new poetic genre.

No translation can fully recreate the particular verbal performance of the original literary work. In translating Horace's *Satires* my goal has been to render Horace's Latin as accurately as I can while, at the same time, producing a verse translation that conveys something of the original style and something of the manner of speaking of the various characters inhabiting the dramatic world of the *Satires*, including the idiosyncratic voice of the narrator whom Horace presents as himself. I have been particularly intent to bring across in my translation the pleasure and meaningfulness of Horatian humor. These poems with their comic situations, cast of wacky characters, jokes, puns, lampoons, and parodies, including a talking statue, a voluble penis, many references to Greek and Roman comedies, animal fables, vulgarity, hyperbole, bathos, irony, farce, caricatures, praise and put-downs, and, not least, self-mockery, are funny and fun to read. Yet "it isn't enough to make the audience / gape with laughter, however good the joke" (*Sat.* 1.10.10–11). There is indeed more to Horatian humor than a good joke. The *Satires* are perhaps the best (certainly the most nuanced) example we have from antiquity of what critics called *spoudogeloion*, a mixing up of the laughable and the serious.

Horatian humor is nicely illustrated in a passage that some critics take as a programmatic preamble to the first book of *Satires*:

What stops a laughing man from speaking straight?
A laugh might even help—like treats in school
That made us want to learn the alphabet.
But jokes aside, let's look at things that matter. (*Sat.* 1.1.26–29)

The Latin of the last line reads: *Sed tamen amoto quaeramus seria ludo*
(1.1.27).[1] The flexibility of Latin syntax permits meaning to be con-
veyed in a way that is not possible in English. The satirist claims that
it is time to stop joking and now to get serious about serious matters,
yet Horace by placing the words in a certain order tells his reader
something quite different. The *amoto . . . ludo* ("joking having been
put aside") typographically frames the *quaeramus seria* ("let's look at
things that matter"), while *ludo* ("joking") stands cheek by jowl with
seria ("serious stuff"). In this line, Horace humorously lets us in on
two vital points about these poems: the comic packages the serious in
the *Satires*, and Horace's own voice is marked by its playful irony. As
Reuben Brower neatly put it: "Horace can be convincingly serious
only when it is certain that no one will take him quite seriously."

An equally important quality of the *Satires* is their literary form.
There was a type of satirical writing, usually referred to as Menippean
satire after its originator Menippus of Gadara (third century BCE),
which was composed in a hybrid form mixing prose and verse. Varro,
Horace's older contemporary, wrote 150 books of Menippean satires,
of which roughly 600 fragments survive. Horace quite deliberately
chose to follow the Roman Lucilius (last half of the second century
BCE), who, after some metrical experimentation, wrote his *saturae*
in dactylic hexameter, a meter most closely associated in the Greco-
Roman world with epic (e.g., the *Iliad* and Virgil's *Aeneid*) and wis-
dom literature (e.g., Hesiod's *Works and Days* and Lucretius' *On the
Nature of Reality*). There's some humor intended in casting satire's
farrago of topics, most of them quite non-epic in nature, in such a

---

1. A variation of this idea is found at the beginning of Horace's first *Epistle*
(1.1.10–11)—"*Nunc itaque et versus et cetera ludicra pono;/quid verum atque decens curo
et rogo et omnis in hoc sum*"—"And so now I am putting aside poetry and other
amusements; what is right and true is the object of my attention and inquiry,
and am I totally absorbed in this." Both here and at *Satire* 1.1.27, the irony is
undisguised. Far from putting aside writing verse (*versus*), the poet continues
writing the *Epistles* in dactylic hexameters (the same meter as the *Satires*), and,
similarly, despite his claim at *Satire* 1.1.29 to put aside *ludus*, humor and Horatian
playfulness are everywhere in the *Satires*.

pedigreed meter. And there's some humor intended when the satirist claims he's willing to take his name from the ranks of poets in order to defend himself against the charges of his putative critics:

> I'm no poet. You'd say it's not enough
> To clap some words in meter. Anyone
> Like me, who writes like people talk, you'd not
> Consider worth the name of poet. (*Sat.* 1.4.42–45)

Some translators of the *Satires*, perhaps taking these lines too much at face value, have produced English versions that show very little, if any, metrical form; some even choose to translate the *Satires* into prose. The satirist is quite emphatic about the importance of writing well-crafted verse (*carmina . . . bona* at *Sat.* 2.1.82–83 and *Sat.* 1.4 and 1.10 *passim*) and if the satirist's word is not enough to establish this point, the *Satires* themselves are proof of Horace's skills as a poet. In appreciating the *Satires*, it is more important to register how something is said than simply what is said. In my view, translating Horace's *Satires* into English verse is a sine qua non for any translation of them into English. What the Romans could and did legitimately claim to have invented was *verse* satire.

But what kind of English verse? It's not impossible to write dactylic hexameters in English (e.g., Longfellow's *Evangeline* and Clough's *Amours de Voyage*). But a major consideration argues against trying to reproduce the rhythms of Horace's verse in an English translation. Dactylic hexameter was a meter very familiar to the Roman reader. He had literally had the rhythm beaten into him as a school boy by a cane-wielding schoolmaster teaching Ennius' *Annales*. Dactylic hexameter, however, is not a meter familiar to contemporary English-speaking readers; we have to make a concerted effort to hear and feel its rhythm. This, together with the length of the hexameter (up to seventeen syllables), inevitably encourages reading the lines as if they were, in effect, prose.

Another choice that some translators have made is to cast the *Satires* in heroic couplets (pairs of end-rhymed iambic pentameters).

> There are (I scarce can think it, but am told)
> There are to whom my Satire seems too bold,

So Alexander Pope, translating the opening lines of *Satire* 2.1, began his *Imitations of Horace* and set a model in the eighteenth century to be followed by several nineteenth-century translators, and, most recently, by A. M. Juster (2008). While recognizing the vagaries of taste, I think there are some objective reasons for treating the rhymed couplet as less than the ideal choice for a twenty-first-century translation of the *Satires*. The fact that Greek and Latin poetry did not have formal rhyme patterns is not a decisive point. What does matter is the sound, tone, and phrasing of the line and the ethos it projects. The heroic couplet seems most naturally suited to the parry and touché of wit. Clever, light, and skipping along, the end-rhyme adding to its neatness, the couplet is governed by an etiquette quite alien to Horace's *Satires*, or *sermones* ("conversations") as he called them. Nor can the couplet convey the range in Horace's special brand of humor, much less the temperament, the quirks, mannerisms, and moods, of the Horatian protagonist.[2] There certainly is cleverness in the *Satires*, but Horatian humor, as a rule, is not so explicitly witty as to call attention to itself and demand applause (cf. the criticism of the *scurra*, or wit, at *Sat.* 1.4.103–4, "who craves / loud laughter's roar, the wit's celebrity"). Finally, the heroic couplet wears its poetic credentials on its sleeve; it cannot, even if it tries, approximate the color of conversational language in the twenty-first century.

In my view, blank verse—unrhymed iambic pentameters—best serves Horace's *Satires*. This meter has the flexibility to accommodate both Milton's great epic *Paradise Lost* and the plain storytelling of Robert Frost. It nicely handles the range of styles in the *Satires*. That range is considerable (see *Sat.* 1.10.12–21): there are long, periodic sentences; poetic language; the quieter tones of reflection and prayer; the rare outburst of pique or frustration; and, on occasion, a mimicking of epic's grand sounds; but overall the style in these poems is informal, conversational, even rambling and discursive. This style goes a long way in bringing the protagonist to dramatic life.

2. The limitations of the heroic couplet in conveying such a range of tone is illustrated by Pope's *Essay on Man* (*Epistle* 4.377–82), where his verse, drawing its precepts from Horace's *Satire* 1.10, fails to convey convincingly the variation of mood and style it purports to illustrate:

Teach me, like thee, in various nature wise,
To fall with dignity, with temper rise,
Formed by thy converse happily to steer,
From grave to gay, from lively to severe;
Correct with spirit; eloquent with ease,
Intent to reason, or polite to please.

In these translations, I have tried to stay true to the *mediocritas* ("moderation," "the mean") that characterizes the Horatian satirist and his language. I have tried to maintain throughout a solid iambic rhythm while, at the same time, taking care to avoid monotonous predictability. It helps that in English the iamb is the basic rhythmic unit of speech. I have imitated Horace in giving freedom of movement to the caesurae (natural pauses) within lines and in the frequency of enjambment (one line running over into the next without pause). Like Horace, I sometimes begin a new sentence or clause in the last foot of a line. And with all this, I have tried to be true as possible to the economy of Horace's style.

Satire by its nature has a lively topical dimension and this, together with the ostensibly autobiographical slant Horace takes in these poems, provides readers of the *Satires* with a view of Roman life and manners during one of the most interesting periods of Roman history. It is a complex world and one needs an expert guide. David Mankin's introduction and detailed commentary provide just that. The reader can explore the commentary in as much depth as he or she chooses. Mankin's notes, with their wealth of information and insight, will answer readers' questions and suggest further lines of inquiry. Most exciting of all, his commentary opens doors to the "behind the scenes" world of these poems. In one sense, the *Satires* are a self-contained literary world—the poems exist in their own time and space. Here it is especially rewarding to follow Mankin's cross-referencing among the satires. Horace clearly intended his reader to pay attention to how he enhances dramatic effects and meaning through the repetition of key words and the arrangement of poems in relation to one another, both within each of the books and in the collection as a whole. At the same time, Horace's *Satires* take their place in the long Greco-Roman literary tradition and are an important bridge to the subsequent modern literary tradition of verse satire. By the time Horace wrote these poems, the Greco-Roman cultural and literary tradition was wonderfully rich and Horace knew that tradition backwards and forwards. Just as interestingly, the *Satires* reflect a particular time, indeed one of the most cliff-hanging periods in Roman history. In such times, matters of great moment shared the stage with the absurd. When Octavian, for example, returned as the victor from the battle of Actium, he was greeted in Brundisium by an enterprising man who had trained a magpie to croak "Hail, Caesar!" It was later revealed that the same man, anticipating all contingencies, had also trained another bird to croak "Hail, Antony!" Mankin's references to points of historical information and to the works of other Latin and Greek authors will make the reader's experience all the richer. This book is intended for several audiences. The college classroom is an excellent place to be introduced to Horace. The more one knows about Rome in the second half of the first century BCE, the more one gets out of reading Horace. We hope this book serves students of Latin and English literature both at the undergraduate and graduate levels, and especially those interested in satire. Students studying Latin in the *Oxford Latin Course* may find these translations of Horace's *Satires* an enjoyable path to getting to know Quintus Horatius Flaccus, the hero of that series. For centuries Horace has had devoted readers who discover in this Augustan poet an amicus. The poet Joseph Brodsky found himself writing a long letter to Horace late one night. Robert Pinsky in *An Explanation of America*, a poem addressed to his daughter, translates and incorporates one of Horace's *Epistles*. Horace's literary friends are legion. We hope a new verse translation and a detailed commentary will please a new generation of readers and writers. Horace is a writer worth getting to know.

For the most part, the manuscript tradition of the *Satires* presents relatively few textual problems. In this translation, I have followed Klingner's 1959 Teubner edition. I have benefited from the learning and insights in the commentaries by A. Palmer (1883), P. Lejay (1911), M. Brown (1995), F. Muecke (1997), and D. Mankin.

The first-century CE satirist Persius (*Pers.* 1.116) famously characterized Horace as *vafer* ("subtle," "crafty," "sly," "an artful dodger"). It is worth keeping Persius' characterization in mind when reading Horace's *Satires*. For all the fun and humor in these poems, the issue that the satirist keeps returning to is a serious one: how can a person live life well? We know from our own experience how easy it is for this sort of question to yield hackneyed and vapid pronouncements. Horace knew as well. He sends up practitioners of pop philosophy and self-help programs in more than one poem, and, with some self-mockery, he catches himself drifting in that direction at times. It is in the *Satires* that Horace developed a knack he would later employ in the *Odes* and *Epistles*, a knack for taking commonplace ideas and handling them in an unusual, sometimes quirky, and always interesting manner. Horace is not as simple and straightforward as he may sometimes appear. He is *vafer*. Mark Twain's tongue-in-cheek warning to the readers of *Huckleberry Finn* might also serve for Horace's

Satires: "Persons attempting to find a motive in this narrative will be prosecuted; persons attempting to find a moral in it will be banished; persons attempting to find a plot in it will be shot."

Acknowledgments

Earlier versions of *Satires* 1.1 and 1.4 were published in *Literary Imagination* and *Arion*, respectively. It is a pleasure to thank those who have made the completion of this project possible. Editor Brian Rak of Hackett Publishing Company has led this work to completion with his sound advice and remarkable patience. I am grateful to project editor Mary Vasquez for her editorial advice and the meticulous care she has given the manuscript. A sabbatical leave granted by Transylvania University helped to speed this project along. I could not ask for a better collaborator than David Mankin. My translations have benefited from his suggestions. In this work, as in everything else in my life, I owe a great deal to my wife, Diane Arnson Svarlien. Her fine ear and sharp critical eye have improved my efforts.

HORACE

Satires

BOOK 1

SATIRE 1.1

How come, Maecenas, folks get out of sorts
With life, dissatisfied with what they've planned
Or miserable at the way their luck turned out?
To hear them talk, everyone's blessed but them.
The veteran, feeling used by years and wrecked   5
By back-breaking toil, says, "Merchants are lucky."
"The soldier's better off," the merchant says,
When southern gales whip up and toss his ship.
"Just look. A battle happens fast. Within
An hour, you're dead or flush with victory."   10
The well-trained lawyer rhapsodizes on
The farmer's life (when clients knock at dawn).
The farmer's served a writ. He's dragged to Town.
No sooner there he snorts, "I've lived a pig's life!"
Et cetera. To run through even half   15
The catalog of discontented men
Would wear out Fabius the chatterbox.
I'm not about to waste your time. *In nuce,*
Imagine this: a god appears and says,
"I answer prayers. Fed up with army life?   20
Well, you're in retail. Lawyer, take this hoe.
Change costumes. Go. What's stopping you?" They won't.
Yet happiness was theirs. You can't blame Jove
If he's pissed off. Never again, he swears.
I know it's not a laughing matter, but   25
What stops a laughing man from speaking straight?
A laugh might even help—like treats in school
That made us want to learn the alphabet.
But jokes aside, let's look at things that matter.
The man pushing his plow in stony ground,   30
Dishonest tradesmen, soldiers, men at sea:
It's counting on retirement's golden years
That keeps these people working every day.
Like ants, they'll say. Those tiny dynamos

3

Don't recklessly ignore their future needs: 35
They stockpile food they've dragged by mouth indoors.
The new year enters dark Aquarius.
And ants? They've stores and wisely stay inside.
Not you. The torrid days of summer, ice
Or fire, the force of sea or arms can't stop   40
Your greediness while someone else has more.
What good is all that cash in heavy bags
You've buried underground? You're terrified
That if you spend one cent, you'll spend it all?
What's great about a treasure left untouched?   45
Your floors produce a hundred thousand bushels.
Your stomach can't hold *that* much more than mine.
Imagine you're the slave it falls upon
To lug the bread basket. Your fellow slaves
And you get equal shares, though you're the one   50
Who bore the heavy load. Or tell me what's
The difference, given nature's limits, plowing
A thousand rather than a hundred acres.
"I like," you say, "to take my bit from big reserves."
But if you grant to me an equal bit,   55
Why praise your granaries more than my cupboards?
You're thirsty. Here's a water jug and cup.
"No thanks, I'd rather dip my goblet in
A river, not some piddling spring." When folks
Enjoy excessiveness, the Aufidus   60
Sweeps them and riverbank into its flood.
The man who wants no more than need requires
Won't taste the river's mud or drown. A lot
Of people, tricked by sheer blind greed, believe
You'll never have enough; you're ranked, they say,   65
By what you have. How can you help such folks?
Prescribe anxiety: that's what they crave.
Some years ago a miser lived in Athens.
He didn't give a hoot what people said.
"The rabble heckles me. At home I clap   70
My hands in glee, just looking at my loot."
A river flees from thirsty Tantalus.
Now that's a funny myth, you smirk. Guess what:
You're Tantalus in all but name. You sleep

On piled up sacks of money, mouth agape.   75
Your rule: Don't touch, just look. It's like your coins
Were sacred things or priceless works of art.
You don't get it. I mean, what money's for.
It buys some bread, a dish of greens, and wine,
And things whose loss would make our nature ache.   80
Or do you like the terror robbing you
Of sleep, tormenting you all day and night,
That burglars, fire, and slaves will rip you off?
For me, I'd rather do without such *goods*!
What happens when a chill or accident   85
Keeps you in bed? Will someone sit up with you,
Count out your pills, or pay for specialists
In hopes you'll live? I wouldn't bank on it.
Your wife? She doesn't wish you well. Your son
Is less concerned. Acquaintances, your neighbors,   90
Their kids don't like you very much. Surprised?
But money's what you value most. Why should
They be concerned? You haven't earned their care.
Relations are a bonus nature gives.
Suppose you tried to cultivate those ties.   95
Would that investment prove as profitless
As teaching dressage to some ornery mule?
In short, it's time to bridle acquisitiveness.
Now that you're richer, fear the poorhouse less.
And once you have the things you craved so much,   100
Rein in yourself, slow down, relax. Or else
You run the risk of faring like Ummidius.
His story's short: so rich he had to weigh
His money. But his clothes! He looked a slave
And died in fear of dying poor. An ex-   105
Slave brave as Helen's twin axed him in half.
"What! You'd have me live the life of Riley?"
Hardly. You've got my verses butting heads
Like two halfbacks. I veto greed; I'm not
Commanding you to be a bum or playboy.   110
You'll find some middle ground between a eunuch
And Don Juan. Things are measured. Go beyond
Or fall short, you will fail to get it right.

I'm back to where I started: greed makes men
Dislike themselves and praise another's fortune.   115
They get depressed because a neighbor's goat
Has swollen udders. Never taking time
To think how others have it worse, they rush
To get ahead of one and then another.
There's always someone richer in their way.   120
The gates swing open. Chariots fly out
Behind the pounding hooves. Each driver whips
His horse to catch the ones in front. For those
He's passed, he doesn't give a second thought.
Just so we seldom find a man who says   125
He's lived a good and happy life and, pleased
With how he's passed the time, gives up his seat
At life's table like a sated dinner guest.
Enough. I'll stop, or else perhaps you'll think
I've plagiarized some sermonizing hack.   130

SATIRE 1.2

The exotic dancers' union, snake-oil men,
Panhandlers, starlets, stand-up comics—this
Whole crowd is dressed in black and all choked up:
Tigellius the pop artiste is dead.
Without a doubt, the man was generous.   5
Contrasting this, another man would balk
At chipping in to help a needy friend
Fight off cold or get a meal. He's worried
People think him prodigal. Ask another
How come he's gobbled up the fine estate   10
His dad and granddad built, and still must have
(With borrowed money now) fine caviar.
  "Let no one say I'm stingy," he replies.
For this, he's praised by some, by others blamed.
Now take Fufidius. [The man is rich   15
In real estate and banking.] Still he fears
He'll get the name of ne'er-do-well or worse,
And so he charges five times normal rates
Of interest and takes the first installment off

The principal. The more you need the cash,   20
The more he hassles you to ante up.
He preys upon the young, the sons of tough,
Unyielding fathers, boys who've just put on
The *toga virilis*. "Dear Lord," you think,
"With what this guy has made, he must enjoy   25
All that wealth!" That's where you're wrong. The fellow
Picks at his feast and tortures himself more
Cruelly than that masochistic father
Who ostracized his son in Terence's play.
If anyone is wondering where this talk   30
Is leading, ponder this: your average fool
Attempts avoiding one offense by doing
The opposite. Maltinus goes out dressed
In baggy clothes. Another dandy hikes
His tunic halfway up his ass. Rufillus   35
Smells of peppermint, Gargonius of goat.
No middle course. Some men won't touch a woman
If any ankle shows; another man
Will only touch the stinking whorehouse type.
"Mazel tov," said Cato's godlike wisdom   40
To one he knew just leaving such a den.
"What fine behavior! When abhorrent lust
Has filled a young man's veins, he better sow
His wild oats here than in another's wife."
Cupiennius disdains the praise of prudes.   45
He likes his piece of ass all flounced in white.
O Romans—you who wish disaster on
Adulterers—lend me your ears. Consider
How they toil and suffer lust, their pleasure
Laced with pain and rarely snatched from peril.   50
One throws himself from someone's roof. One's flogged
To death. Another flees but falls among
A savage gang of thieves. One pays to save
His life. The hired help rape another. Some
A knife lops off a lustful cock and balls.   55
"That's fitting," people say, but Galba cavils.
There's safer sex at bargain rates—I'm talking
About ex-slaves—the sort that Sallust craves
No less insanely than adulterers

Some other fellow's wife. Now he could pay   60
The market price for sex, in keeping with
His means, and still be thought quite generous,
Fair, and good. He needn't let libido
Disgrace and bankrupt him. But no, the man
Is full of self-congratulations, preens   65
And smugly counts himself a paragon
Of rectitude: "I never touch a wife."
So too Marsaeus, famous once for being
Origo's paramour. That starlet took
Him for the family house and farm. He says   70
"It'd never cross my mind to mess around
With married women." But you mess around
With actresses and prostitutes and so
Have harmed your reputation even more
Than pocketbook. Or do you think it quite   75
Enough to shun the name "adulterer"
But not the sexual drive that messes up
So many lives? To wreck a reputation,
To squander one's inheritance is wrong
In every case. Why bicker over whether   80
It's prostitutes or Roman wives at issue?
Take Villius. In Fausta he became
The son-in-law of Sulla. Snared by the name,
How dear he paid for that affair! Attacked
By fist and sword, the door slammed in his face,   85
While Longarenus had her in the house.
Suppose the fellow's Dick announced, "What's up
With you? I'm hard but not unreasonable.
I only ask for cunt. I'm not concerned
About its pedigree or dress." How would   90
He answer Dick? "Her father's prominent!"
Now nature, well endowed to furnish what
One needs, gives better council quite opposed
To this misguided tack, if only you
Weigh matters properly and not mix up   95
The things one ought to seek with what should be
Avoided. Do you really think it makes
No difference whether troubles come from your
Mistakes or from the human situation?

Avoid the sort of sex that you'll regret.   100
I mean adultery. The thrill's not worth
The hardship. Snow-white pearls and emeralds
Can't, no matter what you think, Cerinthus,
Make the lady's thigh more satiny, can't
Give her lovelier legs. A prostitute's   105
The better deal. And add to this: she shows
Her goods without deception. What you see
Is what you get. And if she has some charms,
She doesn't lay them on to mask her flaws.
Rich people, when they bid on thoroughbreds,   110
Have the steeds they're looking at be covered.
This way the buyer won't be taken in
By lovely horseflesh, finely tapered head,
And towering neck, and miss the weak, soft hoof.
That's smart. Don't be a sharp-eyed Lynceus   115
When looking at the best her body boasts,
But then be blinder than Hypsaea when
It comes to seeing things that mar her looks.
"What lovely legs! What arms!" But don't omit
To note the runty ass, enormous nose,   120
Truncated torso, those prodigious feet.
With married women, everything is veiled
Other than the face (excepting Catia).
But if you crave forbidden sex, the sort
Surrounded by defensive walls—the harder   125
It is, the crazier you are—so much
Will block your progress: bodyguards, her litter,
The lady's hairdo people, hangers-on,
Her ankle-length outfit and heavy stole.
So many things will block your view of her.   130
The other route is clear and unobstructed.
A diaphanous chemise of Coan silk
Can't hide uncomely legs or ugly feet.
Your eye can measure her from top to bottom.
But maybe you enjoy the part of patsy,   135
The sap who pays before inspecting goods.
The lover sings of how the huntsman tracks
A hare through drifts of snow, but will not touch
A rabbit put in front of him. He adds,

"Just so my passion loves the chase and flies   140
Past whatever's nigh." You hope a clever
Epigram will somehow cool erotic
Fever, or help you staunch the seething wound
Desire has dealt your heart? Would not it serve
You better if you explored these inquiries: 145
What limit nature sets for passion, what
You wouldn't miss, and what, if lost, would cost
You dear. You'd then distinguish void from solid.
When you're parched, you need a golden goblet?
When starved, a turbot grilled or roast peacock?   150
When a certain body part swells up and
A servant girl or houseboy's right at hand,
You'd rather burst than pounce? I sure wouldn't.
I love an easy Venus, one who comes
At call. A woman stringing you along   155
With "Wait a little" or "I'd like another
Gift" or "Only when my husband's out" is,
As Philodemus writes, fit only for
The Galli. All *he* asks is that a woman
Not cost a lot nor make you wait whenever   160
You order sex. She ought to be good looking
And glamorous but not made up so much
You think she's better than she really is.
When such a woman slips her body under
Mine, she's Ilia or Egeria;   165
I give the tart whatever name I like.
While fucking her, I needn't fear a husband
Suddenly returning from the country,
The dog barking, the door torn off it hinges,
The house in wild uproar, the woman pale   170
With panic jumping out of bed, her maid
(My accomplice) shrieking—everyone in
Terror: one of being whipped, the other
Of losing dowry, I of losing life.
Barefoot, tunic half on, off I scramble   175
To save my ass, my cash, and reputation.
Getting caught is really bad. I'd wager
That even Fabius would second that.

SATIRE 1.3

All singers have this fault: when asked to sing
Among their friends, they always make excuses;
Unasked, they open up and can't be stopped.
That famed performer from Sardinia,
Tigellius, was typical. If Caesar,   5
Who could have forced the man to sing, instead
Had asked the favor of hearing him perform,
In keeping with the bonds of friendship
The man enjoyed with him *and* his father,
He'd have wasted his time. But when the Sard   10
Was in the mood, he'd sing "Io Bacchae"
Nonstop from egg course through the fruit dessert.
He crooned a tenor part one moment, then,
The next, he hit the lowest note a bass
Can drop. The man was inconsistent. Often   15
You saw him racing off like one pursued
By foes; more often, slow and solemn, like
A basket-bearer climbing Juno's temple.
Two hundred slaves attended him at times.
On other days, there might be only ten.   20
He loved to talk of kings and potentates.
But then you'd often hear him say, "Give me
A small, three-legged table, salt enough
To fill a shell, an inexpensive toga
To keep cold weather off—that's all I need."   25
Yet if you gave this frugal man a million,
It'd all be gone before six days were out.
He never slept at night, but went to bed
At dawn and snored the day away. No man
Alive could be more fraught with contradictions.   30
"Okay," you interrupt, "but what about
Yourself? You haven't any faults?" I do,
But of a different sort, perhaps less grave.
The time when Maenius took Novius
To task behind his back, someone said,   35
"Hey, are you really that obtuse about
Yourself or do you think you have us fooled?"
"I give myself a pass," said Maenius.
Such stupid self-love warrants ridicule.

When diagnosing faults in *your* own life   40
Your bleary eyes can't see the obvious.
Yet, when criticizing friends, your vision
Suddenly is sharper than an eagle's,
More piercing than the snake's at Epidaurus.
It works, of course, the other way. Your friends   45
Have eyes. They notice every flaw in you.
He's somewhat quick to lose his temper; folks
Look down their nose at him. His hick haircut,
The floppy shoes, his toga hanging wrong—
What a clown! You're laughing. Wait one minute.   50
Is anyone a better man? You call
This guy your friend. Enormous talents hide
Within that unsophisticated frame.
Wise up. Inspect yourself. Did nature plant
Bad seeds in you, or did pernicious habits?   55
Neglect your own estate and weeds will choke
Your acres. Better burn the bracken off.
Let's focus now on how a lover's blind
To his girlfriend's imperfections. Hagna's
Sebaceous cyst Balbinus thought a mark   60
Of beauty. Wouldn't it be nice if friends
Erred like this in judging friends, and ethics
Had coined a proper term for this mistake.
We ought to practice friendship like a father
Embraces fatherhood and not get hyper-   65
Fastidious in finding fault. Suppose
His boy's a squinter: Daddy calls him "hood-eyed."
A runty kid, the size of Sisyphus,
The dwarf, is "Chickee." Doting fathers name
Bow-legged youngsters "Pigeon-toes." A boy   70
Too lame to stand is papa's little "Gimpy."
This fellow here is tight: let's say he's "frugal."
Here's one who's gauche and talks about himself
Too much: well, he expects his friends will find
Him sociable. The too free-spoken type,   75
The truculent: consider "honest," "fearless."
Hot-headed men are really "passionate."
In my opinion, here's the way to make
And keep good friends. But in our madness we

Turn virtues upside down, corrupting what   80
Was clean before. For if an unassuming
And honest man is living in our midst,
We call him "slow," a regular dummkopf.
Or if another, in this world so full
Of bitter grudges and slurs, protects himself   85
Against the traps of treachery and never
Lets down his guard, we call him "insincere"
And "crafty" when, in fact, we really should
Commend his sanity and cautiousness.
Still others, a little too straightforward—like   90
The unaffected sort of guy I've hoped
You've often seen in me, Maecenas—barge
In and interrupt someone with chatter
Who's deep in thought or reading. "What a pain!"
We say, "He plainly lacks all social skills."   95
How fast we sanction laws unjust to us.
For everyone is born with imperfections.
The best is one who suffers from the least.
The gracious friend should weigh both good and bad
In me—that's fair. And if he wants my friendship,   100
He'll be inclined to emphasize my virtues—
Assuming virtues *do* surpass my faults.
In turn, I'll weigh him in the self-same scale.
Whenever someone thinks a zit or two
Should not put off a friend, he can't complain   105
About the other's warts. It's only fair
To pardon others, if they pardon us.
In short, it's quite impossible to cut
Out anger plus the other problems so
Ingrown in fools. Why doesn't reason use   110
A calibrated scale to check offenses
With punishments that justly fit each wrong?
Suppose a master crucified a slave
For snitching food—a bite of fish, a lick
Of tepid sauce—the dinner guests had left   115
Half-eaten. Any sensible man would think
This master crazier than Labeo.
Consider how much more deranged and grave
A fault is this: a friend has rubbed you wrong;

A gracious man would let it go, but you   120
Despise your friend and shun his company,
Just like a debtor dodging Ruso when
The gloomy Kalends fall: he's terrified
Of Ruso reading him (as if a knife
Were at his throat) his dreadful "History,"   125
If he can't scrape together what he owes.
What if a man has drunk too much and wets
The couch or drops a bowl—some valuable
Antique Evander's hands wore thin—or helps
Himself (he's ravenous) to chicken served   130
To me. Am I to like him less for this?
Then what am I to do if he commits
A theft, betrays a trust, or breaks his word?
If people think all crimes deserve the same
Desert, they're forced to stretch the facts to fit   135
Their theory. Common sense and custom balk;
Utility herself protests, the mother,
So to speak, of equity and justice.
When life crawled forth upon primeval earth,
The herds of speechless, ugly creatures fought,   140
At first with claws and then with bloody fists,
For nuts and shelter. Soon, they wielded clubs,
Advancing step by step to better arms,
Until at last they found the words and names
To score their caterwauling cries with sense.   145
They then began to shy away from war.
They walled their towns and set down laws to curb
Marauders, petty thieves, adulterers.
For long before the time of Helen, cunt
Was warfare's most foul instigator. Then   150
Men fought and died in unrecorded battles,
Nameless. In beast-style fights to seize a mate
The strong prevailed, like bulls in herds today.
The fear injustice brought discovered justice.
This fact, I think, you must acknowledge, if   155
You take the time to study history.
The laws of nature can't distinguish right
From wrong in moral terms, but only fix
What's good for us, what's not, and what to seek

And what to shun. If anyone should steal   160
A baby cabbage from his neighbor's yard,
No reasoned argument can demonstrate
This act is just the same as breaking in
A temple after dark to rob the gods.
There should be a rule that gives just penalties   165
For each and every crime. For some deserve
A savage lashing, some a teacher's cane.
The times I hear you say that piracy
And petty theft are much the same, and how
You'd punish arbitrarily all crimes—   170
The great, the small—by one efficient blow,
If you were given regal power, I don't
Have any fears you'd let a person off
With milder punishment than he deserves.
If the man who's wise is rich and first-rate   175
At making shoes; if he alone is handsome,
And a king, why seek what's yours already?
"You've missed the point," the Stoic says. "Our father
Chrysippus means that even if the sage
Has never made a sandal for himself,   180
He's still a cobbler." How is that, I ask.
"Well, even when Hermogenes is mute,
He's still a stunning vocalist. So shrewd
Alfenus sold his tools and closed his shop,
But still remained a cobbler. There, you see   185
The sage has mastered every art: the best
At everything—so he alone is king."
O mightiest of mighty kings, street brats
Pull at your beard. You better use that staff
To beat them off, or else be mobbed and burst   190
Your lungs from barking at the scalawags.
In short, while you, a king, are off to some
Inexpensive public bath, with only
That oaf Crispinus at your side, my dear
Good friends forgive the fool mistakes I make,   195
And I, in turn, am glad to let theirs go.
Be king. I'm happier a commoner.

SATIRE 1.4

Poets—Eupolis, Cratinus, Aristophanes,
And others writing comedies long ago—
If people played the villain's part: a thief
Or rake, a thug, or some rogue otherwise
Notorious, they freely scourged the scoundrels.   5
Lucilius embraced this model wholly
In everything except the meter; droll
And sharp, yet artless at composing verse.
Here lay his fault. Two hundred lines an hour
He often whipped up—what a tour de force!   10
His language in a muddy rush bore lots
Of stuff you'd edit out. A garrulous
And lazy man, he dodged the toil of writing,
Of writing well, that is. I'm not impressed
By literary girth. Now look—Crispinus   15
Will challenge me. "Just take your tablet! Start
The clock! Let's see which poet writes the most."
Thank god I'm not that gifted. Diffident,
I rarely talk and then I husband words.
Go on and pump your lungs like Vulcan's bellows   20
Until the heat's enough to soften iron.
How blessed is Fannius, getting all his works
Anthologized. My writings no one reads.
I shy away from public recitations
Since some folks don't enjoy this sort of verse: 25
Most warrant ridicule. Pick anyone
From a crowd: he's slave to grim ambition
Or chained to greed. This man's gone mad from love
For married women, this one just as nuts
For boys. The glint of silver captivates   30
One type; for Albius, it's bronze. From east
To where the sun sets, businessmen are blown
Like dust in cyclones, stressed and terrified
Of deficits or losing some sweet deal.
This crowd dreads poetry and hates poets.   35
"There's hay on his horns! Keep away," they warn.
"His friends aren't spared; they're fodder for his jokes.
Whatever stuff he's scribbled down, his heart
Is set that every slave boy fetching bread

Or washer woman at the pump must know."   40
I have a brief rebuttal. First of all,
I'm no poet. You'd say it's not enough
To clap some words in meter. Anyone
Like me, who writes like people talk, you'd not
Consider worth the name of poet. You'd   45
Reserve that rank for souls empowered by genius
With true oracular, symphonic might.
Here's why some critics doubt the comic stage
Is really made for poetry. In diction
And subject matter, comedy lacks force   50
And heady inspiration; just take away
Its feet and what you've got is merely prose.
"But what about," you say, "the scene in which
The angry father fumes at his worthless son
Who casts away a nice, rich bride for some   55
Prostitute, and drunk, is out parading
A torch about the town in broad daylight—
An utter scandal." Pomponius would hear
Some powerful lines if his dad were still alive.
It's clearly not enough to write some verse   60
In unaffected language, which, if you took
The meter out, would sound like any mad
Old man, on stage or off, browbeating his son.
Now take away the steady beat from what
Lucilius wrote and I am writing now;   65
Reorder words so last becomes the first.
Now compare what happens if you jumble
Up this: "When once Discord so fell and foul
Had broke wide open War's strong gates of iron."
It's different, isn't it? For Ennius   70
Is Ennius, no matter how dismembered.
At this point, let's put aside the issue
If satire is or isn't poetry.
We'll hash that out another time. Right now
The only thing I want to straighten out   75
Is: Are you justified distrusting this genre?
Fierce Sulcius and Caprius roam the town,
Armed with little books and hoarse from barking
Out indictments. No wonder bandits cower.

No one need give these two the time of day,   80
Provided that he's living an honest life.
And should you be a bandit like Caelius
Or Birrius, I'm still not a Caprius
Or Sulcius. Why keep on fearing me?
I'd never prostitute my little book   85
In any common shop for customers
Like Tigellius Hermogenes to paw.
As for reciting, I don't do it much;
Not everywhere or to everyone. My friends
Alone occasionally hear some lines,   90
But only when they pressure me to read.
A lot of writers like performing verse
In public baths and market squares. The voice,
Amplified by vaulted space, resonates
And sounds so lovely: empty-headed joy   95
For those who never stop to ask if what
They like to do is sensible and timely.
Now someone says, "You actually enjoy
Inflicting pain. You're twisted." Where on earth
Did you come up with that? Is anyone   100
Who knows me well your source? Whoever bites
A friend behind his back, who won't defend
His pal when others put him down, who craves
Loud laughter's roar, the wit's celebrity,
Who makes things up, who yaps and can't keep still,   105
Betraying secrets told in confidence—
That man is black-hearted! Of him, good Romans,
Beware. You'll often see a dining room
Where twelve are tightly packed on three divans,
With some wag roasting everyone except   110
The host; and once he's drunk, the host as well
Is burned by this initiate of Liber.
Him you think urbane, amusing, liberated;
And you abhor black-hearted men. But if
I laugh because the fop "Rufillus smells   115
Of peppermint, Gargonius of goat,"
You think my little joke is fanged and spiteful?
Here's *you* defending ol' Petillius
When someone mentions him and larceny:

"Petillius has been my closest friend   120
Since we were kids. He's always there for me.
Thank god he's doing well. Don't ask me how
The hell he was acquitted." Isn't there
A fishy smell in words like that, pure venom?
If I can promise categorically   125
One thing about my character, it's this:
I pledge I'm not malicious; this offense
You'll never find in me or in my book.
Now if I speak more freely than you like
And seem too prone to laughter, surely you   130
Can grant a little license here. I learned
This habit from the very best of fathers.
He taught me how to dodge mistakes in life
By marking paradigms of bad behavior.
"Look at," he'd say, "how Albius' boy   135
And Baius, ever short of cash, wrecked life.
You'll learn a lot from them about the virtues
Of thrift and living well within your bounds."
On falling for a whore: "Don't ape Scetanus."
To ward me off affairs with married women   140
When brothels served as well: "Trebonius
Got caught and that destroyed his reputation."
"Philosophers," he used to say, "explain
The reasons why a person must avoid
One thing and seek another. I'll be pleased   145
If I preserve in you the ways passed down
By men of old. So long as you depend
On me to guide your youth, I'll keep your life
And reputation safe. Once age has fired
The mould of mind and body, then you'll swim   150
Without a float." Here's how my father shaped
The boy I was with useful words. And whether
He told me what to do—"See here, you have
A model straight and true"—and singled out
A juryman to be my guide; or when   155
He wouldn't let me loose to do whatever
I liked, he found examples—"Don't fuss. Look
At so and so. That dreadful scandal shows
Compelling proof for why you shouldn't do it."

Just as a neighbor's stark obituary   160
Strikes terror in an ailing epicure
And gets him on a diet, so quite often
Another's shame will turn teenagers off
The path of folly. So my father kept
Me sound and safe from those mistakes that wreck   165
A human life. If now and then I stumble,
It's over moderate faults you wouldn't mind.
Perhaps I'll straighten out these errors too,
With time, the counsel of free-spoken friends,
And by my own attempts at self-repair.   170
For whether I'm at home relaxing or
About the town, I'm always taking stock
Of myself: "This course would steer me straighter
In living life; I know it'd please my friends.
But look at that—that wasn't nice at all.   175
I hope I never act so thoughtlessly."
Here's how in quiet meditation I
Keep occupied correcting imperfections.
Not all the time. Occasionally, I take
A break and then I often end up writing   180
Some lines of verse to entertain myself.
Here's one of those moderate faults I mentioned.
Should you not concede me this, the poets
In battle groups will rally to my aid.
You see, there're more of us—and like the Jews,   185
We'll make you yield your ground and join our mob.

SATIRE 1.5

Left majestic Rome and made Aricia.
Found some modest lodgings. Heliodorus
Came along, the rhetorician, smartest
Of Greeks by far. Next stop Forum Appi:
Bargemen everywhere, dishonest barkeeps.   5
Real travelers make this stretch in one day. We
Took two. Why rush? The Appian is less
Exhausting at an easy pace. But here
The water isn't good and war breaks loose

Between my stomach and me. My travel mates   10
Have supper, I . . . I suffer. Now night drops
Its shadows earthward and fills the sky with stars.
Then shouting. Slaves and bargemen yelling at
Each other. "Park her here." "You're packing in
Three hundred!" "Whoa! She's full." It takes an hour   15
To gather fares and harness up the mule.
Mosquito bites and loud marsh frogs make sleep
Impossible. The bargeman, soused, belts out
Some song about his girl; a passenger
Starts at it too, but louder till at last   20
He tires and drops off. Our slouch of a sailor
Has set the mule to graze, the tow ropes tied
To a rock, and now, flat on his back, snores.
Already day had dawned before we grasp
The boat isn't moving. A man on board,   25
Enraged, jumps out and takes a willow branch
And whacks the head and rump of mule and sailor.
Half the morning gone before we landed.
Feronia, your sacred water cleansed
Our hands and faces. After breakfast, up   30
The three-mile path we crawled to Anxur, perched
On cliffs so white you see the place far off.
Maecenas, best of men, Cocceius too,
Would join us here, ambassadors adept
At reconciling friends who've fallen out.   35
Their mission now was urgently important.
I'd got some inflammation in my eyes
And daubed on black salve. Meanwhile Maecenas
And Cocceius arrived, together with
Fonteius Capito, the spitting image   40
Of tact and dearest friend of Antony.
We're quite relieved to leave the town of Fundi
In the year Aufidius Luscus held
The praetorship. This batty bureaucrat
Made us laugh: the fancy robe, medallions,   45
A senator's broad stripe, his pan of charcoals.
Mamurra's town is where we stop again,
Worn out. Here Murena's villa offers
Rest, and Capito provides his kitchen.

The next day we're in heaven: Plotius,   50
Varius, and Virgil meet up with us
At Sinuessa. Earth has never seen
Men more true-blue—how overjoyed we were
To be together. While I'm compos mentis,
I'll value nothing more than a good friend.   55
A small layover near the Campanian bridge
Provides a roof; the staff bring salt and wood.
At Capua the mules unwind, Maecenas
Gets to play some ball, while I and Virgil
Siesta: exercise is not for those   60
With rheumy eyes and fussy stomachs. Next
Cocceius' villa, amply stocked, atop
The ridge above the shops of Caudium.
Muse, I'd like to have recalled the battle
Of Sarmentus, the witty clown, and Messius,   65
Nicknamed "The Cock." Be brief. The lineage
Of both recount. How Messius was sprung
From famous Oscan stock; Sarmentus' mistress
Still quite alive. They entered battle, boasting
Such ancestors. Sarmentus struck the first: 70
"You look like a rhinoceros." We laugh.
"I'll grant you that," the other snorts, his head
Thrown back. Sarmentus adds, "You're scary enough
Dehorned." An ugly scar, in fact, disfigured
The bristly brow on Messius' left side.   75
After lots of jokes about his looks and
The man's Campanian malady, Sarmentus
Asked him to hoedown like a Cyclops. He fit
The part. No need for mask or high-heeled boot.
At this the "Cock" let loose. He asked Sarmentus   80
If he'd fulfilled his vow and dedicated
His shackles to the Lar. What of his job
As clerk? The law still gave his mistress rights.
A parting shot: "So why'd you run away?
A pound of grain would feed a squirt like you."   85
Such fun it was, we stretched our dinner late.
From here we traveled straight to Beneventum
Where our over-zealous host, while turning
Some skinny thrushes on a spit, came close

To burning down the house. For Vulcan flew   90
Off the hearth across and up the ancient
Kitchen wall to lick the roof. You'd have seen
Some hungry guests and panicked slaves! We save
The meal; all work at putting out the blaze.
Now Apulia unveils the mountains   95
I know so well. We'd never have crawled across
Those hot and windy heights had we not found
A villa near Trivicum. How the tears
Filled our eyes from all the smoke the fireplace
Puffed forth (the fuel was sodden wood and leaves).   100
I lay awake till midnight, dumb enough
To think the girl would come. At last sleep came
To take me off, still cocked, to dirty dreams
That splotched my stomach and pajamas too.
Next day, for thirty-six kilometers,   105
We're swept along in carriages toward
A little town whose name won't fit the meter,
But certain features clearly point it out.
Here water, nature's cheapest good, is sold.
The bread, however, beats the best I've had.   110
Savvy travelers pack some loaves for later.
For once you reach Canusium—they claim
Brave Diomedes built the place—the bread
Is gritty. Water's hard to come by too.
Here Varius must leave us. Everyone   115
Depressed. But on to Rubi, which we reach
At last, exhausted. Heavy rain had damaged
The highway. Next day's weather cleared. The road,
Was worse, however, all the way to Bari,
A fishing town. Then Gnathia, a place   120
The water nymphs have cursed. We had to laugh
When town folk tried convincing us that myrrh
Miraculously melts without a fire
On their temple's threshold. Jew Apella
May swallow rot like that, not I. I've learned   125
That immortal gods lead carefree lives and
Whatever strange event occurs in nature,
No moody god in heaven sent it down.
Brundisi ends this lengthy tale and trip.

SATIRE 1.6

No Lydian, Maecenas, living now
In Tuscany can boast a nobler house.
Your mother's ancestors, your father's too,
Commanded mighty legions once. Most men
Turn up their noses at the likes of me,   5
An ex-slave's son. You're different. Provided
A man's freeborn, you're not concerned about
His parentage. You rightly note that once,
Before the reign of humble Tullius,
A lot of men from undistinguished homes   10
Led exemplary lives and held high office,
While someone like Laevinus, proud to claim
Valerius his ancestor (the man
Who drove Tarquinius Superbus out),
Was never valued more than pocket change.   15
Thus popular opinion branded him.
The same opinion, as you know, elects
Worthless candidates to office, prostrates
Itself before celebrity, and gapes
At funeral masks and fulsome epitaphs.   20
We're far above all that. So what suits us?
No doubt the mob would vote Laevinus in
Before supporting some upstart Decius.
The censor Appius would blacklist me
If I didn't have a freeborn father.   25
He'd be right, if I'd outgrown my breeches.
Vainglory drives a gleaming chariot
And drags behind the high and lowly born
Decked out in chains. Please tell us, Tillius,
To what good end did you put on again   30
The broad, purple stripe to be a tribune?
Resentment swelled. A private life is kinder.
No sooner has a lunatic bound black
Laces halfway up his shins and added
A senator's broad stripe than he begins   35
To hear: "Who *is* that man?" "Whose son is he?"
Say someone's sick with what afflicts Barrus:
That vanity to be thought beautiful.
Girls everywhere he went would have to know

About his face, his calves, feet, teeth, and hair.   40
The statesman too, who vows to safeguard Rome,
Her citizens, the empire, Italy,
And temples, forces everyone to ask
Just who his father was, or whether mom
Has spoiled his name by her obscurity.   45
"Do you," a person shouts, "the son of Syrus
Or Dama or Dionysius, do you dare
Throw Roman citizens down from the Rock
Or hand them over chained to Cadmus?" "But,"
You plead, "my colleague Novius is there   50
One row behind my row because he's what
My father was." "You think that you're Messalla
Or Paullus? As for Novius, well he
At least commands attention. Take the noise
Two hundred wagons make crashing into   55
Three huge funerals rumbling through the Forum:
His voice will trump trumpets, horns, and riot."
But back to me, the son of some ex-slave,
Whom people mock as "son of some ex-slave"
Because these days I'm on familiar terms   60
With you, Maecenas; formerly because
A Roman legion followed me, their tribune.
But these two matters aren't at all the same.
I'm not surprised my officer commission
Would rouse resentment, but it makes no sense   65
Why anyone begrudges me a friend
Like you, especially when you're such a cautious
And careful judge of character and shun
Ambitious self-promoters. It wasn't luck
Or accident that brought me to your door.   70
For Virgil, best of men, explained to you
The sort of man I was and Varius
Corroborated. When we first met face
To face, I stammered out some broken lines;
Sheer deference cut short my saying more.   75
I didn't talk about a famous father.
I didn't boast of riding over vast
Estates on some Satureian farm horse.
Instead, I told you what I was. You said

A few words. That's your way. I took my leave.   80
Eight months went by before you called me back
And bid me join your company of friends.
I take great pride in having won your favor.
For you know how to segregate the true
From counterfeit by judging character   85
In action, not a man's paternal claims.
Now if my faults are few and rather middling
And compromise my otherwise good nature
No more than birthmarks mar a handsome man;
If no one can in fairness charge that I'm   90
In love with wealth, or vile, or lecherous;
If I may take some pride in living a clean
And honest life and say my friends are fond
Of me—all this I owe my father. He
Was poor, with little land, but still refused   95
To pack me off to Flavius' schoolhouse
Where big centurions enrolled their big sons,
Slates and satchels slung across their shoulders;
Each Ides they handed Flavius eight coppers.
Instead he dared to take his boy to Rome   100
To learn the arts a senator or knight
Expects his son to master. Anyone
Who saw my clothes and noticed how I had
Some slaves to carry school supplies might well
Have thought that I, like other boys attending   105
A school in Rome, had great ancestral wealth.
My father, an incorruptible guardian, went
With me himself to each and every class.
What more to say? My sense of decency,
The first of virtue's goods, my father kept   110
Uncompromised by shameful deed or scandal.
He didn't fear the criticism people
Might voice if I became an auctioneer
Who made just small commissions, or turned out,
Like him, a broker. Had that been the case,   115
You'd not hear me complaining. Given how
Things went, I praise and thank him even more.
No sensible man could ever be ashamed
Of such a father. I will not defend

Myself, as many others do, by making   120
Excuses like "it's not my fault my parents
Weren't free-born and famous." Such complaints
Have never crossed my mind or lips. But if
At a fixed age Nature were to send us
Back in time to start our lives again and   125
Order us to choose the sort of parents
Ambition craves, I'd disobey. For I'm
Content and wouldn't trade my parents, even
For ones who'd held the staffs and seats of power.
The common crowd will think me mad, but you,   130
I'd wager, think me sensible for not
Accepting dull responsibilities
Completely new to me. I'd have to change
The way I live: enlarge my revenues,
Receive more morning callers, make more calls,   135
Ensure that one or two companions come
With me on trips abroad or when I go
Out of town, provide for more retainers
And horses, not to mention carriages.
I'm better off the way things are. Let's say   140
Tarentum's where I want to be. I throw
A pack across my gelded mule and off
We go, the luggage bouncing on its rump,
And I, the knight, bouncing on its withers.
No one accuses me of being vile.   145
What happens, Tillius, when you head off
To Tibur? Slaves attend—all five of them—
To carry chamber pot and jugs of wine.
But people jeer because you don't quite cut
A praetor's style. I reckon, senator,   150
My life's a better fit than yours—for this
And countless other reasons. Nothing stops
Me walking out alone to any place
I choose. I pause to ask about the price
Of garden greens and spelt. When evening comes   155
I'm often at the Circus, strolling through
The seedy stalls, or at the Forum where
The fortune tellers catch my ear. Then home
To supper: a bowl of bean noodles, leeks,

And chickpeas cooked and served by three slave boys.   160
A white stone table holds two cups, a ladle,
One cheap all-purpose dish, a flask and saucer,
The whole set mass produced in Campania.
I'm soon in bed and sound asleep. Instead
Of getting up at dawn to hurry off   165
To confabs at the Forum where the statue
Of Marsyas is tortured by the sight
Of Novius the younger doing business,
I stay in bed till ten. Once up, I take
A stroll or sometimes entertain myself   170
Reading quietly or writing something;
Then a nice massage. Unlike vile Natta,
I needn't rob some grimy lamp for oil.
A game of ball soon wears me out. I leave
The Campus Martius, feeling overheated   175
And ready for the public baths. I get
A bite to eat, enough to keep my stomach
Quiet. Then, at home, I take it easy.
You see laid out before you here the life
Of those set free from all the misery   180
Ambition loads upon a man. I count
My blessings every time I think how much
I'm better off the way things are. Thank god
My granddad wasn't quaestor, nor his sons.

SATIRE 1.7

How Persius, a mutt of a man, avenged
Himself on the pus and poison of proscribed
Rupilius Rex is a tale, I'd wager,
Known in every drugstore and barbershop.
This Persius was rich, with huge investments   5
At Clazomenae. He faced some tiresome
Legal case involving Rex. He wasn't
A man to yield; in animosity
He had the upper hand of Rex; his bluster,
His arrogance, and biting words packed more   10
Horsepower than a Barrus or Sisenna.

But back to Rex. When neither man agreed
On terms—for quarrelsome contestants act
Like heroes on the battlefield: between
The fierce Achilles and Priam's son, the rage   15
Was so destructive, Hector had to die:
No other course, when bravest of men clash.
Not so when Discord riles cowards, or two
Poorly matched contenders joust (like Glaucus
The Lycian and Diomedes). Then   20
The weaker man unasked will proffer gifts,
Bow, and yield in battle. Well, when Brutus
Was praetor over wealthy Asia, Rex
And Persius had at each other, paired
As perfectly as Bacchius and Bithus,   25
The gladiators. Into court they rush,
Their fury truly marvelous to see.
Now Persius lays out his case. The whole
Assembly laughs. He praises Brutus, then
His entourage. "O sun of Asia," he calls   30
Brutus. "O propitious constellation"
He calls the staff, excluding Rex. With Rex
The Dog Star rose, the star all farmers hate.
So on he rushed like some wild winter flood
Through forests seldom touched by axe. Against   35
This salty cataract Praeneste's champ
Shoots back a blast of vintage sass and scorn,
Invincible as any vineyard hand
Who gives back better than he gets when some
Wayfarer heckles him and yells out "Cuckoo!"   40
Then Persius the Greek, completely drenched
In Italian vinegar, exclaims: "Great gods
Almighty, Brutus! Why not assassinate
This Rex. You're good at getting rid of kings.
Believe me, here's a job just made for you!"   45

SATIRE 1.8

Not long ago I was a useless piece
Of wood, a fig tree's trunk. A carpenter

Debated what to make of me. I might
Have been a stool; instead he fashioned me
A god, Priapus. Awesome now, a god,   5
I panic thieves and birds. No thief gets past
My raised right hand. My crotch is armed with this
Obscenely long and red protrusion. Birds
Don't bother me. A reed stuck in my head
Spooks the pests and keeps them off this modern   10
And lovely park. A cemetery once
Disgraced this hill. The corpses carried here
Belonged to slaves. Their fellow slaves arranged
For cheap interment. Poor folks shared this ground
Within a common grave. That party clown   15
Pantolobus and bankrupt Nomentanus
Were buried somewhere in this paupers' field.
That pillar over there marks out the lot:
A thousand feet in front, three hundred back,
And indicates that this grave monument   20
Does not descend to heirs. Today, however,
The Esquiline is quite transformed. The bones
And litter swept away, the view is lovely:
A wholesome place to live or promenade
Some afternoon along the bright embankment.   25
I haven't any problem handling thieves
Or wildlife prowling round up here. The hags,
However, worry me. Their chants and potions
Harry human hearts. I've tried again and
Again to drive them off and stop their coming   30
Up here on moonlit nights to dig up bones
And baneful herbs, but nothing seems to work.
These eyes of mine have seen Canidia
Rushing about barefoot, her black robe tucked
Up, and her hair disheveled. How she howled!   35
Sagana, an older hag, joined her wailing.
Their pallor made the very sight of them
Enough to curdle blood. They started digging
Into the ground with nothing but their nails,
Then tore apart a black lamb with their teeth.   40
Its blood gushed down into the ditch—an offering
To conjure forth the dead to rise and speak.

They held two dolls, one made of wool, the other
Wax. The first was big and seemed to threaten
The one who had its waxen arms upraised   45
In supplication like a slave afraid
Of death. One witch addresses Hecate;
The other summons cruel Tisiphone.
Then you'd have seen the dogs of Hell abroad
And serpents. Moon, her face all red, refused   50
To witness such a sight and hid behind
A massive sepulchre. Now if I lie
In anything I'm saying, let my head
Be plastered white by crows; let Julius,
Miss Pediatius so fine, and that thief   55
Voranus pee on me and take a crap.
But why tell everything—how shrill and sad
Hung the sound of dead voices answering
Sagana's words, or how the witches worked
So furtively to bury beard of wolf   60
And tooth of spotted snake, how high the flame
Exploded from the waxen doll, or how
I shuddered, witnessing all the Furies said
And did that night? Still I settled the score.
My figwood ass split out a fart. The blast   65
Of snapping timber boomed just like a popped
Balloon. The hags ran off in panic, back
To Town. You should have seen Canidia.
Her teeth fell out. Sagana's wig flew off
And all the magic herbs and voodoo charms   70
They'd dropped lay scattered wide across the land.
It was enough to make you roar with laughter.

SATIRE 1.9

I'd turned by chance onto the Via Sacra,
Absorbed, the way I get, in something not
Important (probably some verse). Just then
Up runs this man I barely know and grabs
My hand. "Great to see you! How's it going?"   5
"So far, just fine," I say, and wish him well.

He's right behind me when I look again.
"There's nothing else," I quickly ask, "is there?"
"We really ought to get acquainted," he says,
"I'm literary." "Great," I tell him. Mad   10
To free myself, I quicken my pace, then stop
Abruptly, then start walking fast again,
I whisper something to my slave—the sweat
Had reached my ankles. "O Bolanus, what
I'd give to have your temper now," I mutter   15
Under my breath, while on this fellow blathered
In praise of Rome, the neighborhood, whatever.
When I said nothing, he put in, "You're mad
To get away. Don't think I didn't notice.
But it's no use, really. I'm not about   20
To lose you now. I'll follow you wherever
You're headed." "Please," I said, "no need to go
Out of your way. I'm off to see a man
You wouldn't know. He's sick at home across
The Tiber, far off, near the park of Caesar."   25
   "No problem," he replies. "I'm fit. I've time
To kill. I'll tag along." My ears flopped down
Like a mule's a man has overloaded.
He starts again. "I'll bet you'll reckon me
As good a friend as Viscus or Varius.   30
I'm fast at writing poems, lots of them.
I'm really quite the dancer. Hermogenes
Would die to sing like me." I seize the chance
To interrupt. "You have a mother, don't you?
Or other relatives concerned about   35
Your welfare?" "No," says he, "there isn't one
I haven't laid to rest." How blessed the dead!
I'm stuck among the living. Finish me!
This must be the doom a Sabellan crone
Foretold with her divining urn when I   40
Was still a boy. The words she sang proved true:
   "No deadly drug, no sword in battle's fray,
      No hacking cough, no crippling illness slow,
      But someday someone's wordiness will be
      The death of him. So when he's come of age   45
      Let him beware and shun long-winded men."

We'd come along to Vesta's temple, half
The morning gone. It happened he'd been called
To court. The case was lost unless he went.
"Be a pal," he says, "I need a little   50
Support." "May I drop dead if I can stand
Before the bench or know a thing about the law!
And anyway I'm late already. Must
Be off to you know where." He looked distressed.
"I can't make up my mind. Do I lose you   55
Or lose my court case?" "Me," I volunteered.
"No," he said. "I won't do that," and started
Up the street. A conquered man, I followed.
"How are things," he asks, "between Maecenas
And you? So very few get close to him.   60
His judgment's excellent! No one I know
Has turned his plain good luck to better use.
Just think how useful *I* could be. You need
A crony. Sponsor me, and damn me if
You couldn't clear the field of competition."   65
I try explaining, "But we don't behave
The way you think. No house is more upright
Or freer from that sort of meanness. Look,
It doesn't bother me if someone has
More money or if my learning might not match   70
Another's. Each of us respects the rest."
"You're kidding me," he laughs. "Believe it," I say,
"Or not. That's how it is." "Well, get me in.
I'm even more intrigued by this Maecenas."
"You only have to wish it," I rejoined.   75
"Your force of character will take his house
By storm. Maecenas is the sort of man
People can win over. That's the reason
He's guarded and makes the forays difficult."
"I'll not sell myself short," he lets me know.   80
"I'll bribe his slaves. And if I don't succeed
Today, I'll not give up. I'll bide my time.
I'll find him in the street. I'll wait on him.
To mortals, life gives nothing without great toil."
As he was talking, Fuscus Aristius   85
Happened by, a man I think the world of.

He had this fellow's number. Here we stopped.
He asked about my journey, I of his.
To save myself, I started pulling at
His tunic. I pinched his arm. To no avail.   90
I rolled my eyes and nodded at the pest.
No acknowledgment of my annoyance
Did Fuscus make, but having fun, the smartass
Laughed and let me squirm. I lost my temper.
"Aristius," I hissed, "isn't there some   95
Important news you wished to share with me
In private?" "Yes, there is," he smiled, "but it
Can wait. Today's the thirtieth Sabbath.
We better not fart at the gelded Jews."
"Well, I'm not superstitious!" I reply.   100
"I am," he smirks. "I'm more conventional
Than you. Another time we'll have that talk."
I never thought so dark a day would dawn
For me. The shameless man walks off. I'm left,
A sacrificial victim under the knife.   105
Just then by sheer good luck the man's opponent
Runs up and shouts, "Hey, stop, you son of bitch!"
He asks if I will stand as witness. "Yes,"
I say, and let him touch my ear. He hauls
The fellow off to court. There's hullabaloo   110
All round and people charging in from here
And there. That's how Apollo rescued me.

SATIRE 1.10

Yes, I said Lucilius' verse runs
On flat, ungainly feet. Is anyone
Out there so nuts about Lucilius
He can't see that? But on the very page
I criticized his style, the man was praised   5
For scouring Rome with lots of verbal salt.
To recognize one virtue doesn't mean
Commending everything. Laberius' mimes,
I grant, are funny; opera they're not.
It isn't enough to make the audience   10

Gape with laughter, however good the joke.
A writer needs concision. Words should speed
The thought along, not tangle up ideas
And bore the listener. Depending on
The part that's played—the orator, the poet,   15
Sometimes the urbane wit who doesn't waste
Forensic power but lightly scores his point—
The style will modulate: at times severe,
More often humorous. A good joke cuts
Through weighty matters more effectively   20
Than sharp invective. This was how the Greek
Playwrights of Old Comedy won success.
In this they set a model writers ought
To heed. A pity swell Hermogenes
Or Johnny-one-note there who apes Catullus   25
And Calvus haven't read these older Greeks.
"Ah," you say, "but mixing Greek and Latin
Showed off his virtuosity." How slow
You are to learn! You really think the stuff
Pitholeon of Rhodes tossed off demanding   30
And awesome? "But, doesn't it sound divine
When Greek and Latin vowels harmonize?
Falernian's sweeter mixed with Chian wine."
I have to ask, does this apply just when
You're writing verse or also hold when you   35
Must plead a case as tough as Petillius'?
Corvinus and Pedius Publicola
Toil at their legal briefs. But you, forgetting
Father Latinus and your fatherland,
Prefer, no doubt, to babble polyglot   40
In court like some bilingual Canusian.
Although Italian, I experimented
At writing some light verse in Greek. But then
Appeared Quirinus when midnight had passed
And dreams are true. He chided me: "You're mad.   45
You'd do better lugging logs to a forest
Than enlisting in Hellenic legions."
So while that turgid Alpine poet cuts
Memnon's throat in epic style and muddies
The Rhine's headwaters, I enjoy my sport   50

Of writing lines like these. Let others go
Audition songs for Tarpa; *my* lines aren't
Performing acts on stage all season long.
Fundanius, of men alive today,
You're best at writing humorous librettos   55
For comedy's conniving courtesan
And Davus who bamboozle old Chremes.
Pollio sings of kings in trimeters.
High-strung Varius commands the epic
Like no one else. Our native muses love   60
The countryside and grant a tenderness
And charm to Virgil's song. This kind of verse,
Which Varro Atacinus and others tried,
I thought I'd write with more success, though no
Lucilius. I'd never dare to wrest   65
From off the founder's head his crown and praise.
Still, I said, his verse runs muddy; often
There's more in him you'd edit out than keep.
Does Homer's greatness silence learned critics?
Did Lucilius not twit dour Accius   70
With parody and lampoon Ennius
For writing lofty lines that fizzle out,
Though never once upstaging those he faults?
What's wrong if we, his readers, want to know
Whether Lucilius' own temperament   75
Or what he wrote about can best explain
Why his verses aren't more finely made and
Scutter on as if it were sufficient
To harness thoughts in six-foot lines and trot
Two hundred verses out before you eat   80
And then another ten score after lunch?
So poems poured from Tuscan Cassius,
His genius mightier than roaring rivers.
People still go on about his funeral:
Books in boxes make an excellent pyre.   85
Lucilius could be amusing; how
Urbane he was I won't dispute. I grant
He wrote more polished lines of verse than what
An author might produce when fashioning
A brand new kind of work without a Greek   90

Model. I grant he's finer than the whole
Pack of older Roman poets. Still, had
Lucilius been born in our own age,
He'd be filing down his verse and pruning
His rambling lines to fit their proper form,   95
And all the while he worked at making verse
He'd often scratch his head and gnaw his nails.
To write lines worth a second reading, you
Must often use the flat end of your stylus.
Forget about appeasing every taste.   100
Less is more when it comes to readership.
Or have you gone completely nuts and fancy
Your poems taught in run-down schools? Not I.
As the mime Arbuscula said, undaunted
Before the hooting, hissing mob she scorned,   105
"The knights applauded me; I'm satisfied."
Do you believe that bug Pantilius
Irks me? Or that I'm tortured thinking how
Demetrius abuses me behind
My back? Or dopey Fannius, who hangs   110
Around Hermogenes, could hurt my feelings?
Let Plotius, Varius, Maecenas,
Virgil, Valgius and Octavius,
Fuscus, and both the Viscus brothers praise
My work. It's not to curry favor if   115
I add you, Pollio, and you, Messalla,
Your brother, and Bibulus and Servius,
Along with true-blue Furnius and lots
More learned friends I purposely leave unnamed.
If my verse, whatever it's worth, amuses   120
Such men, I'm happy; grieved, if what I write
Defeats my hopes of pleasing friends like these.
Demetrius, Tigellius, fare-ill
Amid your school girls perched on cushioned chairs.
Write quickly, boy, and close my little book.   125

BOOK 2

SATIRE 2.1

HORACE: "Some people say my satires are by far
Too violent. They claim I break the law
That reins in this genre. The rest complain
That what I write is nerveless stuff spun off
A thousand lines per day. Trebatius, please,   5
Advise me. What am I to do?"
TREBATIUS: "Lay off."
HORACE: "You mean stop writing altogether?"
TREBATIUS: "Yes."
HORACE: "Damn me, I know you're right, but I can't sleep."
TREBATIUS: "Insomniacs should oil up; then swim
Three laps across the Tibur. At nightfall, dose   10
Yourself heavily with undiluted wine.
Or if you can't control this madcap passion
For writing, gird yourself to write an epic
And celebrate victorious Caesar.
That sort of work will earn you great rewards."   15
HORACE: "I wish I could, good sir, but inspiration
Fails me. Not everyone can marshal words
To fill a page with battle lines alive
With bristling spears, or tell of broken pikes
And dying Gauls or Parthians unhorsed,   20
Much less describe their gruesome wounds."
TREBATIUS: "Okay,
Then write a piece that praises Caesar's just
And valiant character. Recall how wise
Lucilius gave Scipio such praise."
HORACE: "I'm confident that when the right occasion   25
Appears, I'll rise to meet the challenge, but
The timing's crucial. A Flaccus doesn't stand
Near Caesar's ear, and if I rub him wrong,
He'll kick and guard himself on every side."
TREBATIUS: "Still, you must admit this course is better   30
Than slashing out against that party clown

38

Pantabolus and bankrupt Nomentanus
With dark invective. Everyone despises
A poet writing stuff like that, and fears
The poems, whether he is hit or not."   35
HORACE: "But what am I to do? Milonius
Loves dancing once he's lit and sees double.
From Leda's egg two brothers hatched, but Castor
Was into horses, Pollux lived to box.
For every thousand souls, there are a thousand   40
Quite different passions. Like Lucilius,
(A better man than either one of us)
I take delight in putting words in verse.
He, years ago, entrusted to his books
The sort of things you'd only share with friends,   45
And whether life went well or ill for him,
He never found a better confidant.
The old man's whole life is laid out to view
As publicly as what is painted on
A votive tablet. He's my model, whether   50
I'm called Lucanian or Apulian.
For, as you know, the colonists who plow
The fields of my Venusia can see
The bourns of both these districts. Once Sabellan
Tribes were driven out, this land was given   55
To veterans who, old tradition says,
Were settled here to keep the Romans safe
Against incursions, whether violence
Should sweep across Apulian frontiers
Or wild Lucania explode in war.   60
But rest assured, my pen will never harm
A living soul without good cause. It's here
To guard me, like a sword within its sheath.
Why bother drawing it? No thugs are near.
Let me, Jupiter, Father, King, retire   65
This weapon. Rust consume it! May no one
Harm me, a pacifist. But anyone
Who badgers me—watch out!—will rue the day
His name becomes the stuff of pasquinades.
When Cervius gets mad, he threatens foes   70
With laws and juries. Cross Canidia

Will brandish potions she perfected on
Albucius. Turius the judge will slap
A heavy fine on anyone who dares
To challenge him in court. I think you must   75
Conclude, as I have found, that everyone
Will use his natural strengths to frighten off
Potential enemies. It's nature's law.
The wolf has teeth, the bull is armed with horns,
And instinct teaches each to bite or gore.   80
Entrust to bankrupt Scaeva's care his long-
Lived mom. He'll never raise his filial
Right hand to do her any harm. Small wonder!
For would a wolf attack and use its foot
To kill, or would a bull unsheathe sharp fangs?   85
The poor old thing gets honey laced with hemlock.
The point is, whether quiet old age waits
For me, or dark-winged death is circling near;
Be I rich or poor, at Rome or exiled—
Whatever course my life should take, I know   90
One thing: I'll write no matter what."
TREBATIUS: "I fear,
Young man, you haven't long to live. A cold
Reception waits you at some great friend's door."
HORACE: "But why? Lucilius first dared compose
This kind of verse and stripped hypocrisy   95
Off rotten men. Did Laelius or he
Who conquered Carthage take offense or fault
The poet's wit? Did they feel hurt or grieve
Because the poet hit Metellus hard
And buried Lupus under ridicule?   100
Lucilius, in fact, indicted high
And mighty, charged the people, tribe by tribe—
A steady friend to Virtue's bloc alone.
The virtue of Scipio sometimes threw off
The toga, left the public stage and crowds,   105
And joined the gentle wisdom of Laelius
At home, and all three friends would joke around
While on the stove a pot of greens boiled down.
Now, even if I haven't got the gifts
Lucilius had and can't compete in class,   110

Still, Envy must concede, like it or not,
That I have lived among the powerful.
In biting down on me, she'll break her tooth!
Unless, my learned friend, you see an issue."
TREBATIUS: "I can't contest your point. But still, take care.   115
You've been advised now. Don't let ignorance
Of our time-honored legal code land you
In court. Should anyone indite ill verse
Against another, law and judgment wait."
HORACE: "So be it, if the verse is really ill.   120
But what about a man who indites some verse
That's really good, and Caesar judges him
A worthy poet? If this man's above
Reproach, will he be charged for barking at
Some reprobate deserving ridicule?"   125
TREBATIUS: "Then laughter strikes the tablets. You get off."

SATIRE 2.2

Consider, gentlemen, the frugal life:
What its value is, how great that value.
This talk today is not my own. Ofellus
Made these points—a farmer, no disciple
Of any one philosophy, but shrewd.   5
Become his pupils, not symposiasts
At swank soirees where senseless lavishness
Can trick the eye, infantilize the mind.
Let's ponder his discourse together. Lunch
Can wait. You may well ask "Why so?" Attend.   10
I'll do my best to help you understand.

Every judge who's taken bribes will badly
Weigh the truth. A man exhausted, either
From hunting hares or by a stubborn horse,
Or one accustomed to a Greek lifestyle—   15
Who's quite worn out by Roman army drills—
The sports enthusiast who's having too
Much fun to think that playing ball is work;
You like the discus? Hurl it then—but once

The sweat has made you less fastidious   20
About the food you eat, just see if you
Turn up your nose at simple fare, or think
That only sweet aperitifs can slake
Your burning thirst. The butler's gone. The fish
You hoped to eat swims safe in wintry seas.   25
So feed your growling stomach bread and salt.
You'd be surprised how well a modest meal
Can satisfy. The greatest pleasure comes
Not from some rich aroma. No, it's found
Within you. Working out is appetite's   30
Best condiment. So sweat a little. Oysters,
Exotic fish, imported fowl are lost
On someone stuffed and pasty from binge eating.
Yet once the peacock's served, it's all I can do
To rescue you: you want the peacock; chicken's   35
Not good enough to tickle *your* taste buds.
Vanity perverts your better judgment.
The presentation dazzles you, the cost
Is wickedly delicious. What's the point?
You can't consume those plumes. This bird so rare,   40
When cooked, looks plain and tastes like chicken.
Well, let it pass that you want one and not
The other based on nothing else but looks.
What evidence has proved to you that this
Bass was caught at sea or in the Tiber,   45
Swimming up between the bridges or near
The Tuscan river's mouth? You lunatic—
You praise that mullet's bulk (three pounds!) but still
Must cut it up in individual servings.
I see you're led by looks. Then why have such   50
Contempt for long-back bass? It must be that
The bass is *naturally* long, the mullet small:
A well-fed belly scorns the ordinary.
Your Harpy appetite proclaims it'd like
A big fish filling up a giant dish.   55
Come, south winds, blow and taint their fancy feast.
In fact, the boar and turbot, however fresh,
Already stink—for overindulgence cloys:
Stomachs worried sick want elecampine

Or radishes. At feasts, the rich still serve   60
What poor folks live on: inexpensive eggs,
Black olives too. It wasn't long ago
Gallonius, the auctioneer, became
Notorious for serving sturgeon. Why?
Did oceans feed far fewer turbots then?   65
That fish in fact was safe from fishing nets
And baby storks slept safe within their nests
Until a praetor taught you what to crave.
Should someone now decree that roasted gull
Is haute cuisine, the Roman youth, so quick   70
To learn depravity, would order gull.
Ofellus knows the difference separating
Frugalness from living like a miser.
So don't cut off your nose to spite your face.
Avidienus, nicknamed "Dog" because   75
He acts like one, eats olives five years old
And cornel berries from the woods. He's not
About to open wine before it's turned.
You couldn't stand his olive oil—the smell!
When gussied up to celebrate a wedding,   80
A birthday, or another special day,
He himself must pour the oil in driblets
From some two-gallon jug to dress the cabbage;
He's liberal with the ancient vinegar.
Which lifestyle would the wise man follow? Which   85
Man would be his model? As the saying
Has it: one's caught between a wolf and dog.
The wise man is refined, but just enough
To stave off boorishness; he wouldn't be
Unhappy either way. He's not sadistic   90
Like old Albucius when assigning slaves
Their tasks, nor lax like Naevius, whose guests
Must wash their hands in greasy water bowls.
Such social blunders aren't inconsequential.
But now attend to how it profits you   95
To have a simple diet. The benefits
Are quite extraordinary. Health is top
On the list. You surely know the damage
A smorgasbord can do to good digestion.

Remember how the other day you ate   100
A simple snack and how you felt terrific?
A combination plate of roast and stew
Or thrushes chased by oysters turn the stomach
Into a battlefield. Delicious tastes are churned
To bile and in your stomach phlegm brings strife.   105
Chimera meals like this make people sick.
What's even worse, your body, clogged with food
From yesterday's excess, drags down the soul
And nails that mote of heaven's breath to earth.
Another man, no sooner said than done,   110
Has exercised his legs and arms, enjoyed
A good night's sleep, and wakes at dawn's first light,
Refreshed to meet his daily tasks. He can,
However, splurge some times on holidays.
He's not against a little pampering   115
When illness leaves him weak and thin, and when
The years catch up with him, he's quite prepared
To give his feeble body tender care.
But what of you? You're running through your quota
Of self-indulgence as if there's no tomorrow.   120
You're strong today, but what if sickness hits
You suddenly? You won't be young forever.
In bygone days the Romans praised
The taste of boar gone off. Their noses worked.
I guess our ancestors believed that guests   125
Who might arrive a little late deserved
A serving, even if the meat was spoiled.
A host who gobbled up the whole boar fresh
They thought epitomized bad form. I wish
I'd lived when earth was young and men were men.   130
Does reputation register with you?
It plays more sweetly in our ears than song.
That turbot's big enough to feed an army.
The cost alone would make a sane man gag.
Your uncle's mad, the neighbors look askance.   135
You hate yourself, but can't afford the rope
To end your wretched life. To this he says,
"It's Trausius you should be hectoring.
My revenues and wealth can amply match

Three kings'." Then surely you could spend your big   140
Reserves more wisely. Why are you so rich
While worthy people live in poverty?
The ancient temples stand in ruins. Where is
Your sense of patriotism, selfish man?
Give something to your country. You're rich enough.   145
You think that you alone are Fortune's pet?
Your enemies will laugh at you one day.
When bad luck strikes, which type of person shows
More confidence? The man whose sense of self-
Entitlement swells head and body, or   150
The wise and frugal man, who fears the future,
And gathers war reserves in times of peace?

You'll give these words more credence once
You've heard about Ofellus. I've known him
Since boyhood: frugal then as frugal now   155
When harder times have left him less to spare.
Surveyors took his farm. A tenant now,
He, his sons, and livestock work that land.
You'd hear him say, "Most working days I ate
No more than garden greens and smoked ham hock.   160
But if a friend I hadn't seen for years
Showed up or if the rain prevented me
From doing chores, and welcomed neighbors called,
Then we enjoyed ourselves—not eating fish
Brought from Rome, but roasted kid and chicken.   165
Some nuts, split figs, and raisins made dessert.
Then afterwards we'd play some drinking games
But didn't follow formal rules. We prayed
To Ceres, 'Make the grain grow tall this year!'
And she empowered the wine with magic charms   170
To loosen care's tight grip on wrinkled brows.
Let Fortune storm and bring new troubles all
She wants. There's nothing here for her to steal.
You see, my sons, how far we've been reduced
In worldly goods since property changed hands.   175
Consider this, however. Land is held
In usufruct. No landlord really owns
His real estate. The man who drove us out

One day will find himself evicted by
His own unbridled waste or ignorance   180
Of tricky laws or, barring that, his heir
Will take it all away. Umbrenus has
It now. Ofellus used to call it his.
The earth is time-shared. So live, have courage,
And bravely meet adversity head on."   185

SATIRE 2.3

DAMASIPPUS: "You write so rarely now, that one whole year
Has passed without so much as four requests
For parchment. Why, you're actually unstitching
The stuff you've written, angry at yourself
For sleeping late and drinking much too much,   5
And then, for not producing any verse
Worth speaking of. What's happening? You left
Town sober, fleeing Saturnalia.
Now make your promise good: let's hear some verse.
No use, is it? So pointless putting blame   10
On those reed pens of yours. The wall you're pounding
Is innocent and built to stand the spite
Of angry gods and bards. You had the look
Of one who threatens great achievements if
He had a cozy lodge and time enough.   15
What point in packing Plato, Eupolis,
Menander, and Archilochus, and dragging
Them all the way out here for company?
It's too late now to abdicate your talent
In hopes of making folks resent you less.   20
They'll only think the worst of you for that.
You have a choice: avoid the Siren call
Of laziness, or be resolved to lose
Whatever fame you earned in better times."
HORACE: "For that good council, Damasippus, may   25
All the gods reward you with a barber.
But how'd you come to know me this well?"
DAMASIPPUS: "Since
All my assets crashed at the Stock Exchange,

I haven't anything my own to run,
And so I tend to other men's affairs.   30
There was a time I really loved my work:
Inquiring whether wily Sisyphus
Had used a certain bronze receptacle
To wash his feet. My eye was quick to spot
A sculptor's shoddy work or stiff technique   35
In casting bronze; my expertise let me
Appraise a statue worth a hundred thousand.
In high-end real estate I sold more homes
And gardens profitably than anyone.
In fact, I got the name of 'Mercury's man'   40
At busy junctions all around the town."
HORACE: "I know, and marvel more at how you purged
Yourself of money's ills. But still it's funny
How that disorder metamorphosed into
A new dysfunction, just as when a headache   45
Or chest pain moves into the stomach or when
A patient, after a long depression, turns
Manic suddenly and pummels his doctor.
Do as you please, but don't behave like that."
DAMASIPPUS: "Dear man, don't kid yourself. You're quite insane. 50
Yes, you and well nigh all the other fools
Around the world, if what Stertinius
Rattles on about is right. So eager
To learn, I scribbled down his maxims. How
Profound they were! He comforted me that day   55
And gave me these commands: to cultivate
A sage's beard and leave Fabricius' bridge
A happy man. You see, I really thought
That suicide was how to deal with failure.
I'd veiled my head, prepared to throw myself   60
Into the river, when, by sheer good luck,
He happened by. 'You better not,' he said,
'Do anything undignified. The sense
Of worthlessness that's strangling you right now
Is really counterfeit. Why fear the threat   65
Of madmen calling *you* insane? Let me
First clarify what madness is. If it
Turns out to be uniquely found in you,

I'll shut my mouth and let you die a man.
Chrysippus and all the Stoic flock maintain   70
That when a person's driven blind through life
By ignorance of what is real and put
At risk by folly, then that person's "mad."
This definition holds across all ranks,
From mighty kings to commoners. The one   75
Exception is the sage. Now understand
Why folks who call you mad are fools themselves.
It's like what happens in the woods. Sometimes
Miscalculations make men lose their way.
They wander off the path. Some turn off right,   80
Some left. Yet though they cover different ground,
They're all alike in being lost. Don't think
You're more insane than those deriding you.
They're not so wise; they've dragging tails behind.
One kind of lunatic imagines things   85
To fear. He whines that rivers, fire, and cliffs
Block his way. The ground, in fact, is level.
Another kind, quite different but just as mad,
You can't hold back from plunging in a flood
Or holocaust. His own dear mother tries   90
To save the fool. His lovely sister tries.
His father, wife, and other relatives
All shout, "Be careful! Don't you see how deep
That ditch is? How precipitous that cliff?"
To no avail. The man's as unresponsive   95
As Fufius, the drunken actor, when
He played Iliona and missed his cue.
Twelve hundred voices joined Catienus
In shouting "Mother, hark!"—to no avail.
Let me show you how the general public   100
Behaves in much the same unbalanced way.
Damasippus madly buys old statues.
The man who lends this guy the cash is sane?
Be that as it may. What if I said, "Here, take
This money. Never pay it back." Would you   105
Be nuts to take the cash or more insane
For passing up a gift from Mercury?
Write a loan agreement: *Nerius lends*

10,000. Still not secure enough. Use
Cicuta's tamper-proof accounting books.   110
Then add a hundred . . . no, a thousand bonds.
The crook still slips these chains as easily
As Proteus, and laughs throughout his trial,
One minute turning into a boar, the next
A bird or rock, and, when he likes, a tree.   115
If being incompetent is proof you're mad,
And competent, you're sane, then take my word,
Perellius, your brain has lost a screw:
The loans you make can never be repaid.

Come and listen. Straighten out your toga.   120
Any one of you who's sick from vicious
Ambition, pale from greed or feverish
From superstition's woes or some other
Mental illness—gather round and listen
How each and every one of you is mad.   125
The biggest dose of hellebore must go
For people diagnosed with avarice.
Perhaps they'll need Anticyra's whole crop.
Staberius' heirs inscribed upon
His tomb the sum of what he'd left them. Had   130
They not, his will required that they cough up
The cost of entertaining all of Rome:
One hundred pairs of gladiators plus
A public feast (arranged by Arrius)
Requiring all the grain of Africa.   135
"No matter if I'm right or wrong," he'd told
His heirs, "don't act the outraged uncle part."
Staberius, I think, quite shrewdly knew
What he was doing. So why did he insist
They set in stone his total patrimony?   140
Throughout his life the man thought poverty
A monumental fault. He fought it off
At any cost. For had he died one cent
Less wealthy, he'd have thought himself so much
More worthless. "Everything—the excellent,   145
Esteem, the beautiful, both human and
Immortal things, must yield to wealth in all

Its loveliness. The man who's made great wealth
Will rank among the famous, brave, the just . . ."
"But would you call him 'wise'?" "Of course, and he's   150
A king. This man is what he wants to be."
Staberius thus hoped that wealth might win
For him the great respectability
Honest merit earns. Did Aristippus,
The Greek philosopher, do anything   155
Resembling this when he in Libya
Told his slaves to drop the gold they carried?
Its weight, he said, was hampering their progress.
Which one of these two men is more insane?
Null point: one riddle can't clear up another.   160
If some collector bought a lot of lyres,
But didn't like the lyre or music much;
If someone bought a cobbler's knife and lasts
But didn't make a shoe; if he despised
The shipping trade, but handled sailing gear,   165
I'd wager people everywhere would say,
And rightly too, the guy was off his rocker.
So what about the man who's locked away
His cash. He hasn't a clue what money's for;
Afraid to even touch the hallowed coins.   170
You see much difference? Imagine now
A man spread out beside a giant heap
Of grain. He's ever vigilant and armed,
A hefty cudgel at his side. He owns
This grain, and yet, when hunger gnaws at him,   175
He dare not eat one bite of it; instead,
Economizing, he eats bitter herbs.
What if his cellar stored a thousand—no,
Say three hundred thousand—bottles of Chian
And old Falernian, yet he insisted   180
On drinking nasty vinegar? Suppose
A man approaching eighty bedded down
On straw when in his linen closet moths
Were feasting on fine bedclothes? Few, of course,
Would think him mad: most people toss and turn   185
In just the same delirium. You old
God-forsaken fool! Your son and freedman

(You made them heirs) will guzzle all your wine.
You're guarding it for them. Or is it fear
Of poverty that makes you tight? Consider   190
How little capital it'd take each day
To purchase decent oil for salad dressing
And basic hygiene needs. Your hair's a mess!
Now if you really think that less is more,
Why perjure yourself, why swindle folks and steal   195
Each chance you get? You call that sane behavior?
If you had started throwing stones at folks
Or stoned the slaves you paid good money for,
Then every boy and girl would shout "He's mad."
When you garrote your wife and poison mom,   200
You keep your head? Why not? This isn't Argos;
You're not unhinged Orestes—didn't use
A sword. Perhaps you really think Orestes
Lost his mind *because* he killed his mother;
That only after blood had warmed his blade   205
And gruesome Furies hounded him, he snapped.
The opposite, in fact, was true. The while
That people thought his mental health was slipping,
He never did a thing to warrant blame:
He didn't dare to murder Pylades   210
Or knife his sister. All he did was stab
The two with words. He shouted "Fury" at
Electra; black depression made him hurl
Another hurtful word at Pylades.
Then there's Opimius, that poor rich man.   215
On holidays he drank a plain Veientine
And used a cheap Campanian-ware ladle.
On other days he drank a really bad
Excuse for wine. When he began to fail,
His heir, quite overjoyed, went running for   220
The safe deposit boxes, key in hand.
The fellow's staunch physician acted quickly:
He had a table brought in, ordered bags
Of coins poured out, told several men to count
The total. *That* woke up Optimius.   225
"Take care," the doctor said. "An eager heir
Will soon be rich." "Not while I'm still alive!"

"Well, if you want to live, you better be
More vigilant. Now pay attention." "What
Do you advise?" "Your blood is thin; you're weak.   230
You've got to eat to fortify your stomach—
It's shutting down. Why hesitate? Why not
Just take this broth of boiled basmati rice."
"What'd that cost?" "Not much." "How much exactly?"
"Eight *asses*." "Dear me. What's the difference?   235
Death by highway robbery or sickness!"
Who then is sane? The man who's not a fool.
But what about the greedy man? A fool
Gone mad. But does it follow then that folks
Who aren't the greedy type are sane? Oh, no.   240
Dear Stoic, why is that? I'll tell you why.
Imagine Craterus is diagnosing
A patient: "I'd rule out dyspepsia."
"You mean he isn't sick?" "I didn't say that."
["The problem," Craterus replies, "is in   245
The lungs or kidneys. It's quite serious."]
He's not a perjurer, he's not a miser.
Then let him sacrifice a pig and thank
His easy Lares. But say ambition makes
Him reckless. Pack him off to Anticyra.   250
Is there in fact much difference if you throw
The stuff you own into a deep abyss
Or never use whatever's right at hand?
They say that Servius Oppidius,
A rich man by old-fashioned standards, split   255
The property he owned at Canusium
Between his sons. He summoned both of them
As he lay dying. "Aulus, ever since
The time I saw you stuffing knucklebones
And nuts into your tunic's baggy folds,   260
I watched you gamble, lose and give away.
Tiberius, I watched you too add up
And grimly squirrel away the stuff you owned.
I really feared that both of you were mad
In opposite extremes; that one of you   265
Would be another Nomentanus; one
A new Cicuta. Boys, I'm asking you,

Before the gods who guard our house and home,
Don't add a jot, Tiberius; and Aulus,
Don't you subtract from what your father deems   270
To be enough and Nature circumscribes.
And furthermore, I want you both to swear
You'll never let vainglory wind you up
To run for office. If either one of you
Becomes an aedile or praetor, cursed be   275
His name, and let his word be null and void."
You'd waste a fortune, doling out chickpeas,
Lupines, and beans to play the politician
Who preens and promenades around the Circus
And has his figure cast in bronze. For this,   280
You lunatic, you've stripped yourself of all
The land and cash your father saved for you.
You really think that you, a wily fox,
Can masquerade as noble lion and win
The sort of accolades Agrippa earns?   285
O son of Atreus, you interdict
The burial of Ajax? Why is that?
"Because I'm king." Well, I, a commoner,
Won't question you. "My orders are judicious.
If anyone thinks me unjust, I give   290
Him leave to speak." O greatest king of kings,
I pray the gods will let you capture Troy
And bring the fleet back home. Permission, please,
To question you and hear how you respond.
"Proceed." Why Ajax, second to Achilles?   295
He saved the Greeks so often, won great fame.
Why leave his corpse unburied, rotting here?
Is it to make the people Priam rules
And Priam too rejoice at seeing one
Who kept so many sons from finding rest   300
In their ancestral tombs lie here exposed?
"The man was mad. He brought death down upon
A thousand sheep, while shouting he'd killed renowned
Ulysses, Menelaus, and me!" But you,
When *you* at Aulis forced your own sweet daughter   305
To take the heifer's place and sprinkled her head
With spelt-meal mixed with salt before the altar,

Did reason guide your hand, you shameless man?
Did Ajax, mad enough to murder sheep,
Lift up his sword against his wife and boy?   310
Though Ajax cursed the sons of Atreus,
Did Teucer suffer harm? Ulysses hurt?
"But I rescued my fleet held fast at that
Unpropitious beach. Life's blood, I reasoned,
Would satisfy the gods." It was *your* own blood,   315
You madman! "Yes, my own; but I'm not mad."
The man imagining things, mistaking false
For true, disoriented in a fog
Of crime, is judged unsteady, whether it's
Stupidity or rage that's hijacked him.   320
Ajax lost it when he started killing
Those unblameworthy lambs. Now you, to win
An empty title, carry out a crime
With cool deliberation. Who'd contend
That's normal? Is your heart, engorged with pride,   325
So free from fault? Suppose a person loved
To take his cute pet lamb for litter rides,
And dressed the thing in gowns, just like a daughter,
Gave it golden finery, and servants,
Named the animal Posilla or Rufa   330
And planned to marry it to some fine husband:
A judge would intervene and strip that man
Of all his legal rights and put him under
The guardianship of stable relatives.
Well, if a person chose to sacrifice   335
His daughter rather than a lamb, is he
Compos mentis? Now, please don't say he is.
When foolishness turns dark, there looms the height
Of madness. Criminals are lunatics.
Blood-glad Bellona thunders all around   340
The man bedazzling fame has hypnotized.
It's time we take Extravagance to court
And Nomentanus, prince of profligates.
For Reason demonstrates that wasting wealth
Is tantamount to being dumb *and* nuts.   345
This man was left a thousand talents. Right
Away he made a public proclamation:

"Fishmongers, dealers in fruit, perfume, and birds,
You godless riffraff haunting Tuscan Street,
You poultrymen, panhandlers, everyone   350
Who hustles at the produce stalls and on
Velabrum street—come dawn, be at my house."
Well, they came in droves. A pimp spoke for all:
"Whatever, sir, is ours is yours. Just place
Your order now or, if you choose, tomorrow."   355
The equitable young man replied: "*You* pulled
On heavy boots and slept outdoors in snowy
Lucania so I could feast on boar.
You trawl the wintry seas to harvest fish.
I'm busy being lazy, hardly fit   360
To have so much. Enough! Here, take a million.
You get a million too. For you (your wife
Makes house calls late at night), let's triple it."
Aesopus' son decided he could drink
A fortune worth one million in one gulp: 365
He took the stunning pearl Metella wore
In her ear and liquefied the treasure
By dropping it in vinegar. Could he
Have acted more insane if he had flung
That pearl into a cataract or sewer?   370
Or take the sons of Quintus Arrius,
Those brothers people talk about, a pair
Of slackers, frivolous, and quite perverse
In what they like. They lunch on nightingales
Procured at untold cost. What category   375
Do they belong in? Can we chalk them up
As sane or must we mark their names in black?
If building little houses, hitching mice
To wagons, playing games like odds and evens,
Or riding hobby horses fascinates   380
A person old enough to sport a beard,
There's clearly something out of whack in him.
If logic demonstrates that being in love
Is far more juvenile than childish games;
That shedding tears of love for prostitutes   385
Amounts to acting like you're three again
And playing in the sand, then answer this:

Are you prepared to follow Polemon
Into rehab and cast off everything
That marks your illness—stockings, scarves,   390
Plush pillows—like, they say, Polemon did
When, called out by a teacher's stern rebukes,
He sobered up and tore the garlands off
His neck and hoped that none had seen him drunk.
You hand some sulky kid a piece of fruit.   395
The kid's not interested. Try coaxing him.
"Just try it." No, he won't. Of course, he'd want
It if it wasn't offered. How, I ask,
Are lovers different? When the woman's door
Is locked, the lover argues with himself: 400
Should he go back or not? He'd planned to go.
But then she didn't ask. He haunts the door
He's come to hate. "What if she asks me now?
I better go. But maybe ending all
My pain right now is best. She locked me out.   405
She calls me back. Should I go back to her?
Not even if she begged me on her knees!"
The clever slave appears. "When something, Master,
Has neither rhyme nor reason, then it won't
Be made to follow rules or measurements.   410
In Love, these evils coexist: there's war,
Then peace again. Blind chance sets them in motion,
Loose and unpredictable as weather.
If someone tried to organize this storm
For his advantage, he'd no more succeed   415
Than if he tried methodically to lose
His sanity." Now tell me this: when you
Shoot Picenian apple seeds and shout
With joy because one hits the vaulted ceiling,
Are you self-possessed? Do you really think   420
It less insane for thirty-something men
To coo in baby talk than build toy houses?
Add violence to folly—take your sword
And poke the fire. Was Marius insane
When he killed Hellas recently and threw   425
Himself off a roof? But then, maybe you,
Instead of finding him insane, would call

His action criminal. For people use
Related terms in designating things.
A certain freedman once upon a time,   430
An old man, washed his hands and ran around
To all the cross-road shrines to pray at dawn
(He hadn't touched the bottle): "Rescue me from death!
It isn't much," he told the gods, "to save
Just me. That's easy work for gods." This man   435
Had working ears and eyes. As for his mind,
No master would have certified him sane
At time of sale, unless he loved a lawsuit.
Chrysippus groups this crowd of fools among
Menenius' prolific family.   440
"O Jupiter, you give and take away
Huge sorrows," says the mom whose son has spent
Five months in bed. "If only he will stop
This shivering, I'll have him stand at dawn
In the Tiber naked on your fast day."   445
By sheer good luck or doctoring, the boy
Recovers. Mad, his mother murders him:
On Tiber's freezing shore, the fever comes
Back. What evil wrecked her mind? Religion.'"

These words Stertinius, the eighth wise man,   450
In friendship gave to me and armed me well.
Henceforth, if I'm attacked, I'll get revenge.
Whoever calls me mad, will hear the same
Thrown back at him and maybe then he'll learn
To recognize what's hanging from his rear."   455
HORACE: "Well, Stoic, best of luck in selling off
At profit all that's left post bankruptcy.
I know that folly manifests itself
In several ways, so please explain what form
Of nonsense makes me rave? I seem quite sane."   460
DAMASIPPUS: "Did Agave know that she was crazy
The day she ripped apart her luckless son
And carried off his severed head?"
HORACE: "Okay,
I confess I'm foolish, even crazy,
But help me understand what mental flaw   465

Is making me so ill."
DAMASIPPUS: "Then listen. First
Of all, your building plans. A midget two
Feet tall from head to toe, you try to do
What truly big men do. And *you* can mock
How Turbo, once he's armed, acts way too big   470
To fit his body? *You* are less absurd?
You think it's perfectly okay to act
Just like Maecenas, when in fact you're so
Not him? You're way too small to play his game.
One day a mother frog was off somewhere.   475
A calf stepped on her young. Just one survived
And told his mother how a monster squashed
His siblings. She began to puff herself up.
'Was this how large the creature was?' she asked.
'No. Bigger by half.' 'This big?' she asked again,   480
Still puffing even more. And as she kept
On getting bigger, 'Blow until you burst,'
The youngster said, 'You still can't get that large.'
This picture comes quite close to pegging you.
Now throw your poems in as well: more oil   485
To fuel the fire. Was any poet sane?
If any were, you are. I'll not bring up
Your terrific temper."
HORACE: "Stop already!"
DAMASIPPUS: "The way you live quite far beyond your means."
HORACE: "Damasippus, mind your own damn business."   490
DAMASIPPUS: "Lovesick for girls and boys two thousand-fold."
HORACE: "Your royal Madness, spare a common fool!"

SATIRE 2.4

HORACE: "Where, Catius, have you been? Where to . . . ?"
CATIUS: "No time!
I've heard some things I really must write down.
The latest philosophical precepts.
This stuff transcends Pythagoras, the man
Anytus indicted, *and* wise Plato!"   5
HORACE: "I'm sorry now I troubled you. My fault

Entirely. Please, excuse my breaking in.
But don't fret about forgetting something.
Your memory's phenomenal. A gift,
I'd guess. Or did you work at training it?"   10
CATIUS: "I'm wondering how I'll ever keep in mind
Everything I heard. The subject matter
Is intricate, and intricate the style."
HORACE: "What's the teacher's name? From Rome or elsewhere?"
CATIUS: "I'll sing his precepts now from memory.   15
His name, however, must be left unsaid.

When serving eggs, remember oblong ones
Have better taste than round; their whites are whiter.
These eggs are strong and firm and have male yolks.
Dry soil will grow a sweeter cabbage. Closer   20
To town, the over-irrigated plots
Produce washed-out and tasteless vegetables.
Should someone unexpectedly drop by
One evening, drown the roasting hen in wine:
This trick will tenderize the toughest bird.   25
Outstanding mushrooms grow in meadowlands;
One shouldn't put much trust in other kinds.
The man who ends his lunch with black mulberries
(They must be picked before the sun gets hot)
Enjoys good health right through the summer heat.   30
Aufidius took honey mixed with strong
Falernian. That wasn't smart. Take care
That nothing potent fills your empty veins.
A light, sweet wine works best to cleanse the stomach.
For constipation, eat some ocean mussels.   35
Cheap shellfish also open up the blockage.
Low-growing sorrel works as well, but don't
Forget to serve with wine from Cos—the white.
A waxing moon plumps out the slimy shellfish.
Not every sea, however, grows the finest.   40
The Lucrine clam beats Baiae's best. Circeii
Has oysters; get sea urchins at Misenum.
Posh Tarentum boasts its broad-shelled scallops.
Let no one rashly claim he's got the art
Of dining well until he thoroughly   45

Has mastered all the subtle grades of taste.
One trawls the most expensive shops for fish
But hasn't learned which one is best with sauce
And which, if nicely grilled, can get the bored
Dinner guest back up upon his elbow.   50
One won't get tasteless meat, enjoying boar
From Umbria, so fat from holm-oak acorns
It bows the big, round dish. Laurentian pig
Is trash meat—fed on reeds and marshy sedge.
The vine-fed deer can be inedible.   55
The epicure who knows his hare will choose
A pregnant one and only eat the forelegs.
The natural properties and proper age
In fish and fowl had been a mystery
Until my palate set the record straight.   60
Some have gifts for making novel pastries
But nothing else. It's quite inadequate
Exhausting all your efforts on one thing.
Suppose someone makes sure the wine is good,
But soaks the fish in cut-rate olive oil?   65
Set Massic wine out under cloudless skies:
The evening air will thin its heaviness;
The harmful odor disappears as well.
To strain the wine through linen spoils the taste.
The expert adds Falernian lees to light   70
Surrentine wine, then drops a pigeon egg
Into the jar to gather all the dregs.
(The sinking yolk attracts the sediment.)
You'll bring a heavy drinker back to life
With African snails and grilled prawns. Lettuce sits   75
On an acidy stomach undigested
When eaten after wine. An appetite
Once piqued wants ham or sausage. Better yet,
Get something hot from any fast-food joint.
It's worth your while to master recipes   80
For complex sauces. Cold-pressed olive oil
Is where you start. Add undiluted wine
And mix with brine (the pungent stuff the fish
Shipped from Byzantium come packed in). Then
Some herbs (chopped fine), and boil. A pinch of choice   85

Corycian saffron. Now it needs to stand.
The final touch: Venafran olive oil.
Tibur apples can't surpass Picenum's
In flavor, though they look as if they could.
Venuculan grapes are best preserved in jars.   90
Best to dry your Alban grapes by smoking.
I invented serving these with apples.
You'll also find that I initiated putting
Fish paste and wine lees out together; I
First as well to set out cute saltcellars   95
Containing fine white pepper *and* black salt.
It's grossly wrong to drop three thousand at
A shop, then make an ocean-roaming fish
Fit some narrow dish. It turns one's stomach
When slaves, who've stolen licks and nibbled where   100
They shouldn't, serve guests wine in glasses smeared
With greasy fingerprints, or if a thick
Deposit's built up on an old wine bowl.
A broom, some mats, and sawdust—how expensive
Can these be? Skimp on basics, pay the cost   105
In large-scale shame. Imagine sweeping fine
Mosaic floors with some disgusting broom!
Or Tyrian couch covers with valances
No one's ever washed! Have you forgotten:
Neglecting simple, inexpensive things   110
Is less excusable than not providing
What the rich can serve their guests at dinner."

HORACE: "My learned Catius, please, for friendship's sake
And by the gods, remember me next time
You're going to a lecture—take me too.   115
It's nice to hear from memory the whole
Of what you heard, yet still it's not the same
As hearing it firsthand. I didn't get
To read his face or sense the man's gestalt.
You did and take for granted what I missed.   120
I have this great desire to find the source,
No matter what the distance. There I'll drink
What wisdom knows of human happiness."

SATIRE 2.5

ULYSSES: "One thing more, Tiresias. Just tell me
What stratagems, what wiles will get me back
The property I've lost. What . . . what's so funny?"
TIRESIAS: "So, our cunning hero thinks that sailing
To Ithaca and seeing once again   5
His own Penates isn't quite enough?"
ULYSSES: "You've lied to no one. You, the prophet, see
Me returning destitute and naked;
A pack of suitors meanwhile hasn't left
A cask of wine or cattle herd untouched.   10
The fact is, lineage and character,
Minus cash, aren't worth a sack of seaweed."
TIRESIAS: "In plain terms, you're scared stiff of poverty.
Well, here's a method sure to make you rich.
Let's say you're given a thrush or something else   15
You like. Regift it. Send it off to nest
Where wealth lights up an old man's house. Sweet fruit
Or other gems your well-run farm produces
Be sure to give the tycoon first; the Lar
Can wait. Magnates are more revered than Lares.   20
Don't let his perjury, his lack of breeding,
The stain of fratricide, the fact that he's
A runaway slave, prevent your joining him
On public outings every time he asks;
And take the traffic side, escorting him."   25
ULYSSES: "I'm supposed to shield the flank of some . . . some
Disgusting Dama! I didn't act like that
At Troy. I've always vied with better men."
TIRESIAS: "You can, of course, continue being poor."
ULYSSES: "Okay. Buck up, brave heart. You've weathered worse. 30
Now, seer, tell me where the money is.
Tell me how to rake it in."
TIRESIAS: "I've told you;
I'm telling you: be cunning. Hunt the old
Everywhere for legacies. Don't despair
If one or two are sly enough to nosh the bait,   35
Unhooked. Outsmarted, don't forsake this craft.
When lawsuits, large or small, come up, defend
The richer litigant who has no kids,

However bad and shameless he may be
In hauling better men to court. Turn down   40
The reputable citizen, however just
His lawsuit, if he's got a son or if
His wife's still fertile. Talk to him like this:
'Publius,' or 'Quintus' (thin-skinned ears just
Love how nice a first name sounds), 'your virtue   45
Itself has made me love you like a friend.
I know how double-headed law can be.
I'm more than competent at pleading cases.
Should anyone try treating you with scorn
Or making you one nutshell poorer, first   50
Let him rip out my eyes! My job will be
To see that you're not screwed or made a joke.'
Send him home; tell him to take it easy.
Take over defending him. Don't yield an inch
However red the Dog Star glows and makes   55
The speechless statues crack, and Furius,
Stuffed full of tripe, 'spews snow 'cross wintry Alps.'
Then some will nudge their neighbors, 'Don't you see
How patient he can be, how true to friends,
How sharp.' The tuna run; your fishponds fill.   60
And furthermore, let's say a sickly son
Has been acknowledged by his father and
Is being reared in luxury—don't miss
This chance to camouflage your blatant way
Of sucking up to bachelors: just worm   65
In among the beneficiaries
With hopes of being second to the son,
Or, should some accident dispatch the boy
To Orcus, you're already next in line.
It's very rare this gamble disappoints.   70
If someone offers you his will to read,
Refuse and make a fuss of pushing it
Away. But sneak a sidelong glance at what
The second line on page one stipulates.
One quick look will tell if you're another   75
Joint heir or if you stand to get it all.
Frequently a clerk, who started out half-
Baked in minor posts, will trick the raven.

Coranus mocks Nasica chasing wills."
ULYSSES: "You're raving mad. Or are you mocking me   80
With all this hocus-pocus?"
TIRESIAS: "What I say,
Laertes' son, will come to be or not.
Great Apollo's gift made me a prophet."
ULYSSES: "Then why not tell me what you're getting at!"
TIRESIAS: "The day when Parthia will quail before   85
A youth, high-born Aeneas' heir, great
On land and sea, Nasica, apprehensive
At what it'll cost to settle all his debts,
Will give in marriage to the fine Coranus
His tall and stately daughter. Then the man's   90
New son-in-law will do the following: first,
Produce his will, then bid Nasica read it.
The man begs off repeatedly. At last
He reads in silence, fully taking in
That he and his get only lots of grief.   95
Another tip: suppose some scheming dame
Or freedman has a senile fool completely
In their power. Make common cause. Commend them
To him, and they'll return the favor when
You're not there. This strategy works wonders,   100
But better still: besiege the old man's heart.
He's nuts and writes god-awful verse: applaud.
He's into prostitutes: don't make him ask;
Insist that he, the better man, enjoy
Penelope."
ULYSSES: "You think I've got a hope   105
Of working as her pimp? The suitors couldn't
Drive *her* from virtue's path. She's way too good."
TIRESIAS: "Those youngsters didn't come with big enough
Gifts; besides, for them, the food beat Venus.
That's why Penelope stayed true. But once   110
You two team up and she has tasted just
A bit of sugar daddy, she'll be like
A hound who won't let go its greasy bone.
I'll tell you something else. It happened back
In Thebes when I was on in years. An evil   115
Old woman had it in her will that at

The funeral her heir must carry her
Corpse richly oiled upon his naked shoulder.
In death she hoped to give that guy the slip.
I guess he hounded her in life. Take care   120
In how you go about it. Don't hold back
Too much or overplay your helpfulness.
The difficult and peevish sort don't like
A chatterbox. Beyond a 'no' or 'yes,'
Keep quiet. Play the comic role of Davus,   125
Your head bent down like someone used to fear.
Waylay the man with your subservience.
On breezy days, insist he take precautions
And cover his head. In crowds, push a way
Through for him. The times he feels like talking,   130
Strain your ears. Is he a glutton for praise?
Then don't stop puffing up his bulging ego
With long, long-winded compliments until
He lifts his hands to heaven, crying 'please!'
The day he sets you free from your long years   135
Of servitude and care, and wide awake
You hear: 'Ulysses gets a quarter share,'
Then, let people catch you saying, 'Dama,
My good friend, is no more?' And 'Where can I
Find again such constancy and courage!'   140
And now, a tear or two (if you can squeeze
Some out) would help to mask the happiness
Your face betrays. As for the monument:
If you're in charge of this detail, don't scrimp.
Let the neighbors know you're good at funerals.   145
Should any fellow heir, who's older, get
A nasty cough, tell him how pleased you'd be
To let him have the house or farm from your
Share for next to nothing . . . but Proserpina
Is yanking at my chain. Go live. Farewell."   150

SATIRE 2.6

I prayed for this: a farmstead not too large,
A garden plot, a spring that's never dry
Near the house, and just a bit of woodland.
The gods delivered more than what I dreamed.
I'm happy, Mercury, and ask for nothing   5
Except for you to make my blessings last.
If I've not made my wealth dishonestly
Nor rush to waste it through extravagance—
If I'm not one to utter foolish prayers
Like "Why can't my neighbor's corner acre,   10
Which now deforms my little farm, be mine!"
Or "Why can't I get lucky and stumble on
A pot of silver, like the man who found
A treasure, bought the land, and plowed the field
He'd worked for wages: praised be Hercules!"   15
If I'm content and grateful for what's mine,
Hear my prayer, O son of Maia: fatten
My flocks and all I'm master of, but not
My head. Protector, be my strongest guard.

I've left the city, reached the distant hills,   20
My pastoral citadel. What better place
For satire's Muse on foot to celebrate!
No burdensome ambitions crush me now,
No thick sirocco, nor autumnal heat
That makes the undertakers rich in Rome.   25
Father, god of morning's light! O Janus,
If that name please you more—humanity,
As gods decree, begins the day's first work
With you. Begin with me my song. At Rome
You rush me off to testify in court: 30
"Come on! Don't let another get there first."
The north wind scours the land and winter's short
Snow-blown days get even shorter—still, off
I go. And once I've sworn some affidavit
(To haunt me later on), I'm forced to wrestle   35
My way through crowds and bodily harm the slow.
"What's your problem, idiot?" some loser
Cries out at me with angry curses, "Go

Ahead and run us over, if you're minding
Your Maecenas and dashing back to him!"   40
How sweet this sounds to me I can't deny.
But once I reach the doleful Esquiline
I'm swarmed from every side; a hundred chores
Not my own become my headache: "Roscius
Wants you bright and early at the Puteal."   45
"Reminder: new, important business at
The Records Office. Get back to us today."
"Make sure Maecenas signs these papers soon."
When you say, "I'll do my best"—he presses,
Insisting "You can do it, if you want."   50

It's the seventh year and soon the eighth since
Maecenas let me join his group of friends;
I mean, he's taking me along sometimes
On carriage trips and trusting me with chitchat—
"You have the time?" "How about that Thracian   55
Bantam? A match for Syrus?" "My, this morning
Cold really bites, unless you're dressed for it"—
And gossip safely dropped in leaky ears.

Day in and out and hour to hour, the whole
Damned time I'm dogged by jealousy and grudge.   60
If someone spots our man together with
Maecenas at the games or playing ball
On the Campus, I'm "the son of Fortune."
A rumor from the Rostra blows through all
The city's intersections like a chill.   65
Each and every man I meet wants answers:
"Good sir, what's the news about the Dacians?
I bet you know. You're closer to the gods than I."
"Not one thing." "You always have to mock us."
"God damn me if I've heard a word." "Well, what   70
About the vets? Will Caesar settle them
In Sicily or on Italian soil?"
I swear I'm ignorant. They marvel at
My silence like it's signally profound.
This sort of nonsense wastes my day. I get   75
Depressed. I'm often praying: "When will I

See you again, my country home, and read
The ancient authors, nap, do nothing, drink
In life's sweet moments freed from care. Some beans
(Pythagoras' next of kin), some good   80
Bacon fat to give the cabbage seasoning—
When can I sit down to such a supper?"
Immortal dinner parties! Nights my friends
And I enjoy together round my Lar.
Lots left over for the saucy servants.   85
There aren't those drinking bouts with crazy rules:
Each guest can suit himself—the stronger stuff
For heroes; some need less to mellow out.
And we talk. Not about vacation homes
Or who owns this or that townhouse, or how   90
Well or badly Lepos, the famous mime,
Can dance. No. We focus on things that matter—
Those things it's harmful not to know: is wealth
What makes us happy or is it excellence?
What pulls us into friendships: self-concern   95
Or moral sense? What do we mean exactly
In speaking of "the good" or "highest good"?
And in our conversations, Cervius,
My neighbor, shares with us some homespun tale.
He may run on, but never pointlessly.   100
When someone, for example, hasn't a clue
What worries money brings, and starts extolling
Arellius' wealth, our friend begins:
"The story goes that once a country mouse
Was entertaining in his dirt-poor den   105
A city mouse. Both host and guest were friends
From way back. Rough and frugal as he was,
The country mouse could be a bit less tight
When guests arrived. In short, he didn't stint
But served the chickpeas and long oats he'd laid   110
Away and dragged out with his teeth a raisin
And bits of half-gnawed bacon. So he hoped
This smorgasbord might please his fussy friend,
Who barely let a single dish so much
As touch his curled-up lip. The mouse of the house,   115
Reclining on fresh chaff, ate spelt and darnel,

And didn't touch the banquet's finer fare.
Finally the city mouse protested,
"My friend, how can you possibly enjoy
Enduring life on this steep, wooded ridge?   120
Can't you see that wilderness is savage
And can't compare with fine society?
Pack your bags. Let's go together. Trust me:
We're creatures given mortal souls for life.
However great or small, there's no escape   125
From dying. Listen, chum, that's how it is.
Quaff the good life while you can! Live knowing
Life is short." This made a big impression.
The country mouse bounds out the door and off
They set upon their trip to Town and soon   130
Arrived: they didn't want to creep along
The city walls in daylight. Night was at
Midpoint in her journey through the heavens
When the mice walked in a mansion. Brilliant
Red coverlets emblazed the ivory couches,   135
And many dishes, left from some great feast
That evening, still were out, stacked up in trays.
By now, the city mouse has got the bumpkin
Reclining on a purple fleece, while he,
In waiter's apron, runs about and keeps   140
The courses coming—like a home-bred slave,
Who samples each before he serves a dish.
The country mouse lay back enjoying it.
He likes the change. It's fun to live it up
In luxury. When all at once a huge   145
And sudden sound of banging doors had both
Mice scrambling off the couch and down the hall's
Whole length and width. Sheer terror then broke loose.
The barks and growls of big Molossian hounds
Tore through the house. 'I don't need this,' cried out   150
The country mouse. 'Farewell. My forest den
Is safe. And plain old vetch is comfort food!'"

SATIRE 2.7

DAVUS: "You've had my ear for quite some time. I'd like
To say a thing or two, but fear chokes slaves.
HORACE: "Davus?"
DAVUS: "Yes, it's Davus, your possession
And loyal friend and honest . . . well, as good
As one can be and still survive. . . ."
HORACE: "Then take   5
Advantage of December's license. Talk.
DAVUS: "Some people relish vice tenaciously.
But many more swim back and forth—intent
On doing good one moment, then, the next,
They're hooked by something crooked. People marked   10
That Priscus wore three rings or none at all.
So inconsistent that he changed his toga—
From broad to narrow stripe—upon the hour.
One minute leaving a mansion, then the next
He'd hole up in some dive the better sort   15
Of freedman wouldn't be caught dead seen leaving.
In Rome Don Juan, philosopher in Athens.
Vertumni everywhere frowned at his birth.
Volanerius, that party clown, when
The gout he'd richly earned had gnarled his fingers, 20
Paid someone by the day to gather up
His dice and put them in the box for him:
Yet since he sticks wholeheartedly to one
Vice, the less distressed he is; it's better
Than laboring at a chain—now tight, now slack."   25
HORACE: "You plan on telling me sometime today,
Whip-bait, the point of all this crap?"
DAVUS: "You are,
I'd say, the point."
HORACE: "How's that, you piece of scum?"
DAVUS: "You praise the past, the old traditions, but
You'd categorically refuse to budge   30
If all at once some god could take you there.
Either you doubt that what you tout is better,
Or mired in filth, you can't pull out your foot,
And haven't got the strength to champion right.
In Rome, you miss the country; once you're there,   35

The distant city shines more fair than a star.
You're fickle. If you happen not to have
A dinner invitation, you extol
A carefree meal of garden greens; as if
You'd never leave the house except in chains,   40
You say you're blessed and hug yourself because
You needn't be off drinking somewhere. Let
Maecenas summon you to dine (a last-
Minute invitation comes one evening)—
'Hurry! Get the lantern oil! Does any-   45
One hear?' you yammer out in great commotion
And scramble out the door. Here Mulvius
And all the other party clowns take off
Attacking you with unrepeatable
Curses. Mulvius is now confessing: 50
'I'm my stomach's slave. The smell of cooking
Gets my nose aroused. I'm weak and lazy,
And, if you want to add, a glutton. But
You're just like me, and maybe worse. So why
Unprovoked scold *me*—like you're much better—   55
Masking your own faults with polished language?'
Now what if you should be unmasked and found
To be an even greater fool than I
Who cost five hundred drachmas? Stop—don't try
To scare me with that look or hit me. Keep   60
Your temper while I explicate the points
The doorman at Crispinus' taught me.

You're captivated by another's wife;
I'm captivated by a prostitute.
Whose sin is worse? And who gets crucified?   65
When headstrong nature has me craving sex,
It doesn't matter who the woman is
Naked in the bright lamplight I'm banging
With my swollen prick or who has mounted
And rides me wild, her bottom bouncing high.   70
I walk away, with no concerns about
A damaged reputation or that richer
Or better-looking guys should come there too.
But you—you strip off every sign of rank,

Your knight's ring *and* your Roman dress; you hood   75
Your perfumed head, and sally forth not like
A reputable juryman, but like
Some shameless Dama. Don't you turn into
The part you play? In fear, you're led inside,
Your bones shaking as lust and panic clash.   80
What does it matter whether you've sold yourself
To feel the brand, the rod, and fatal sword,
Or end up stuffed in some disgusting chest
By a maid (the wife's confederate in
Vice), your head wedged tight against your kneecaps?   85
Does the cuckold have the legal power
To punish both? Or is seducer dealt more justly
The punishment? The lady after all
Doesn't change her clothes or house, and isn't
On top: [she's scared and doesn't trust your passion.]   90
With eyes wide open you'll submit to base
Punishment and forfeit all your goods and
Lifestyle, with your hide and reputation,
To the whims of one enraged, mad master.
If you escaped, I'll bet you learned your lesson   95
And see the danger. Nope: you're seeking out
Another chance to panic, another chance
To self-destruct: you're such a perfect slave!
What beast, once freed, comes running back
To find its broken chain. That's too perverse.   100
'I'm no adulterer,' you say. Well, nor
Am I a thief, by god, when wisdom guides
Me past your silverware. But take away
The risk, and nature, not reined in, runs wild.
So *you're* my master? You who scrape and bow   105
To circumstance and men of rank. Should you
Be manumitted three or even four
Times over, would you ever shake your fear?
One more point, no less compelling: whether
A slave who carries out a second slave's   110
Commands is called an 'under-slave,' as you,
The masters, like to put it, or 'fellow-slave,'
Precisely what is *our* relationship?
You, who order me around, abjectly

Kowtow to another man and jump like   115
A wooden puppet jerked on someone's string.
Who then *is* free? The sage. He owns himself.
This man not poverty, nor death, nor chains
Can terrify. He bravely challenges
Appetite and scorns acclaim. Completeness   120
In himself. Externals find his roundness
Impossible to stick upon, and each
Time Fortune charges him, it's she who's maimed.
You recognize yourself in anything
I've said about the sage? A woman asks   125
You for five talents, tortures you, and locks
You out, and douses you with ice-cold water,
And calls you back. Throw off that shameful yoke.
Be free at last. 'I'm free.' Come on, say it.
You can't, can you? A master drives your soul   130
Relentlessly: worn out, you feel the goads;
The driver wheels you round—you can't resist.
Or when you're paralyzed with wonder at
A painting signed by Pausias, do you,
Madman, err less than when I strain to see   135
Some scenes dashed off in ocher or charcoal
Of gladiators—Rutuba and Fulvus,
Pacideianus—real men drawn to life,
Wielding weapons, quick to thrust or parry?
So Davus is no good, a slouch, while you   140
Come off a connoisseur of old fine art.
If I am tempted by a steaming hot cake,
I'm worthless. Does your strength of character
Resist the tempting banquet spread? Why is
My bondage to food more self-destructive?   145
I'm whipped, that's why. But is your punishment
Less for craving those expensive tapas?
An endless round of banquets surely sours
The stomach; feet, when hijacked by a vicious
Body, bulk at carrying the weight. Or   150
Suppose a slave one evening swaps some grapes
For a stolen strigil: is this action
A sin? Well, what about the man who sells
His family's land to satisfy his stomach?

He's not a slave? Let's add another point: 155
One lousy hour of your own company's
Too much for you. You're quite incapable
Of using leisure wisely. Like a slave
Who flees his master, you desert yourself
And try to swindle care by wine or sleep   160
In vain. That dark companion never leaves."
HORACE: "Where's a rock?"
DAVUS: "Do what?"
HORACE: "Where're some arrows?"
DAVUS: "The man's insane or else he's writing verse!"
HORACE: "Get the hell out! Unless you want to be
The ninth drudge sent to work my Sabine farm!"   165

SATIRE 2.8

HORACE: "Did you enjoy the dinner party rich
Nasidienus threw? They told me when
I came by yesterday to see if you
Might dine with me, that you were there carousing
From early afternoon."
FUNDANIUS: "That's right. I had   5
The best time ever."
HORACE: "Tell me, if it's not
Too much to ask, what dish first pacified
Your angry appetite."
FUNDANIUS: "Lucanian boar,
Caught, our host disclosed, as south winds blew mild.
As garnish: piquant baby turnips, lettuce,   10
Radishes—good fillips for fed-up stomachs—
Parsnips, fish paste, and lees of Coan wine.
These cleared away, a boy, his tunic hiked
Way up, wiped off the table with a thick
Red towel; another scooped up crumbs and what-   15
Ever else might discommode the diners.
Grave as an Attic maid with Ceres' ark,
Dark-skinned Hydaspes serves the Caecuban;
Alcon brings in Chian, sans seawater.
Here our host pipes up, 'Should you, Maecenas   20

Prefer some Alban or Falernian
To what's been served, we have those wines as well.'"
HORACE: "Killjoy wealth! Fundanius, what I want
To know is who was there. It sounds like fun."
FUNDANIUS: "I had top couch, then Viscus Thurinus,   25
And next, I recollect, was Varius.
Vibidius and Servilius Balatro
Came next, two extras Maecenas brought along.
Nomentanus was above and Porcius,
Who played the clown in gulping down cakes whole,   30
Below our host. If anything escaped
Our notice, Nomentanus had the job
Of pointing out the treat we'd missed. As for
The rest of us—that is to say, the mob—
We tucked in oysters, fowl, and fish whose taste   35
Seemed mysteriously unfamiliar:
I noticed this right off, before he had
Passed me the dish of turbot and flounder loin.
Next, he tutored me on honey apples:
They turn this red, he said, when picked on nights   40
The moon is on the wane. What difference
This makes you better get from him yourself.
Vibidius now says to Balatro,
'Let's drink him dry, or perish unavenged!'
He calls for larger cups. Our caterer   45
At this turns ashen; nothing terrifies
The man as much as serious imbibing:
He fears a drinker's nasty tongue or how
A fiery wine can blunt the palate's edge.
Vibidius and Balatro tipped whole   50
Wine jugs into Allifae-ware wine cups,
As did the rest, except for those who had
The lowest couch; they didn't hit the bottle.
A moray eel is brought in now, stretched out
On a platter, scampi swimming round it.   55
Our lordly host explains: 'This eel was pregnant
When caught. Post partum, eel goes off in taste.
To make the sauce, you need Venafrum's oil
(First pressing), garum (made from Spanish mackerel),
A five-year-old Italian wine (pour in   60

While cooking); Chian (nothing less) is added
Once it's cooked down; white pepper, vinegar
Fermented from Methymnean grapes—add last.
I introduced arugula and tart
Elecampine to the preparation;   65
Curtillus adds unwashed sea urchins: these
Enhance the flavor better than fish brine.'
About this time the heavy tapestries
Came crashing down. The dish was ruined.
Black dust flew everywhere and more of it   70
Than north winds blow across Campania's plains.
We feared the worst but once we realized
There wasn't any risk, we pulled ourselves
Together. Rufus, head in hands, wept so
That you'd have thought his little boy had died.   75
What might have happened, if Nomentanus
Had not so sagely bucked up his ally!
'Alas, Fortuna, who among the gods
Torments us more? The joy you always take
In mocking human efforts!' Varius   80
Grabbed his napkin and scarcely kept from laughing.
Balatro, sniffing out absurdity,
Was saying, 'Such is life. Your industry
Will never get the fame it's earned. To fete
Me aren't you stretched and racked by every kind   85
Of worry? Burnt bread or some bungled sauce
Might be put out; the slaves who serve the guests
Might wear their tunics wrong, their hair not right.
And accidents can happen: tapestries,
Like yours just did, can crash; a numskull slips   90
And breaks a dish. Here's where a host is like
A general: challenges reveal his genius;
Favorable conditions keep it hidden.'
Then Nasidienus says, 'I pray the gods
Accommodate your every wish. You are   95
A good man really *and* a gracious guest.'
He calls for slippers. Now imagine us
Abuzz with whispers like conspirators."
HORACE: "There isn't any show I'd rather see.
Come on, what happened next?"

FUNDANIUS: "Vibidius asked   100
The servants: was the wine jug smashed as well?
(His calls for more had all been left unanswered.)
We improvised some jokes, with Balatro's
Encouragement, to alibi our laughter.
You, Nasidienus, enter, countenance   105
Transformed, determined now to fix
By artistry the mess bad luck had made.
After him came servants with a platter
Quite big enough to hold a crane, a male
No less, already carved, and topped with lots   110
Of meal and salt. And pâté de foie gras from
A snow-white goose well fed on juicy figs,
And rabbit legs, the better tasting for
Having been cut off the loins. Then blackbirds
With char-grilled breasts, and pigeons, rumps removed—   115
Delicious treats—had not our host explained
The provenance and properties of each.
We took revenge by fleeing, all untasted,
As if Canidia had breathed upon the food
Toxin worse than Africa's snake venom.   120

NOTES

Satire 1.1 Notes

1 *Maecenas*: the name so close to the beginning of the book indicates that it is dedicated to him. So, too, the *Epodes* (1.4), *Odes* 1–3 (1.1.1), and *Epistles* 1 (1.3), as well as each book of Virgil's *Georgics* and, it would seem, Propertius' second book of elegies (*Sat.* 2.1.17).

3 *luck*: the Latin word for "luck" or "chance" is *fors*, which, along with its adjective *fortunatus*, "lucky" (6), never loses its association with *fortuna*, a force (or goddess) regarded as fickle, inconstant, unstable, and utterly beyond human control. See *Sat.* 1.6.69, 1.9.1, 2.2.146, 172, 2.6.6, 2.6.63, 2.7.123, 2.8.81, 111nn.; *Odes* 1.35, 2.1.3, 3.29; *Ep.* 1.1.68–69. Lucilius seems to have dealt with the topic in Book 27 of his *Satires* (frr. 769–90 *ROL*).

5 *The veteran*: there were still thousands of men, many with years of service, on active duty in the early 30s BCE, what with war in Syria against the Parthians, Octavian preparing a campaign in Illyria, Sex. Pompeius and his navy still at large (until late 35), and the possibility of more civil war in everybody's thoughts.

11 *The well-trained lawyer*: in Republican Rome the reward for the efforts of an *iuris consultus*, "legal counselor," on behalf of his clients would be (other than aggravation) gratitude and prestige, but not money. See 31n.

12 *the farmer's life*: see *Sat.* 2.2 and especially 2.6. H. mocks this kind of escapist fantasy in *Epd.* 2.

13 *to Town*: in much Latin literature, the word *urbs* by itself often refers to Rome; see 1.8.68, 1.9.17, 1.10.6, 2.3.8, 42, 2.4.21, 2.6.20, 65, 130, 132, 2.7.36, but also 60n. below.

17 *Fabius*: apparently the same man as at 1.2.178. According to Porph., he is "Q. Fabius Maximus from Narbo [modern Narbonne in southern France], born of equestrian rank, a partisan of Pompey, he wrote a number of books concerning Stoic philosophy." The last detail, if true, would make him fitting company for the "sermonizing hack" mentioned in line 130 (see n.).

18 *waste your time*: see 129–30nn. But this could be an early dig against H.'s poetic precursor Lucilius, who was notoriously prolix; see 1.4.8–15, 1.5.130n., 1.10.12.

19 *a god appears*: as if ex machina; so, too, at 2.7.31. H. may have in mind passages such as Cic. *Sen.* 83 and Plato (?), *Alcibiades* 105a (Socrates speaking): "suppose one of the gods should say to you: 'Alcibiades, do you wish to continue to live the life you have now, or to die at once unless it will be possible for you to attain something greater?'"

23 *happiness*: H. uses the Latin word *beatus*, which can mean "happy" but also "fortunate" and, in a more concrete sense, "rich." The difference between these senses was a matter of great interest to philosophers in general and H. in particular (cf. 126, 1.3.197, 1.4.22, 2.4.123, 2.6.94, 127, 2.8.1nn., *Epd.* 2.1, 8.9, 16.41, *Odes* 1.4.14, 2.2.18, 2.3.7, 2.16.28, 2.18.14, 3.9.4, 3.16.32, 3.29.11, 4.9.46; *Ep.* 1.6.47, 1.10.14, 1.16.18, 1.18.32, 2.1.139).

    Jove: there is a similar shift from general to particular at 59–60 "a river . . . Aufidus." Jupiter (the form "Jove" comes from the oblique grammatical cases, which omit the suffix *–piter* = *pater*, "father") is the greatest of Rome's gods (cf. 1.2.24, 2.1.65, 2.3.441), but the colloquial "if he's pissed off" undercuts any solemnity here.

25–29 These lines are often regarded as a statement of H.'s "creed" as a satirist, but there is hardly a poem in either book without its share of gratuitous laughs, and while H. does address important questions about personal and social conduct, he often seems to go out of his way to avoid "things that matter" in the public and political world of the Roman Republic's final crisis.

26 *a laughing man from speaking straight*: the Latin, *ridentem dicere verum*, is one of H.'s most famous tags. It is interesting, in light of a supposed connection between *satira* and satyrs (see the Introduction), that H. recommends something similar for those writing satyr plays (*Ars* 226).

27 *like treats in school*: the treats are *crustula*, "small pastries" (see 2.4.61), either rewards for recitation (cf. Jerome, *Epistles* 107.4) or, possibly, "visual aids" shaped like letters (cf. Quint. 1.1.26).

30 *The man . . . ground*: H. picks up where he left off, with the farmer, but seems to signal his new seriousness with a somber, almost epic-sounding periphrasis.

31 *dishonest tradesmen*: in place of the lawyer mentioned in line 11, who was not motivated by desire for financial gain. But "tradesmen" hardly belong in the serious contexts momentarily suggested by line 30.

34 *Like ants*: it appears that Lucilius made a similar comparison (frr. 586–87 *ROL*): "thus [i.e., like the ant] you should seek those fruits which, when the winter is horrid, / you would be able to use and delight yourself with at home." See also Virg. *G.* 1.186 ("the ant fearful of an old age without resources"), Virg. *A.* 4.402–7, and Proverbs 6:6 ("Consider the ant, thou sluggard").

    they'll say: emphatic, because they *act* otherwise.

35 *don't . . . ignore their future needs*: Ofellus would approve (2.2.151–52), but cf. *Ars* 122: (old age is foolishly) "greedy for the future."

37 *Aquarius*: by Roman reckoning, the sun enters the "house" of the aptly named zodiac sign Aquarius, "water-bringer," on January 16.

38 *wisely*: H.'s first reference in the *Satires* to "wisdom" (*sapientia*), a quality that will be sadly lacking in the humans who populate the poems.

39 *Not you*: H. abruptly shifts from exposition to direct engagement with one of his targets, possibly someone to be imagined as eavesdropping on H.'s conversation with Maecenas.

41   *while someone else has more*: the real reason why folks are dissatisfied turns out
to be envy, something H. is much on guard against (cf. 1.3.84–85, 1.6.32,
65, 2.1.111–13, 2.3.20, 2.6.60), combined with a notion, or rather an excuse
(69–70n.), that "you're ranked . . . by what you have" (65–66).

42–53   Some of the same examples and language will be "appropriated" for
his own argument by the absurd Damasippus at 2.3.120–24.

43   *buried underground*: possibly to become another man's "treasure trove"
(2.6.12–15).

46   *floors*: threshing floors (*areae*), where the grain was separated from the chaff
and the bounty of the harvest would be on display. See 2.6.103n.
   a hundred thousand bushels: perhaps imitating Lucil. frr. 581–82 and 583
(if those fragments belong together and are emended as Palmer suggests),
"While you harvest a hundred thousand bushels of grain, / a thousand jars
of wine, I [though less wealthy] enjoy things just as much as you do."

48   *the slave*: in Rome, as in most societies until the late eighteenth century,
slavery was an accepted, if not always comfortable, fact of life.

49   *fellow slaves*: see 1.8.13, 2.7.116–17n.

52   *nature's limits*: probably alluding to Epicurus' view that humans ought to
desire things that are natural and necessary for existence rather than those
that are natural but superfluous (as here) or, worse yet, unnatural and unnec-
essary. See 80, 94, 1.2.92, 146, and Epicurus, *Key Doctrines* 15, "the bounty of
nature has its limits and is therefore readily accessible," and id. 21, "the one
understanding the limits of life knows how easy it is to remove pain arising
from need and to make an entire life complete." This is the first of many
references in the *Satires* to "nature" (*natura*, Greek *physis*); in most of the
other contexts there is also an Epicurean or at least Lucretian resonance. The
image of "limits" or "restraints" is continued in lines 98, 101, and 112–13.

59   *a river*: the image may anticipate H.'s attack on his precursor Lucilius
(1.4.11n.); if so, it would seem to add a literary dimension to H.'s moral/
ethical criticism.

60   *Aufidus*: see 23n. But the sudden reference to the principal river of H.'s home-
land Apulia (1.5.44n.), many days' travel southeast of Rome (13n.), is jarring.

62   *no more than need requires*: cf. Epicurus, *HP* 21B4, and the proverb, "that
mortal lacks least who desires least" (Publ. Syr. 286). But there may be a
word play in the Latin, with the word for "no more," *tantuli* (literally "so
small an amount"), anticipating the example of Tantalus below (72–74).

65–66   *you're ranked . . . by what you have*: the other shoe drops (41n.). H. seems
to echo Lucil. frr. 1194–95 (text uncertain), "gold and obtaining votes are
proof of excellence and of manhood; / you are and are considered to be
worth as much as you possess."

67   *they crave*: H. flirts with a paradox: these "folk" seem to find satisfaction
(cf. 2) and even "glee" (71) in being miserable.

68   *a miser . . . in Athens*: usually identified as Timon, who during the
Peloponnesian War lived in isolation from his fellow Athenians, although
in the fullest accounts (Plut., *Life of Antony*. 70, Lucian, *Timon*—the main
source of Shakespeare's *Timon of Athens*) he is driven by misanthropy, not by

a Fafnir-like "glee" over his "loot." After the defeat at Actium, Mark Antony would for a time emulate Timon.

69–70 The miser's open contempt for public opinion contrasts with the notion that "you're ranked . . . by what you have" (65–66).

72 *Tantalus*: in Greek myth a son of Zeus (Jupiter) who tried to steal from the gods; after death, he was punished by being "tantalized" with water that dribbled away before he could drink and fruit that blew out of his reach before he could eat (Hom. *Od*. 11.582–92). He is mentioned in an unknown context at Lucil. frr. 136–37 *ROL*, "Tantalus, who for his unspeakable deeds / pays penalties, penalties." See also *Odes* 2.18.36–38.

73 *a funny myth*: according to Cicero, *Tusc*. 1.10–11 (45 BCE), sophisticated Romans of his time considered myths like those about Tantalus mere "fantasies of poets and artists," although in Epicurean thinking they retained some value as allegories for ways in which humans torment themselves (Lucr. 3.978–1023).

77 *sacred things*: echoed by Damasippus (42–53n.) at 2.3.169–70.
     works of art: cf. 1.3.128–29, 2.3.32–37, 2.7.18–19.

79 *greens*: garden greens (Latin *holus*) were a staple of a modest and moderate diet; cf. 1.6.155, 2.1.108, 2.2.160, 2.7.43.

80 *our nature*: see 52n.

83 *slaves*: runaways; see 2.5.23, 2.7.159.

84 *such* goods: ironic, of course. The term "goods" (Latin *bona*) is often used in philosophy of the things that humans ought to seek (2.96–97n.). The different ideas about what these were and what the highest of them might be is the subject of Cicero's *De finibus bonorum et malorum* ("concerning the extremes of good things and bad things"). See 1.3.157–58, 2.6.95nn.

94 *a bonus nature gives*: see 52n. But H. departs here from Epicurean doctrine, in which human ties are based chiefly on culture and utility, not on nature. See 1.3.137–60, Lucr. 5.1011–27, and *HP* section 22.

102 *Ummidius*: otherwise unknown, but the name may be a play on *homo*, "man," and *medius*, "middle (of)," anticipating the wretch's fate (106).

103–4 *weigh / his money*: proverbial; cf. Cic. *Phil*. 2.97, "such great piles of coins are stacked at this man's house that now they are weighed, not counted."

104 *a slave*: see 48n. At Rome, with the exception of the toga, which was reserved for male citizens (1.2.24, 1.3.24, 49, 1.6.31n., 2.1.105, 2.3.120, 2.7.12–13), slaves wore clothing that was similar in make and style to that of free and freed persons but that tended to be cheaper, drabber, and shabbier.

105–6 *An ex- / Slave . . . axed him in half*: see 102n. The ex-slave (Latin *liberta*; see 6.6n.) was perhaps his heir, tired of waiting for the money.
     Helen's twin: Clytemnestra, the infamous sister of Helen (1.3.149), who, when her husband Agamemnon (2.3.286) returned from the Trojan War, either killed him herself with an ax, or, in other versions, assisted her lover Aegisthus in the deed, which was avenged by her and Agamemnon's son Orestes (2.3.202n.).

107 *live the life of Riley?*: H. allows his target (39n.) to respond. The proverbial "Riley" is an apt equivalent for two Roman stock figures mentioned in the Latin, Naevius and Nomentanus, high livers also mentioned by Lucilius (frr. 80–82, 1257–58 *ROL*) and again at 2.2.92 (Naevius) and 1.8.16, 2.1.32, 2.3.266, 343; cf. 2.8.32n. (Nomentanus).

110 *bum or playboy*: the Latin terms are *vappa*, literally "wine gone flat," and *nebulo*, "cloud man." The latter occurs at Lucil. fr. 500 *ROL*.

111 *some middle ground*: the idea of a happy medium or, as H. memorably put it (*C.* 2.10.5), a "happy mean," is especially associated with Aristotle (e.g., *EN* 2.6.15) but by H.'s time had long since passed into popular philosophy. See 1.2.37, 1.3.33, 1.4.167, 182, 1.6.87, 2.2.73, 2.5.121–22, and *Ep.* 1.18.9 ("Virtue is a mean between vices").

111–12 *a eunuch / and Don Juan*: H.'s Roman examples are Tanais whose name, Greek for the River Don, suggests foreign origin, and "some sources" cited by Porph., not implausibly identified as an ex-slave of Maecenas (cf. 2.8.19n.) and "the father-in-law of Visellius," whom Porph. says was *hirneo-sus*, "afflicted with a ruptured scrotum."

114 *where I started*: not the poem, but where he identified greed as the cause of people's dissatisfaction (39–41).

116 *a neighbor's goat*: a kind of *reductio ad absurdum* of "the grass is greener"; cf. *Ep.* 1.2.57 ("the envious man wastes away with another's prosperity") and Ov. *Ars* 1.349–50 ("the crop is always more fertile in other folks' fields, / and the neighboring flock always has larger udders").

118 *how others have it worse*: cf. what may be an Epicurean view in Plut., *De tranquillitate animi* 10, "in regard to contentment, it is especially important to look to oneself . . . or, failing that, to contemplate those with less and not, as many men, compare (oneself to) those with more."

121–24 The image and language have an epic resonance; cf. Enn. *Ann.* 463–64 [= 443–44 *ROL*], (the movement of warships is similar to) "when, poured from the starting barrier, / chariots with a great resounding vie to hurl [themselves through the track]" (supplement by Skutsch). Both Ennius (4.70n.) and H. seem to have influenced Virgil's famous comparison of the world at war to chariots rushing out of control (*G.* 1.512–14).

126 *happy life*: see 22n.

128 *sated dinner guest*: although the idea of life as a "banquet" (cf. 3.127–28n.) is commonplace, H. here imitates Lucr. 3.938, "Why not withdraw (from life) like a dinner guest fed full of life?"; cf. 3.956–60, "because you always crave what is absent, / . . . death stands by your head unexpected before / you are able to depart satisfied and fed full with the good things of life." Some see a word play in H.'s version between "satisfied" (Latin *satur*) and "satire" (*satira*; see 2.1.1n.), although Lucr. also uses the term *satur* in the second passage.

129 *Enough*: H. avoids a Lucilian excess (18n.).

130 *sermonizing hack*: H. names a particular "hack," Crispinus, a tenth-rate windbag poet and Stoic philosopher also mentioned at 1.3.194, 1.4.15, and 2.7.62.

Satire 1.2 Notes

1 *exotic dancers'*: Latin *mimae*, actresses, dancers, and singers in short plays with comic or mythological themes (1.10.8n.) and in enactments of literary texts. From the 80s BCE on, mime was popular at Rome, and a number of performers achieved "celebrity status." These included Origo (69), Arbuscula (1.10.104), Lepos (2.6.91), and Cytheris, an ex-slave (58n.) notorious as the mistress of Mark Antony and then of the poet Cornelius Gallus, who referred to her in his elegies as "Lycoris" ("wolf-girl").

4 *Tigellius*: mentioned again in the past tense, at 1.3.4–30. Although a native of Sardinia (1.3.4n.), the form of his name indicates that he was a Roman citizen. He was friendly with Julius Caesar and, later, Octavian (1.3.5–10), but was disliked by Cicero (*Fam.* 7.24–25, *Att.* 13.49–51) and the poet Calvus (1.10.25–26n.); cf. fr. 3 *FLP,* "the stinking head of Sardinian Tigellius is for sale." He is not to be confused with another singer, possibly a relative or an emulator, Tigellius Hermogenes (1.4.87, 1.10.109–11n.), also referred to as Tigellius (1.10.123) or as Hermogenes (1.9.32, 1.10.24), a musician and also, it seems, a poet (1.10.24n.), who was still living at the time of *Satires* 1.

9 *people think him prodigal*: this miser, the spendthrift mentioned next, and Fufidius (12) are all driven by concern for public opinion (see 1.1.65–66), but with very different results.

Ask another: the imperative is the first indication of an addressee, the "you" of 24–26, who remains unidentified. H. interrupts the conversation with an intrusion by a third person (30), exclamations by various characters (40–44, 56, 67), apostrophes to others (47–50, 72–81, 103), and an imagined dialogue (87–91) before resuming it at 92 (but see 137n.).

10 *gobbled up the fine estate*: cf. 1.4.135–36, 2.3.345–63, 371–75, 2.7.159–60.

14 *praised by some, by others blamed*: depending on whether they are themselves misers or spendthrifts.

15 *Fufidius*: a rapacious banker/usurer, possibly the same man mentioned at Cic. *Pis.* 86 and Q. *Fr.* 3.1.3. H. targets other usurers at 1.3.122–26, 1.6.166–68, and, possibly, 1.7.5–6 (see n.); see also *Epd.* 2.67–70, *Ep.* 1.1.80.

15–16 *[The man . . . banking.]*: the brackets indicate that the phrase, which occurs with more point at *Ars* 421, was probably not put here by H., but by someone copying the text at a later time.

17 *ne'er-do-well or worse*: see 1.1.110n.

18–19 *five times normal rates . . . first installment*: the legal rate had been fixed in 51 BCE at 1% per month. By taking the first 5% from the principal, Fufidius gets away with advancing less money.

22–23 *tough, / unyielding fathers*: tightwads, as so often in Roman comedy.

24 *toga virilis*: a male citizen was recognized as a legal adult when he exchanged his child's clothes and regalia for a "grown man's toga." See 1.1.104n.

27 *tortures himself*: metaphors involving torture and other corporeal punishment (the Latin term here is *crucio*, "crucify") were probably more vivid to the Romans than they are (or ought to be) to Americans because real torture, especially of slaves, was not uncommon at Rome. See 1.3.113n., 2.7.131.

29   *Terence's play*: *Heauton Timorumenos* ("The Self-Avenger"). The father could not forgive himself because he ran off his son Clinia when the young man fell in love with a pauper girl.

30   *If anyone is wondering*: 9n.

32–33   *one offense . . . the opposite*: this philosophical-sounding adage is a kind of red herring, as H.'s focus will not be on (moral) "offenses" (Latin *vitia*), but on avoiding pain and humiliation.

33   *Maltinus*: the name is probably meant to suggest Greek *malthakos*, "soft," "effeminate." See Lucil. fr. 744 *ROL*, "They call him insane whom they see is spoken of as a softy-girl [*maltha*, a variant of the Greek term] and a woman." According to Porph., some early interpreters thought Maltinus here was a teasing pseudonym for Maecenas, "who always strutted into Town with his tunics hanging low" (Sen. *Ep.* 114.6). For men not on active military service, the tunic, the basic all-purpose garment and undergarment of the ancient world, was supposed to hang to the knee: "below that suits married women [see 122–23], above that, centurions" (Quint. 11.3.138).

35–36   *Rufillus . . . goat*: quoted by H. himself at 1.4.115 and by Sen. *Ep.* 86.13, where instead of *Rufillus* the MSS give *Bucculus*. The former, "little redhead," could be a nickname for someone with the surname Rufus, such as the poet Ser. Sulpicius (1.10.117n.) or the unlucky host Nasidienus (2.8.74); the latter means "big cheeks."

36   *Gargonius of goat*: Cicero (*Brut.* 180) mentions a C. Gargonius as an inept orator of Sulla's time, Seneca the Elder (*Controuersiae* 1.7.18, etc.), a like-named teacher of rhetoric in H.'s generation with a famously raucous voice.

　　　goat: a euphemism for body odor at least as early as Old Comedy (1.4.2n.); also in H. at *Epd.* 12.4–6 and *Ep.* 1.5.29. Cf. Catul. 69.5–6: (Rufus can't get a girl because) "it is alleged that / a nasty goat dwells in the valley of your armpits."

37   *middle course*: see 1.1.111n.

38   *if any ankle shows*: i.e., if she is not a married woman (*matrona*). In public, a matron was expected to wear a white (46) floor-length outer garment called a *stola* (translated as "dress" at 90, "outfit" at 129; see also 122).

40   *Cato's godlike wisdom*: cf. Lucil. fr. 1240 *ROL*, "Valerius' godlike wisdom." Both H. and Lucilius parody a kind of periphrasis common in epic and other elevated poetry, e.g., Hom. *Il.* 5.71, "the might of Diomedes" = "the mighty Diomedes" (1.5.113n.); cf. 1.7.2–3, 2.1.104–6nn., *Odes* 3.21.11–12, "the virtue of ancient Cato," Cic. *De Or.* 3.168, Virg. *A.* 11.354, "the violence of Turnus." M. Porcius Cato (234–149 BCE), sometimes known as "the Censor" not just because he held that office (184–183 BCE) but because he was regarded in his own time and persisted in collective memory as a paragon and guardian of old-fashioned Roman virtue. See *Odes* 2.15.11–12, *Ep.* 1.19.13–14. His relaxed attitude about bordellos was shared by many other Romans, including H.'s father (1.4.140–41); cf. 2.7.71–78, Pl. *Curculio* 33–38, Cic. *Cael.* 48: "if there is anyone who thinks even affairs with prostitutes are forbidden to young men, he is stern indeed—I cannot deny it—but he is at odds not only with the license of this time but even from the custom and allowances of our ancestors."

45 *Cupiennius*: the name, although attested (Porph. identifies this bearer of it as friend of Augustus), sounds like a compound of *cupio* ("I desire") and Ennius, the poet whose verses are about to be parodied (47–48n.), something like "Skirtchaucer" might be in English.

47–48 *O Romans . . . lend me your ears*: the translation echoes Antonius' funeral oration in Shakespeare's *Julius Caesar* as H.'s Latin parodies two verses by the great epic poet Q. Ennius (1.4.70n.), *Ann.* 494–95: "Now hear this, you who wish god speed / to the Roman state and increase to Latium." The second verse is also parodied in one of Varro's Menippean satires (fr. 542 Astbury).

48 *adulterers*: translating *moechi* (literally "urinators"), a slangy Greek loan word common in satire and other "low" verse (e.g., 59, 2.7.17, 106, Pl. *Amphitryo* 135, Lucil. fr. 1048 *ROL*, Catul. 37.16) but jarring in this "Ennian" context (above).

49–50 *pleasure / laced with pain*: H. adopts an Epicurean argument against illicit sex (*HP* 21 G3, 22 Q4; cf. 21 B3, D1, 3).

51–55 There are serious accounts of the punishment of adulterers (e.g., Val. Max. 6.1.13), but more often they are played for laughs as at 168–76, in Roman comedy (e.g., Pl. *Miles* 1395–1426), satire (2.7.79–90, Juv. 10.310–23), epigram (Mart. 2.47, 60, 83), and, it would seem, mime (1n.).

51–52 *flogged / to death*: the Latin could also mean "almost to death," which would make more sense if Porph. is right in identifying this man as the historian Sallust (c. 86–35 BCE), since he managed to pay off and outlive his flogger, T. Annius Milo, who had caught Sallust with his wife Fausta (82n.), by some 13 years (see Gel. 17.18). In 50 BCE he was expelled from the senate by the censors after admitting to adultery ([Cic.] *Sal.* 16), but it is not clear if the two incidents were related. See also 58n.

56 *"That's fitting," people say*: in Republican Rome there seem to have been no laws concerned specifically with adultery (Sallust [above] was expelled from the senate on moral, not legal grounds), but under the principle of "self-help" there were few limits to what a citizen could do in cases of invasion of his space and property. Octavian late in life was concerned enough about adultery, especially in his own family, to enact a *Lex Iulia de adulteriis* (18 BCE) prescribing but also limiting the violence of punishments.

Galba: presumably a member of the Sulpicii Galbae, a distinguished patrician clan, and either a jurist or an experienced adulterer or both.

57 *at bargain rates*: this and the phrase "market price" would seem to refer to the cost not of a bordello, since that has already been mentioned as an alternative, but of gifts and other favors for unmarried "mistresses" of a higher status than common prostitutes.

58 *ex-slaves*: Latin *libertinae*, although the word did not have the associations that "libertine" has in English. Slaves emancipated by their owners automatically attained full citizen status in Rome and in much of Italy at all periods (1.6.7n.), but in the Republic relatively few (1.6.24, 51–52nn.) attained high rank and many worked in what we would call "entertainment and service industries" that were traditionally considered beneath Roman dignity. There was no stigma attached to consorting with such people, only with being too obsessed with them, as H. admits of himself in *Epd.* 14 and *Odes* 1.33.

    Sallust: not the adulterer historian (51–52n.), but probably his great-nephew and heir of the same name, who died in 20 CE. This would make him quite but not impossibly young in the mid-30s BCE. He grew up to become an important advisor to Octavian and Octavian's successor Tiberius. *Odes* 2.2 is addressed to him.

59   *adulterers*: 48n.

61–62   *in keeping with / his means*: and thus likely to be thought neither a miser nor a spendthrift (14, 37).

67   *"I never touch a wife"*: spoken by Sallust.

68   *Marsaeus*: otherwise unknown.

69   *Origo's*: 1n.

72–81   A kind of extended apostrophe to Marsaeus.

82   *Fausta*: the daughter of (in)famous L. Cornelius Sulla, who set a kind of precedent for Julius and Octavian Caesar by twice turning his armies against the Republic (88 and 82 BCE), eliminating his enemies through proscription (1.7.2n.), and seizing dictatorial power to restore the state. His successes led him to call himself *Felix*, "lucky," and his children *Fausta* and *Faustus*, "fortunate."

83   *son-in-law*: ironic; Fausta's real husband was T. Annius Milo (51–52n.).
    the name: both for its pedigree and for its literal meaning (82n.).

86   *Longarenus*: otherwise unknown. The name is attested, but it might be meant here to evoke the Latin words *longauo*, "sausage," and *longao*, "rectum."

87   *Dick announced*: H. echoes a famous passage in Lucretius (3.931–51), where personified Nature lectures a man on the silliness of his fear of death. The word for "dick" here, *mutto*, is very rare and probably borrowed from Lucil. fr. 335 *ROL*, "but with her left hand the girlfriend rubbed [its? her?] tears off of the dick."

89   *cunt*: H.'s term, *cunnus*, is as obscene in Latin as this is in English; cf. 1.3.149.

90   *pedigree or dress*: 38, 83nn.

92   *nature*: 1.1.52n.

94   *you*: H.'s original addressee (9n.), who turns out to be an adulterer. See 137n.

95–154   Addressed, with a brief interruption (137n.), to a contemporary adulterer.

96–97   *things one ought to seek . . . what should be / avoided*: alternatives often mentioned in Greek philosophy, including Epicureanism (e.g., *HP* 21B2); cf. 1.3.159–60, 1.4.96–97.

103   *no matter what you think*: apostrophe. If Cerinthus is a Roman adulterer, the Greek name, which means "honeycomb," would seem to be a suggestive pseudonym, as it probably is for the lover in the elegies by and about the woman poet Sulpicia ([Tib.] 3.8–20). But H.'s text can also be translated "no matter if it [the thigh] is yours," in which case Cerinthus could be a handsome male mime (1n.) or "boy-toy" (so Porph.). See 151n.

110–14   *Rich people . . . soft hoof:* A somewhat complicated analogy, but the idea
seems to be that whereas a woman might parade her "endowments" to distract
scrutiny of other parts just as or even more important for sexual pleasure, rich
men buying horses avoid such distraction by covering the superficial features
of the animals and focusing on those essential for utility. The comparison of
women with beasts is not unusual for satire and other "low" genres; see *Epd.*
8 and 12, but it also occurs in the more elevated *Odes* 1.23 and 2.5.

115   *Lynceus:* a hero in Greek myth proverbial for his keen eyesight; see *Ep.*
1.1.28, Cic. *Fam.* 9.2.2.

117   *blinder than Hypsaea:* the blindness of lovers and of love itself is proverbial
(e.g., 1.3.39, 58), but for Lucretius also the first symptom of a bad case
of "lovesickness" (Lucr. 4.1149–70). Hypsaea (a real surname) is otherwise
unknown.

119   *"What lovely legs! What arms!":* a parody of Greek poems such as
Philodemus (158n.), *A.P.* 5.132.1–2, "O foot, o shin, o thighs at the sight of
which I rightly / perish!"

122   *everything is veiled:* with the *stola* (38n.).

123   *Catia:* according to Porph., a matron "who because of the beauty of her
legs wore a short dress in defiance of modesty. Moreover she was so degraded
that she committed adultery with Valerius Acisculus, a tribune of the plebs,
behind a curtain in the shrine of Venus at the Theater of Pompey." A man
named L. Valerius Acisculus was an overseer of the Roman mint in 45 BCE,
but there is no record of him attaining the tribunate of the plebs.

127   *litter:* the rich and indolent in Rome often moved about the city in
enclosed litters (*lecticae*); see 2.3.327, Catul. 10.

128   *hangers-on:* the Latin (or, actually, Greek) term is *parasitae* (masc. *parasitoi*),
from *para,* "alongside," and *sitos,* "food." See 2.5.17, 2.6.136, 2.7.51, 2.8.28,
87–88nn.

129   *ankle-length outfit and heavy stole:* 38n. The "stole" (Latin *palla*) was a large,
usually woolen cloak worn in bad weather by both women and men.

132   *Coan silk:* a cloth woven on the Greek island of Cos from the cocoons of
wild silkworms. It was highly prized but considered inferior to the product
brought to the Mediterranean region from China (see *Epd.* 8.15) on the
famous Silk Road.

137   *The lover:* with the abrupt shift to the third person, H. seems to turn away
from the adulterer (92–154n.) and hold him up to the inspection of the wider
audience of the poem's readers. See 1.1.39, 1.3.178, 1.4.98, 2.5.4nn.

   sings: his song is based on and quotes an epigram by the third-century
BCE Hellenistic Greek poet Callimachus of Cyrene (epig. 31 *LCL* = *A.P.*
12.102), "The hunter, Epicydes, in the mountains searches for / every hare
and for the tracks of every doe-antelope, / enduring frost and snow. But if
someone should say / 'Look, this beast has been wounded,' he does not bag
it. / Such is my love. It knows how to pursue what flees, but flies by what
is lying at hand."

142–43   *erotic / fever . . . seething wound:* traditional metaphors for infatuation;
cf. *Epd.* 11.13–16, *Odes* 1.27.12, 20, and Lucr. 4.1048–90.

146 *what limit nature sets*: 1.1.52n.

148 *void from solid*: "the words are playfully transferred to morality from Epicurean physics, which made matter . . . and void . . . the two ultimate constituents of the universe" (Brown). See Lucr. 1.419–44.

149 *goblet*: see 1.1.57–59.

150 *turbot . . . peacock*: prized delicacies at Rome; see 2.2.34–35, 48–52, 133, 2.8.38, *Epd.* 2.50.

152 *a servant girl or houseboy's*: Roman law protected slaves (as property) from sexual abuse by strangers but not by their owners. For "house boys" (Latin *vernae*), see 2.6.85n. H., like many in his time, was casually what would now be called bisexual; see 1.4.30, 2.3.491, 2.8.18–19, *Epd.* 11, *Odes* 4.1.

154 *Venus*: metonymy for "mistress," "squeeze"; cf. *Odes* 1.27.14, 33.13, Lucr. 4.1185. But H.'s audience would be aware that both Julius and Octavian Caesar made much of their supposed descent, through her son Aeneas and grandson Iulus, from the real Venus.

158 *Philodemus*: an Epicurean philosopher from Gadara in Syria who in the mid-first century BCE lived at Rome and Herculaneum, where fragments of his books have been discovered under the volcanic ash of Mt. Vesuvius' eruption in 79 CE. A number of his poems also survive in the *Greek Anthology* (119n.), but not the one cited here.

159 *the Galli*: two meanings are possible: "Gauls," as typical barbarians, or "Galli," the term for the men who castrated themselves in order to become priests of the Asian goddess Cybele; see Catul. 63.

165 *she's Ilia or Egeria*: Ilia, a Vestal Virgin (!), was a descendant of Aeneas, and thus a relative of the Julian clan (153n.) as well as the mother of Rome's founder, Romulus (see *Odes* 3.9.7–8); Egeria, a Latin nymph or goddess, was said to be a counselor and mistress of the second king of Rome, Numa Pompilius (Enn. *Ann.* 113, Liv. 1.21.3, Juv. 3.12). H. may owe something here to the Cynic poet Cercidas (fl. 225 BCE) of Megalopolis in central Greece (*Meliambi* 3.27–32 *LCL*): "The Aphrodite [= Venus] from the marketplace / and attached to no one in particular, / whenever you wish and however you desire her, / there is no fear or aggravation; / bedding her for a small fee, / you seem to be the son-in-law of Tyndareus [the stepfather of Helen of Troy; see 1.3.1149n.]."

167–76 See 51–55n.

167 *fucking*: H.'s word, *futuo*, is just as obscene in Latin.

172 *my accomplice*: as in Davus' complaint (48n.) about H.'s supposed adulteries (2.7.89–90) and often in love poetry (e.g., Ovid, *Am.* 1.11).

174 *losing dowry*: it is not clear how much she could forfeit during the Republic (cf. Val. Max. 8.2.3), but the *Lex Iulia* of 18 BCE (56n.) set the amount at one-half of the total value.

175 *tunic*: 33n.

178 *even Fabius*: that is, even a Stoic philosopher (1.1.17n.), who might be expected to insist that the wise man is immune to pain and suffering. The humor would be more pointed if this Fabius was himself an adulterer (so Porph.).

Satire 1.3 Notes

4 *Sardinia*: identifying this particular singer (below), but possibly alluding to an ethnic stereotype, that Sardinia, a poor and unhealthy place, produced nothing but slaves, but those slaves were practically useless; cf. Cic. *Fam.* 7.24.2.

5 *Tigellius*: the man whose death was announced at 1.2.4; see note there.
Caesar: here Octavian; see 9n. below. This is the one direct reference to him in the first book of *Satires*, but see 1.5.34–36n.

6 *who could have forced the man*: this clause can be interpreted in two distinct ways. One, it could go closely with the ensuing clause, "who could have forced . . . if (only) he had asked . . ."; that is, Octavian, although he chose not to, could have gotten Tigellius to sing simply by appealing to their long relationship. This seems apt for conditions in the mid-30s BCE, when it is unlikely that Octavian, still far from secure in his power, would or even could have exercised any "compulsion" on a citizen (1.2.4n.) not under his military command. Two, it could be absolute, as a harsher alternative to "if (instead) he had asked . . ." (so most commentators). But this would be better suited to the early 20s, after Octavian/Augustus had attained an overt and unassailable authority in the state (cf. *Ep.* 2.1.228).

9 *his father*: Julius Caesar's will, executed in April 44 BCE, made his great-nephew C. Octavius his heir and adopted son with the new name C. Julius Caesar Octavianus.

11 *"Io Bacchae"*: a summons to the Bacchae, also known as Maenads, female votaries of the Greek god Bacchus (= Dionysus and, at Rome, Liber [1.4.112n.]); see *Odes* 1.18, 2.19, and 3.25. Tigellius could have been singing a dithyramb, a type of Greek song associated with Bacchus known for its lascivious rhythms (cf. *Odes* 4.2.10–12, *A.P.* 85, 202–19) and, as Brown points out, hardly appropriate for a banquet.

12 *egg course . . . fruit dessert*: Roman meals typically began with eggs, sucked raw from the shell, and concluded with apples or other fruit.

15 *inconsistent*: the Latin, *nil aequale homini fuit illi* ("nothing was consistent about that man") seems to raise the expectation that H. will now discuss the merits of *aequabilitas*, which in its sense of "consistency of mind and conduct" was counted by the Stoics among the cardinal virtues (e.g., Cic. *Off.* 1.90, 111) and which H. would admit was not one of his own strong points (2.7.29–47, *Ep.* 1.1.97–100). But the intervention of his addressee (26, 31nn.) throws him off track, and he ends up advocating *aequabilitas* in another sense borne by the word and words related to it (75, 95, 134–35, 138, 169nn.), of "fairness," "justice," or "tolerance." See also 30n.

17 *slow and solemn*: cf. 2.8.17.

18 *Juno's temple*: probably the one on the Aventine Hill, where Romans brought offerings to avert the influence of bad omens.

19 *Two hundred*: probably an exaggerated round number, as at 1.4.9, 1.5.15, 1.6.55, 1.10.80, Lucil. frr. 511–13 *ROL*, etc.
slaves: 1.1.48n.

20   *only ten*: H. seems to have kept three slaves at his townhouse (1.6.160) and eight at his modest Sabine estate (2.7.165n.); five are too few for the dignity of a praetor (1.6.146–47; cf. 160).

23   *small, three-legged table*: as opposed to the fancier tables used in Greek-style banquets; cf. 127–28, 1.4.109n., 1.6.161, 2.4.50, 2.6.116, 135–45, 2.8.17.

24   *a shell*: extreme, as even moralists did not consider a saltcellar a luxury item (*Odes* 1.16.14).

   toga: cf. 49, 1.1.104n.

26   *if you gave*: the first indication in the poem of an addressee, who will interrupt and criticize H. (31–33) and himself be singled out for criticism of his foolish conduct and Stoic dogma (40–57, 108–26, 155–97). See also 58, 92, 178nn.

30   *fraught with contradictions*: the Latin, *impar sibi*, can mean either "inconsistent with himself" or "unfair to himself"; see 15n., but also 134–35, 169nn.

31   *you interrupt*: 26n.

33   *of a different sort*: H. does not get around to detailing these faults explicitly (but cf. 47–50n.) until 90–95, but the harangue on which he now launches could certainly be considered "a little too straightforward" (90) and might strike some listeners as annoying "chatter" (93).

34   *Maenius*: a notorious "wit" (*scurra*; see 1.5.65–66n.) and prodigal (1.2.9, 1.4.54) also featured at *Ep.* 1.15.26–41. He seems to have been mentioned by Lucilius (frr. 1136–37 *ROL*) in connection with a structure, the *columna Maenia* on the Capitoline Hill, which he supposedly kept when he sold off the rest of his property because it afforded a good view of gladiator shows in the Forum (Porph.). Ironically, in the late Republic this *columna* was used to display the names of delinquent debtors (Cic. *Sest.* 18, 124).

   Novius: presumably a man similar to Maenius, but cf. 1.6.50n.

35   *behind his back*: see 1.4.101–7, 1.10.109–10.

39   *self-love*: cf. 58, *Odes* 1.18.14, *caecus amor sui*, "blind love of oneself."

41–44   A variation on the adage "we cannot see our own faults, but as soon as other people foul up, we are censors" (Phaedr. 4.10.4–5); cf. Cic. *Tusc.* 3.73, *Off.* 1.146.

41   *bleary eyes*: here metaphorical, but cf. 1.5.37n.

43   *an eagle's*: cf. Hom. *Il.* 17.67, (Menelaus [149n.] advanced into battle) "glancing about him like an eagle, whom they say / sees the most acutely of all sky-dwelling birds."

44   *the snake's at Epidaurus*: the ancients thought all snakes were keen-eyed, but this one, associated with a famous Greek temple of the healing god Aesculepius (Asclepius), would presumably also be, like the god himself, a "sharp diagnostician."

47–49   *temper . . . haircut . . . shoes . . . toga*: faults that H. elsewhere attributes to himself; cf. 2.3.488, *Odes* 1.16.22–28, 3.9.23–24, *Ep.* 1.20.25 (succumbing to anger), *Ep.* 1.1.94–97 (addressed to Maecenas; see 15n.), "if with my hair poorly cut / I run into you, you chuckle indulgently; if by chance a shabby undershirt peeks out / under my threadbare tunic or if my toga is in disarray, / you chuckle indulgently." Some ancient commentators cited by Pseudacro thought the "hick haircut" a dig at Octavian, who was famously careless about his tonsure (Suet. *Aug.* 79.1), and the "toga hanging wrong" a swipe at the poet Virgil, a man "of unseemly appearance and garb."

54 *nature*: 1.1.52n.

58 *Let's focus*: with the shift to the first person plural, which is continued, except at 92 (see n.), until 118, H. seems to try, at least temporarily, to make common cause with his thus far unfriendly addressee. See 26n.

  a lover's blind: cf. 39, 1.2.117n.

59 *Hagna's*: the common Greek name ("holy woman") would suit a slave or freedwoman (1.2.58, 151nn.), but it also suggests the Latin word *agna*, "young ewe" (cf. 2.3.327–30).

60 *Balbinus*: a common Roman surname, but possibly L. Saenius Balbinus, a senator proscribed by the triumvirs in 43 BCE (1.7.2n.), who survived to be reconciled with Octavian and attain the consulate in 30 BCE (App. *B.C.* 4.50). Cf. 4.58n.

63 *this mistake*: in the case of a lover, it really is a "mistake"; cf. Plato, *Republic* 5.474d–475d, Lucr. 4.1160–70; only Ovid (*Ars* 2.657–72—wickedly echoing H.) has the nerve to recommend it (but cf. *Rem.* 315–40, where he reverses his advice). But many philosophers considered the use of flattery (Greek *kolakeia*, Latin *assentatio* or *obsequium*), even if directed toward friends, a serious fault; see Theophrastus, *Characters* 2, Cic. *Amic.* 88–100, *Off.* 1.42, 91.

67 *squinter . . . "hood-eyed"*: the first term, *strabo*, is direct and derogatory, the second, *paetus*, less so, as shown by its use as an epithet of the love goddess Venus (e.g., Var. *Men.* 344; cf. Ov. *Ars* 2.659). But both, like other terms in 69–72 (see nn.), occur as Roman surnames (e.g., Cn. Pompeius Strabo, the father of Pompey, L. Autronius Paetus, substitute consul in 33 BCE), which, with a sensibility hardly imaginable in twenty-first-century America, were often based on physical deformities.

68 *Sisyphus*: this "dwarf belonging to M. Antonius the triumvir is said to have been about two feet tall but of a lively intellect" (Porph.); the latter quality may account for his name (see 2.3.32).

69 *"Chickee"*: Latin *pullus*, literally "small fowl" (130, 2.2.165), is a term of endearment (Pl. *Casina* 138) but also a surname (e.g., Q. Numitorius Pullus, the father of Antony's father's first wife).

70–72 *"Pigeon-toes" . . . "Gimpy" . . . "frugal"*: *varus* (e.g., *Epd.* 5.73, *Odes* 1.18.1), *scaurus* (*Odes* 1.12.37), and *frugi* (Cic. *Tusc.* 3.16) were also (67n.) common surnames at Rome.

75 *too free-spoken*: the Latin *plus aequo liber*, "more than fairly [15n.] frank," evokes the concept of *libertas*, "freedom," including "freedom of speech," the hallmark of the Roman Republic, which seemed to be in decline during the triumviral period and would be in very short supply under the emperors.

83 *dummkopf*: rendering Latin *pinguis*, literally "fat(headed)"; cf. 2.6.17–19n.

84–85 *so full / of bitter grudges and slurs*: see 1.1.41n.

90–91 *too straightforward . . . unaffected*: see 33, 75nn.

92 *Maecenas*: since Maecenas was not, as far as known, a Stoic (15, 134–35nn.), H.'s address here is probably a momentary apostrophe, as if Maecenas were "eavesdropping" (39n.). But if he is the addressee throughout, H.'s very freedom to criticize him could be meant to show that, contrary to what their enemies might say, he and the men in his circle (including Octavian?) were not completely opposed to such freedom. See 75n., 1.9.66–71, Cic. *Off.* 1.88.

96   *"unjust"*: Latin *inaequus* (15n.).

97   *everyone is born with imperfections*: a commonplace; cf. Catul. 22.20, Prop. 2.22.17, "to each man as he is created nature has given a fault," Tac. *Hist.* 4.74.2, "there will be faults so long as there are humans."

99–103   *weigh . . . scale*: the image of "weighing on a scale" was ancient even in H.'s time; cf. Cic. *Fin.* 5.91–92, *Tusc.* 5.51; see also Daniel 5:27, "thou hast been weighed in the balance and found wanting."

100–106   *that's fair . . . It's only fair*: the Latin is *aequum est* (15n.).

104–6   *zit . . . warts*: the thought is similar to that at 41–42 and likewise proverbial; see Sen. Dialogues, 8.27.4, "you comment on other people's pimples, yourself infested with sores."

109   *anger*: in ancient philosophy anger (*ira*) was considered especially "problematic" because it could not only lead to irrational acts (113–17) and disruption of friendship (118–26), but, when afflicting powerful men, bring great harm to a community; see *Odes* 1.16, Cic. *Tusc.* 48–55, *Off.* 1.88–89, 132–37. But H. may also single it out because it was a dominant emotion in Lucilian satire, not to mention one of his own faults (47–50n.).

110   *fools*: possibly a sarcastic reference to the Stoic tenet—the main theme of Damasippus' rant in *Sat.* 2.3—that all humans are "fools" (*stulti*) or even "madmen" (*insani*) except the ideal (Stoic) "sage" (*sapiens*). Cf. 134–35, 175–77, 195nn., 1.4.143.

113   *crucified*: not metaphorical here (but cf. 1.2.27n., 1.10.108); hanging on a cross (*crux*) was an accepted, if extreme, punishment at Rome for slaves who had committed crimes. See 2.7.70, *Ep.* 1.16.46–48.

114   *snitching food*: Lucilius may refer to this "crime" at fr. 629 *ROL*, "and a slave who had licked up with his mouth the tasty cakes." See also 2.7.142–43.

117   *Labeo*: possibly an example borrowed from Lucilius, who was still writing in 131 BCE, when the tribune of the plebs C. Atilius Labeo "insanely" tried to have one of the censors executed because the man had failed to include him in the list of new senators (Liv. *Epit.* 49). H. can hardly mean, as Porph. thinks, the famous jurist M. Antistius Labeo, an outspoken critic of Octavian during the principate (Tac. *Ann.* 3.75) but barely a teenager at the time H. wrote *Satires* 1.

118   *more deranged and grave*: i.e., than torturing a slave for a small offense. H.'s commentators explain this as hyperbole or "badinage," but see 1.1.48n.

119   *you*: 58n.

122   *Ruso*: a Roman surname, but this particular moneylender (1.2.15n.) is otherwise unknown.

123   *Kalends*: the first day of any Roman month. Money lent out or the interest on it could be collected legally only on this or on the other named days, the Nones and the Ides.

124–25 *reading . . . his dreadful "History"*: authors often tried out works prior to public performance (*recitatio*) on smaller audiences made "captive" by friendship, greed, or obligation; cf. 1.4.22–24, 88–97, 2.7.1, 58–60, *Ep.* 1.19.41–42, 2.1.223, 2.2.92–98, *Ars* 419–37, 472–76.

127–28 *wets / the couch*: at a Greek-style banquet, where guests reclined on couches or divans (*lecti*); see 1.4.109, 2.3.393, 2.4.50, 2.6.116, 135, 147, 2.8.25. At Trimalchio's infamous banquet in Petronius, the host tells his guests to relieve themselves on the couches if they feel the need (47.5), but also declares "water [= urine] outside, wine inside" (52.7).

129 *Evander's hands*: showing the fabulous antiquity of the bowl; Evander was the king of the Arcadians whom Aeneas found living at the future site of Rome (Virg. *A.* 8). Cf. 2.3.32–34, Gel. 1.10.2 (a man speaks such archaic Latin that) "it's as if you are talking with Evander's mother," Mart. 8.6.10.

133 *betrays a trust*: see 1.4.105–6.

134–35 *all crimes deserve the same / desert*: a Stoic paradox (see Cic. *Fin.* 4.55, 75–78, *Parad.* 20–26), opposed by the Epicureans (Diog. Laert. 10.120). The word for "same" here and at 169 is *par* (30n.).

137 *Utility*: in Epicurean thought, "utility" (*chreia* or *to sympheron*) is the basis of all attributes that distinguish humans from animals as well as from the gods, who in their carefree existence (1.5.126n.) have no need for justice or the like.

mother: for this type of personification, cf. *Ep.* 2.2.119 (new ways of expressing things) "which father Need has sired," Cic. *Leg.* 1.47, "pleasure, the mother of all ills."

138 *equity*: the Latin word is *aequum* (15n.).

139–56 H.'s account of the evolution of human society, with its emphasis on utility (137n.) and the role of language, is thoroughly Epicurean and in places closely echoes (and also "lightens up") Lucretius' far grander and more detailed narrative at 5.925–1457; see also Virgil's somewhat more "religious" version at *G.* 1.121–59.

142 *nuts*: acorns (*glandes*), often mentioned as the staple of human diet prior to hunting and agriculture. See Lucr. 5.939, 965, 1416, Virg. *G.* 1.8, 148, 159, and Juv. 6.10, (a "cavewoman") "shaggier than her acorn-belching husband."

147 *They walled their towns*: making war more difficult, but not ending it; many readers would no doubt recall the horrific civil war siege of Perugia (41–40 BCE), which ended with Octavian's troops massacring numerous Roman senators and equites after they had surrendered. H. seems to echo Virg. *Ecl.* 4.31–34, where the poet predicts that a new "Golden Age" will be interrupted when "some traces of ancient wrong will creep in, / which will bid men . . . to gird towns / with walls." According to Lucretius (5.1108–60), it was the foundation of walled cities, which led to greed, murderous ambition, and civil strife, that forced men to establish laws.

148 *marauders*: Latin *latrones*, a term that can denote "bandits," "pirates," or, in propaganda, civil war enemies (e.g., *Epd.* 4.19), all of them serious threats to public safety. See 168–69.

petty thieves, adulterers: surprisingly minor offenders, and in Republican Rome, at least, there do not appear to have been "laws" deterring adultery (1.2.56n.). But the bathos, if it is that, allows H. to "back off," as it were, from civil war (above) and focus on the distant past and the always amusing subject of sexuality.

149   *Helen*: in the most famous of all Greek myths, Paris' theft of her from her husband Menelaus and their adultery led to the Trojan War. H. retells the story at *Odes* 1.15; cf. *Odes* 3.3.25–26, 4.9.13–16, *Epd.* 17.42, and *Ep.* 1.2.6–8.

  cunt: the vulgarity (1.2.89n.) seems to jerk the reader back from didactic epic (139–56n.) to satire. Cf. *Priap.* 68.9, "Hey, if Trojan dick hadn't pleased Spartan cunt, / Homer wouldn't have had a poem to sing."

151–52   *unrecorded battles, / nameless*: a variation on a theme H. expresses more grandly at *Odes* 4.9.13–28, esp. 25–28, "There lived mighty men before Agamemnon, / many of them, but all of them unwept / and unknown are smothered in the long / night, because they lack a sacred bard."

152   *beast-style*: the Latin phrase, *more ferarum*, occurs at Lucr. 4.1256, where it is equivalent to American "doggy-style," 5.932, (early men) "lived in the wide-wandering style of beasts," and 6.198, (winds) "roar with beast-style menacing."

154   *fear . . . discovered justice*: i.e., justice arose as a useful (see 137) answer to injustice, not from any natural or divine impulse. See *HP* 22A.1–5.

155   *you must acknowledge*: Latin *fateare necesse est*, a formula occuring 11 times in Lucretius (e.g., 3.766, 5.343).

157   *nature*: 54n.

157–58   *right / from wrong*: the Latin word here for "right" is *bona* (1.1.84), that for "wrong" is *iniqua* (= *in*, "not," + *aequum*); see 15n.

159–60   *seek . . . shun*: philosophical language (cf. 1.2.96–97).

160–64   *steal / a baby cabbage . . . rob the gods*: H. may allude to the infamous early Athenian law code of Draco (whence "draconian"), in which "those who stole vegetables or fruits were punished in the same way as committers of sacrilege [164n.] and murderers" (Plut. *Life of Solon* 17.1; cf. Gel. 11.18.3). At Rome, the difference between these crimes is not just a question of decree, but of category: theft of private property was a matter for civil law or, just as often, "self-help" (1.2.56n.), while sacrilege, an offense against the state, was a matter for public (criminal) law.

164   *after dark*: at Rome a thief caught at night could legally be killed on the spot (*Lex XII* 8.12 *ROL*).

  rob the gods: the most basic form of *sacrilegium* (from *sacrum*, "holy object," + *legere*, "take"). But in Epicurean thinking (139–56n.) the gods themselves ought to be indifferent to such a crime, since "it is necessary that the whole nature of the gods in and of itself / enjoys immortal life in the highest state of tranquility / distant and far removed from our [human] affairs" (Lucr. 1.44–46); see 1.5.127n.

165   *There should be a rule*: H. means "rule" in the sense of (moral) standard or norm (= Greek *kanon*, "canon"), not of legal regulation, a sense of *regula* (literally "measuring stick") not attested in Republican Latin.

168 *piracy*: 148n.

169 *the same*: 30, 134–35nn.

172 *If you were given regal power*: H.'s addressee (26, 92nn.) probably means this literally (= "if I were in charge"), but H. pretends to interpret it as a reference to Stoic doctrine (175–77n.).

175–77 *the man who's wise . . . alone is . . . a king*: another (110, 134–35nn.) Stoic paradox (cf. Cic. *Parad.* 42–52) to which H. will again allude at 2.3.75, 150–51, 2.7.122–28, *Odes* 2.2.21, *Ep.* 1.1.106–8, and *Ep.* 1.10.8. According to Porph., it had already been mocked by Lucilius (frr. 1189–90 *ROL*), "not yet even he who will possess all these things / will be reckoned [? (the text is corrupt)] handsome, wealthy, free [110n.], and alone a king." See also Var. *Men.* 245 Astbury (possibly echoing Lucilius), "he alone is king, he alone is eloquent, he alone is handsome, strong, . . . spic and span. If someone matches this definition of Cleanthes [179n.], don't go near the man!"

178 *the Stoic says*: with the shift to the third person H. seems to turn away from his addressee (26n.) and acknowledge the wider audience of his readers. Cf. 1.2.137n.

179 *Chrysippus*: Chrysippus of Soli in Asia Minor (c. 280–207 BCE) was the third head of the Stoic school at Athens, having succeeded Cleanthes (331–232 BCE; see 175–77n.), who had succeeded the school's founder Zeno of Cyprus (335–263 BCE). See 2.3.70, 439.

182 *Hermogenes*: 1.2.4n.

184 *Alfenus*: Porph. identifies this as P. Alfenus Varus, a native of Cremona, who gave up his shoe-making business there to emigrate to Rome, where he achieved distinction as a legal expert (cf. Gel. 7(6).5.1, *Dig.* 1.2.2.44) and served as (replacement) consul in 39 BCE. He may be the Alfenus of Catul. 30 and, possibly (cf. 70–72n.), the "Varus" of Catul. 10, 22, H.'s own *Odes* 1.18, and, what seems less likely, of Virgil's *Ecl.* 6 and 9.

188 *street brats*: the "urchins" of Rome, as of other towns, were not shy about mocking oddballs; cf. 1.4.39–40n., 2.3.199, *Ars* 455–56, "intelligent folk fear and avoid encountering the crazy poet, / kids recklessly tease him and chase after him."

189 *your beard . . . that staff*: the stereotypical or at least "street" philosopher (usually a Cynic [see below] rather than a Stoic), had an unruly beard (2.3.57, Pers. 1.133; cf. *Ars* 298) and his only possessions were a walking stick and a satchel (Petr. 14.2.3, Mart. 4.53.3, 14.81.2).

191 *barking*: H.'s Stoic, instead of "stoically" enduring the abuse, acts more like the Cynic philosophers, who got their name (Greek *kunikos*, "doggish") from their snarling tone and "dogged" attacks on people and things that displeased them.

193–4 *inexpensive public bath, with only . . . Crispinus*: The "philosopher king" is short not only of money, but of friends.

194 *Crispinus*: 1.1.130n.

195 *fool*: 110n.

197 *happier*: 1.1.23n.

Satire 1.4 Notes

1   *Poets*: emphatic here, at 35, and at 186, but raising the question, to be explored in 41–73, of whether comic writers and satirists truly merit this appellation. See 42n.

   Eupolis . . . Aristophanes: the "big three" of Athenian Old Comedy (below) in the fifth century BCE. The oldest, Cratinus (cf. *Ep.* 1.19.1–3), died around 423, Eupolis (cf. 2.3.16) around 415, and Aristophanes, the most famous, in 388 BCE. Between them they wrote about 90 comedies, but although there are many fragments of these plays, only 11, all by Aristophanes, survive intact.

2   *comedies long ago*: the plays of Aristophanes et al. were called "Old Comedy" (cf. 1.10.22, *Ars* 281–84) to distinguish them from the "New Comedy" of Menander (2.3.17) and others that came into vogue after Athens' defeat in the Peloponnesian War (404 BCE). The former was highly political, scathingly abusive of public figures, and relentlessly bawdy; the latter, which would be the model for Plautus (*Ep.* 2.1.58, 170–76), Terence (2.29, *Ep.* 2.1.59), and other comic poets writing at Rome, found a gentler humor in the mishaps of private life and in the faults and follies of stock figures.

5   *freely scourged*: cf. 1.3.75n.

6   *Lucilius embraced this model wholly*: the idea of Old Comedy as a literary model or, at least, an inspiration for Lucilian satire (H. ignores here earlier Roman satire, but cf. 70–71n.), seems to have been widely accepted in H.'s time and may have come from Lucilius himself (see fr. 411 *ROL*).

7   *except the meter*: Lucilius wrote some of his earliest poems (books 26–29) in meters used in Greek and Latin comedy (and tragedy), but the rest, like H.'s *Satires* and *Epistles*, were in dactylic hexameters, the measure of Greek and, beginning with Ennius (67–71), of Latin epic.

9   *Two hundred lines an hour*: see 1.10.77–81.

10   *what a tour de force!*: H. is being sarcastic, but not a few Greeks and Romans were impressed by this kind of thing; cf. Cic. *Arch.* 5–6, *De Or.* 3.194.

11   *muddy rush*: cf. 1.10.67. Lucilius' poetry is a kind of metaphorical version of the dangerous river Aufidus (1.1.59–61). Some commentators detect here a reference to an aesthetic associated with Hellenistic (Alexandrian) poetry and especially with the poet-critic Callimachus (1.2.137n.), who denounced overly long and carelessly written poems and praised those that were brief and artfully polished; see *Hymn* 1.105–12, which may be H.'s model for the image a dirty river, *Epigr.* 28, *Aetia* fr. 1, and fr. 465 *LCL*, "a big book is the same as a big evil." But the metaphor figures elsewhere in H. (1.7.34–35, 1.10.48–50, 83, *Odes* 4.2.5–8, *Ep.* 2.2.120–21) as well as in Latin literary criticism seemingly independent of Callimachus (e.g., Cic. *Brut.* 316).

12   *stuff you'd edit out*: the first indication of an addressee, who is not named but is clearly not a friend (89–90, 100–1, 169). Although here the man seems to share H.'s qualms about Lucilius' sloppiness, it will emerge that he is one of those who "dread poets and hate poetry" (25–35n.) and that he distrusts satire as a genre (76) without either knowing much about it or recognizing his own hypocrisy in this (113–24). See also 42, 98nn.

garrulous: like Fabius (1.1.17).

15 *Crispinus*: 1.130n.

16 *tablet*: a Roman writer composed his rough draft with the sharp end of a small metal stick (*stilus*, "stylus," "pen"; see 2.1.61) on wooden tables covered with wax that could be smoothed over for reuse with the blunt end of the same stick (1.10.99).

18 *not that gifted*: more sarcasm (8).

19 *I rarely talk*: but cf. 1.3.90–94.

20 *Go on*: probably addressed to Crispinus (apostrophe), although H.'s addressee could also be a windbag poet (12n.).

Vulcan's bellows: at the smith-god's forge under the volcanic Mt. Aetna in Sicily (*Odes* 1.4.6–7).

22 *blessed*: the Latin is *beatus* (1.1.23n.), here sarcastic.

Fannius: possibly the "dopey Fannius" mentioned at 1.10.110–11 as a maligner of H. and companion of Tigellius Hermogenes (1.2.4n.). There was a C. Fannius among the supporters of Sex. Pompeius (1.1.5n.) who abandoned him just before his final defeat and death in 35 BCE (App. *B.C.* 5.139).

24 *public recitations*: see 88–97 and 1.3.124–25n.

25–35 *some folks . . . This crowd*: this group would seem to include H.'s addressee (12n.), to whom he directs his "rebuttal" (42–72).

27 *grim ambition*: H.'s first mention of this fault, of which he is anxious to claim innocence (1.6.26, 1.9.65, 1.10.115nn., 2.6.23; cf. 1.3.147n., 2.3.121–22, 249–45, 2.7.110–11).

28–29 *greed . . . married women*: as in *Sat.* 1.1 and 1.2.

30 *for boys*: 1.2.151n.

30–31 *silver captivates . . . bronze*: the men are antique nuts, the sort that the absurd Damasippus made money off of (2.3.31–37). H.'s slave Davus accuses him of this fault, among others (2.7.136); see also *Ep.* 1.16.17–18.

31 *Albius*: possibly the same man as at 136, but certainly not the elegist Albius Tibullus, who would have been a small boy in the early 30s BCE. There could be a play on the name, which suggests *albus*, "pasty-faced" (cf. 2.2.33).

32 *businessmen*: also a target in *Sat.* 1.1.

35 *poetry . . . poets*: 1n.

36 *hay on his horns*: "Even nowadays at Rome we see hay placed in a kind of loop on the horns of a steer so that passersby can be warned to avoid him" (Porph.). Cf. 2.1.79–80, *Odes* 3.21.18, Plut. *Quaest. Rom.* 71. At *Epd.* 6.11–12, H., in his pose as an iambist (2.3.17n.), describes himself as a bull with "horns readied to thrust at evil-doers."

39–40 *slave boy . . . washer woman*: purveyors of gossip, but also a far cry from the kind of people likely to attend a public recitation (24).

41 *brief rebuttal*: H. may echo Lucilius, who seems also to have replied to an attack on his satire in a poem in his book 30 (frr. 1061–91 *ROL*); cf. fr. 1063, "Nevertheless I will try to write briefly in refutation," and 98–99, 99–100nn. below.

42 *I'm no poet*: this answer to the haters of poets (35) is so silly that it seems best taken as an alert to H.'s readers that his rebuttal, or at least the first part of it (up to 72), is largely ironic. (The 1950's movie star Victor Mature, when refused membership in a country club on the grounds that they did not admit actors, replied: "I'm no actor! I have the reviews to prove it.")

You'd say: H. again (12n.) depicts his addressee sharing his view, at least until he seems to go too far (53–58).

44   *who writes like people talk*: an allusion to H.'s own term for his satires, *sermones*, "conversations." See the Introduction.

46–47   *souls . . . genius . . . symphonic might*: the language is suitably grandiloquent.

48   *the comic stage*: H. starts with satires's supposed model (6n.) before turning to satire itself (64–71).

53   *you say*: H. has gone too far for his addressee (12, 42nn.), who is made to express a commonly held view that even comedy can "rise" to poetic heights; cf. *Ars* 93–94, "now and then Comedy lifts up her voice, / and an angered Chremes [1.10.56–57n.] quibbles in fulsome phrases."

the scene: from a lost play, but it sounds more like New Comedy than Old Comedy (2n.).

57   *a torch . . . in broad daylight*: torches were necessary for night travel in ancient cities, which rarely had streetlights (cf. 2.7.45, Prop. 1.3.9), but to use them by day (except in religious contexts) was considered so absurd that it was proverbial for a useless action (e.g., Cic. *Fin.* 4.29).

58   *Pomponius*: possibly the son of a Pomponius who escaped proscription (1.7.2n.) by the triumvirs in 43 BCE by joining Sex. Pompeius (App. *B.C.* 4.45).

68–69   *"When once Discord . . . iron"*: from book 7 of Ennius' *Annales* (225–26). The gates are those of the Temple of Janus (2.6.26nn.) at Rome, which had been closed as a symbol of peace at the end of the First Punic War in 241 BCE but were soon reopened for another war and would not be closed again until 29 BCE, after Octavian's victory over Antony and Cleopatra (see *Ep.* 2.1.255, *Odes* 4.15.8–9).

68   *Discord*: a kind of Fury (cf. *Ann.* 220–21), the model for Virgil's Allecto in *A.* 7, although in his imitation of the Ennian passage there (7.620–22) it is Juno who opens the gates. The word might have had a different resonance for H.'s readers than for those of Ennius, since by the late Republic *discordia* had become almost a technical term for "civil strife" (e.g., Cic. *Phil.* 7.25, Virg. *Ecl.* 1.72, *G.* 2.496, *A.* 8.702). Cf. 7.18n.

70   *Ennius*: Q. Ennius (239–169 BCE), a native of Rudiae in H.'s own Apulia (1.5.95) who became Rome's first great epic poet (1.10.71–72) but also wrote drama, a poem in praise of Scipio Africanus, and the first literary satire. See 68–69, 1.1.121–24, 1.2.45, 47–48, 1.10.71, 90–91nn.

71   *no matter how dismembered*: the rather nasty image evokes the fates of Pentheus (2.3.305n.) and the mythical Greek poet Orpheus (Virg. *G.* 4.520–22), but it may also be meant to suggest the idea, common in ancient literary theory, of a poem or other work as a kind of "living body" (e.g., Aristotle, *Poetics* 7.8–10, 8.4, Cic. *De Or.* 3.96).

74   *another time*: cf. 1.10.15–16n..

77–79   *Sulcius . . . indictments*: at Rome and in the Greek world, where there were no offices of "state's attorney," it was up to private citizens, encouraged by the prospect of social and political advancement and monetary rewards, to serve as *accusatores* ("prosecutors") of criminal offenders. See Cic. *Off.* 2.49–51, *S. Rosc.* 8, 83, *Verr.* 1.21, 5.173, *Sul.* 50, etc.

77 *Sulcius and Caprius*: otherwise unknown, but their names may be meant to suggest varieties of fig tree, *ficus sulca* and *caprificus*, and thus allude to the Greek term for prosecutors, *sycophantes*, literally "fig-revealers."

78 *little books*: either dossiers of their targets' alleged crimes or formal "court briefs," but in any case not to be confused with H.'s sort of "little book" (85).

79 *bandits*: 1.3.148n.

82–83 *Caelius . . . Birrius*: genuine names, but otherwise unknown. Lucilius may have mentioned a Caelius in connection with a fight or battle (fr. 1008 *ROL*), but the text is uncertain.

85 *little book*: 78n.

87 *Tigellius Hermogenes*: 1.2.4n.

88 *reciting*: 24n.

93 *public baths*: where the acoustics were like those in a modern gym's shower room. Cf. Petr. 73.3, "lured on by the sound in the bath chamber he raised his drunken voice all the way to the ceiling and began to mutilate songs."

96–97 *who . . . timely*: i.e., who are "pains" and "lack social skills" (1.3.94–95).

98 *someone says*: for the shift to the third person, see 1.2.137n. But some of the MSS have *inquis*, "you say," instead of *inquit*, "he [the man] says."

98–99 *"You . . . enjoy / inflicting pain*: addressed to H. by his addressee (12n.). H. again (41n.) seems to echo Lucilius' *apologia*: cf. fr. 1085 *ROL* (also addressed to the poet; cf. 1075), "You enjoy it when you scatter about these libels about me in your conversations."

99–100 *Where on earth . . . with that?*: cf. Lucilius' reply to his attacker (98–99n.) in fr. 1078 *ROL*: "You have the nerve to allege these things against me? Don't you turn things over in your mind first?"

101–8 *who knows me . . . beware*: H. turns his concern that someone he knows may have ratted him out (100–1) into a tirade against "backbiters" (cf. 1.3.35) in general. But some editors assign these lines to H.'s addressee, with H. turning the man's own view against him in the lines that follow, 108–24.

107 *black-hearted*: see line 114. The Latin word, *niger* (literally "black"), is in this sense an antonym of *candidus* (literally "white"), "true-blue" (1.5.53 and 1.10.118). For the Romans there would be no racial implications in this language, since they did not really define groups in terms of color (but cf. 2.8.18n.).

    good Romans: apostrophe (see 12n.).

109 *twelve . . . on three divans*: not only are the guests objectionable, but the dinner party is in poor form: Greek and Roman custom assigned no more than three people to a couch, and, according to Varro, *Men.* 333 Astbury, the number present should be no fewer than that of the Graces (three) and no more than that of the Muses (nine). Nasidienus' fiasco in *Sat.* 2.8 at least followed the rules (2.8.28–34).

111 *once he's drunk*: as Nasidienus fears in regard to two of his guests (2.8.51).

112–13 *Liber . . . liberated*: Liber, the Roman name for the Greek god of wine Dionysus/Bacchus (1.3.11n.), refers to his power to make people free (*liber*; see 1.3.75n.) of inhibitions. See *Ep.* 1.19.1–5, 2.2.78.

113 *urbane*: Latin *urbanus*, literally "from the City" (cf. 1.1.12, 13nn.), can also indicate sophistication, cleverness, and subtlety; cf. 1.10.115–16n., *Ars* 273, Cic. *Cael.* 9, Catul. 22.2.

114 *black-hearted*: 107n.

115–16 *"Rufillus . . . goat"*: quoting 1.2.35–36.

117 *fanged*: the Latin, *mordax*, "biting," continues the image of "back-biting" (101–2).

  spiteful: something H. is much on guard against from others (1.1.41n.).

118 *Petillius*: also mentioned at 1.10.36. A Petillius Capitolinus (his family surname, not an epithet; see below) was an overseer of the Roman mint (cf. 1.2.123n.) in 43 BCE, but it is not known what "larceny" he was acquitted of. Porph. says it was taking the golden crown from the statue of Jupiter in the Capitoline Temple, but this seems to be an invention based on the surname and on the proverbial description of a bold theft as "stealing the holy crown of Jupiter" (cf. Pl. *Menaechmi* 941, *Trinummus* 83–84).

129 *more freely*: 112–13n. There may be irony here, since, although H. has not yet mentioned it, his father was not "free" by birth (1.6.25, 58–59).

132 *the very best of fathers*: H. talks at length about his father in *Sat.* 1.6 and mentions him at *Ep.* 1.20.20, in what may be his last hexameter poem.

134 *marking paradigms of bad behavior*: and some of good (152–55). He may have done this "marking" while escorting H. to school (1.6.107–8). The method of instruction resembles that of Demeas, a father in Terence's New Comedy (2n.) *Adelphi* (414–19): "I let nothing slip by, I get him used to the idea, / then I bid him look, as though into a mirror, into the lives of everybody else / and take from them examples for himself of / 'do this' . . . 'don't do that' / 'this merits praise' . . . 'this is a fault.'"

135 *Albius' boy*: evidently a chip off the old block.

136 *Baius, ever short of cash*: unknown, but H. probably plays on his name, which in Greek means "short," including "short on resources" = *inops*, his Latin epithet here.

139–41 *falling for a whore . . . married women . . . brothels*: H. explains where he learned the advice he dispenses at 1.2.37–81. There is no contradiction between lines 139 and 141: brothels are fine for release (1.2.40n.) but not the place to find true love.

139 *Scetanus*: otherwise unknown, as is the name. Some MSS have *Sectanus*, which could be a play on *sectari*, "chase after," "stalk."

141 *Trebonius*: also unknown, but a member of a distinguished clan that included C. Trebonius, the substitute consul in 45 BCE, who was the first of conspirators against Julius Caesar to pay with his life (Cic. *Phil.* 11).

143 *Philosophers*: possibly dismissive; cf. 1.3.110, 175–77nn.

144–45 *avoid . . . seek*: philosophical language (1.2.96–97n.).

146–47 *ways passed down / by men of old*: H.'s father, an ex-slave whose own father was a slave (129n.), could not use the Roman formula *mos / mores maiorum*, "way(s) of our ancestors."

151 *float*: a Roman life preserver made from the bark of a cork tree (*cortex*); cf. *Odes* 3.9.22, Pl. *Aulularia* 595–96, Liv. 5.46.8.

155 *a juryman*: men of the equestrian order who were chosen to be eligible for jury duty in criminal cases were expected to be of the highest character (Cic. *Clu.* 121). H. himself attained this status by the time of Book 2 of the *Satires*, if not earlier (2.7.77).

160–64 *Just as a . . . path of folly*: The simile furnishes a concrete example of the proverb "it's good to recognize things to be avoided from another person's misfortune" (Publ. Syr. 46).

167 *moderate faults*: cf. 182, 1.1.111n., 1.3.33, 1.6.87.

169 *free-spoken*: 1.3.75n.

180–81 *writing . . . to entertain myself*: rendering the verb *illudere*, literally "play around." The simple form *ludere* and its noun *ludus* are often used in connection with "light verse" (e.g., 1.10.50, *Odes* 1.32.2, Lucil. frr. 1039–40), but the latter can also mean "stage play" (2.6.62, 2.8.68n.); cf. 1–2 above.

182 *moderate faults*: 167n.

183 *poets*: see 1n.

185 *there're more of us*: either because the number of poets is commensurate with the number of people who "warrant ridicule" (26), or because almost everybody thinks he or she can be a poet; cf. *Ep.* 2.1.117, "skilled and unskilled, all over the place we [humans] scribble poems."

   like the Jews: the poets are like a crowd of Rome's many Jews, who were notorious for getting their coreligionists to act and express themselves publicly in a solid bloc (see Cic. *Flac.* 66). Some commentators take this as a reference to Jewish proselytizing, but although Jews were ridiculed for their supposed superstition (1.5.125n.) and for the custom of circumcision (1.9.99n.), there is no other evidence that they either solicited conversions in Republican Rome or that the Romans thought they did so.

Satire 1.5 Notes

1–2 Not surprisingly for a poem full of (mock) epic touches, H. follows the Homeric model for his narrative and, skipping preliminaries, "carries his listener right / into the middle of things" (*Ars* 148–49); more specifically, he seems to echo the equally bare-bones start of the account Odysseus (Ulysses) gives the Phaeacians of *his* journey (*Od.* 9.39–40): "From Ilium a carrying wind brought me to the Cicones / at Ismarus." But the result is that an uninformed "listener" (92n.) at first would have no idea why H. was traveling, and even when there is a reference to the purpose of the trip it is remarkably vague (34–36n.). According to Porph., H.'s satire is an attempt to "rival" a much longer satire (it filled a whole book) by Lucilius, in which he described a journey to southern Italy but also to Sicily (frr. 94–148 *ROL*).

1   *majestic Rome*: inviting comparison between Rome and the mostly backwater stops on the journey about to be described.

  Aricia: at the foot of the Alban Hills, the site of two important temples of Diana and the birthplace of Octavian's mother Atia.

2   *Heliodorus*: possibly a) the author of a Greek poem called "The Wonders of Italy," of which a fragment survives (= Stobaeus, *Florilegium* 100.6) describing a warm spring at Puteoli effective for eye ailments (see 36–39), or b) an alias for Apollodorus (the name does not fit into dactylic verse; see 29, 31, 107, 2.4.4nn.) of Pergamon, a teacher of rhetoric who had been Octavian's tutor (Suet. *Aug.* 89).

4   *Forum Appi*: a small town named for Appius Claudius Caecus (7n.) at the edge of the Pomptine Marshes, a malarial swamp that could be crossed either on the Appian Way or, more easily, by barge on a canal constructed in 160 BCE.

6   *Real travelers*: as opposed to "tenderfeet." The Latin *praecincti* means girded-up (as in "gird up thy loins") = ready to walk vigorously.

7   *The Appian*: i.e., the Appian Way (*Via Appia*), the great road running from Rome southeast to Capua, then south-southeast to Brundisium (Brindisi), named for Appius Claudius Caecus, who was censor when construction began in 312 BCE. Its original purpose was to provide ready access to the territories of Rome's fierce enemies the Oscan-speaking (68n.) Samnites and their allies; nearly every stop on it had been at one time or another a battlefield.

9   *The water isn't good*: see 29, 109, and 114.

11–12   *Now night . . . stars*: an epic-sounding introduction to a most "unepic" interchange of travelers' slaves and bargemen.

16   *the mule*: like Sal of the Erie Canal, she pulls the barge from a towpath at the canal's edge.

17   *loud marsh frogs*: their presence as a "choir" indicates that it is spring, probably early May (see Cic. *Fam.* 7.18.3).

26   *willow branch*: from the bank of the marshy canal.

28   *Half the morning gone*: literally "in the fourth hour [after sunrise]," which in spring would be between 9 and 10 a.m.; cf. 1.6.54–55n., 169, 1.9.47–48, 2.6.45, 2.7.45.

29   *Feronia*: a Sabine goddess (Varro, *Lingua Latina* 5.74) regarded as a protector of ex-slaves such as H.'s father (*Sat.* 1.6); the apostrophe, while metrically expedient (the possessive form of the name cannot fit into dactylic verse), may also imply familiarity.

31   *we crawled*: translating *repimus*, a word normally used of "creeping things" (late Latin *reptiles*). But it turns out they are traveling by mule cart (58).

  Anxur: the ordinary Latin name Tarracina does not fit into dactylic verse (see 47 and 108), but H.'s use of the Volscian name may also be meant to recall ancient wars between the Volscians and Rome and also to hint that he and his friends are somewhat "anxious" (Latin *anxius*).

32   *cliffs so white*: a picturesque detail but possibly contributing to H.'s eye trouble (37–38).

33 *Cocceius*: L. Cocceius Nerva, consul in 39 BCE, was a great-great uncle of the future emperor Nerva.

34 *would join us here*: it is not clear why H. and Heliodorus or, for that matter, Plotius, Virgil, and Varius (50–51), left Rome separately from Maecenas and were not part of his official retinue (see 1.6.136–38).

34–36 *ambassadors . . . mission . . . urgently important*: this is as close as H. gets to explaining the purpose of the journey. The spring setting (17n.) suggests that the year was 37 BCE, and the "ambassadors" were on their way to Tarentum to meet Octavian and Antony, who would there reach a new agreement (the Treaty of Tarentum) superseding the Treaty of Brundisium (fall 40 BCE) and renewing the triumvirate for another five years. See the Introduction.

35 *reconciling friends*: they had helped negotiate the Treaty of Brundisium (see above) between Octavian and Antony.

37 *inflammation*: making him "bleary eyed" (*lippus*); see 1.3.41.

40 *Fonteius Capito*: consul in 33 BCE. He was Antony's legate in the East and would bring Cleopatra to him at Antioch some time after the likely date of this poem (Plut., *Life of Antony* 36.1).

42 *Fundi*: another formerly Volcian town (31n.), as was Formiae (47n.). Both places were famous for their wines, Caecuban (2.8.21) from Fundi, and Falernian (1.10.33, 2.3.180, 2.4.32, 70) from Formiae.

43–44 *in the year . . . praetorship*: a mocking parody of the Roman use of the names of consuls to indicate particular years.

43 *Aufidius Luscus*: his name suggests the river Aufidus in H.'s homeland (112n.; see 1.1.60, 2.4.31); his surname, which means "one-eyed," suggests that he, too, has defective vision (37); and his profession ("bureaucrat" translates *scriba*; see 65, 83nn.) is the same as that of H. But unlike H. (*Sat.* 1.6 passim), he flaunts his ambition, even though it is unlikely he had any real claim to (Roman) senatorial regalia or to the title "praetor"; at Fundi, the local magistrates seem to have been called "aediles."

46 *pan of charcoals*: apparently for burning incense (122) at a welcoming ceremony.

47 *Mamurra's town*: i.e., Formiae, another name not suited to dactylic verse (2n.). But the periphrasis has unpleasant connotations: the first Mamurra prominent at Rome was a repulsive character who, thanks to the favor of both Pompey and Caesar, achieved and squandered enormous wealth. See Catul. 29, 41, 43, and 57.

48 *Murena's villa*: one of the many country estates in the area owned by prominent Romans. L. Licinius Varro Murena was the adopted brother of Maecenas' wife Terentia; much later (23 or 22 BCE) he would be involved in a conspiracy against Octavian.

50–51 *Plotius, / Varius, and Virgil*: by the late 30s Virgil was already famous as the author of the *Eclogues* (10.61–62); he and L. Varius Rufus, known for his now lost epic poetry (*Sat.* 1.10.59–60, *Odes* 1.6) and, later, for his tragedy *Thyestes*, introduced H. to Maecenas (*Sat.* 1.6.71–73). M. Plotius Tucca would be, along with Varius, Virgil's literary executor and thus responsible

for preserving, contrary to Virgil's wishes, the unfinished *Aeneid*. All three
are mentioned again among H.'s "ideal readers" (1.10.112–13).

52 *Sinuessa*: producer of yet another excellent wine (42n.), Massicum (2.4.66).

53 *true-blue*: they are *candidus*, the opposite of "black-hearted" (1.4.107n.).

56 *layover*: a stop on what would become the remarkable postal system of the
Roman empire.

　　Campanian bridge: over the river Savo (Saona), the boundary in old times
between Latin territory and Campania.

58 *Capua*: the leading municipality in Campania, it had lost territory to military
settlements in the aftermath of the battle of Philippi; so, too, Caudium (63) and
Beneventum (87), not to mention H.'s own town of Venusia; cf. 1.6.95n.

59 *play some ball*: evidently a favorite pastime of Maecenas (2.6.62; see also
2.2.18).

60 *siesta*: a custom in ancient Rome as in many Mediterranean and (modern)
"Latin" countries. See 2.6.78n.

61 *fussy stomachs*: H.'s own (9–10), but also Virgil's; see Suet. *Vita Vergiliana*
8, "his health was delicate, for often he suffered from stomachaches, sore
throats, and headaches, and he often vomited blood."

63 *the shops of Caudium*: a rather bathetic way to refer to a place remembered
by Romans as the site of humiliating military defeat in 321 BCE. "The
Gettysburg Mall" might strike American ears in a similar way.

64–66 *Muse . . . battle . . . lineage*: a parody of the style of Greek and Latin epic,
in which the Muse or Muses are often invoked to assist the poet in "recall-
ing" names, ancestry, and deeds of ancient heroes. See 1.10.60, 2.6.22nn.;
Odes 1.6.11–12, 4.8.13–29, 4.9.21; *Ep.* 2.1.241–44; *Ars* 141; Hom. *Il.* 1.1–7,
2.484–94; *Od.* 1.1–10; Virg. *A.* 1.8–11.

65 *Sarmentus*: his name, meaning "twig" or "stalk," fits his stature (85). The
scholia on Juv. 5.3 say that he was an Etruscan (like Maecenas), the slave
first of M. Favonius, the husband of his "mistress" (69), then of Maecenas.
When he was freed, he managed to attain equestrian status and, like H., a
position as a "clerk" (84; see 44, 2.6.47nn.). He would seem to be too old
and high in rank to be the Sarmentus mentioned by Plut. (*Life of Antony* 59.8)
as a "boy-toy" of Octavian.

　　the witty clown: translating *scurra*, the exact term for the type of man
contrasted with the (Horatian) satirist at 1.4.108–14; see also 1.8.15, 2.1.31,
and 2.7.21, 52.

65–66 *Messius . . . "The Cock"*: otherwise unknown, although Porph. says that
he, too, was a knight (*eques*). His name suggests Latin *messor*, "clodhopper,"
but his Oscan ancestry (68n.) and nickname Cicirrus (an Oscan word for
"rooster") hint at Atellan Farce, a form of improvised drama originating in
Oscan Italy that featured grotesque stock characters, crude physical comedy,
and scurrilous abuse.

66 *Be brief*: probably a dig at the long-winded Lucilius; see 1–2n., 1.4.9–15.

68 *famous Oscan stock*: ironic; among the Romans, the term "Oscan" (*Oscus*,
Opscus, *Opicus*), used of the non-Greek inhabitants of S. Italy, had a con-

nation of being "backwards," "uncouth," and "oversexed." A number of ancient grammarians derived *obscaenus*, "obscene," from *oscus*. See also 77n.

mistress: the wife of M. Favonius (66n.). Sarmentus' antecedents prior to his becoming a slave are irrelevant.

71 *a rhinoceros*: interpreting *equi* . . . *feri*, literally "wild horse," which could also refer to a unicorn (see Pliny, *Nat.* 8.76). But H. probably alludes to Lucil. frr. 109–10 *ROL* (from the older satirist's "journey poem" [1–2n.]), "the bucktoothed man from Bovilla [a town near Aricia] with his little tooth sticking out, this guy's / a rhinoceros." See also fr. 184 *ROL,* (someone is or acts) "just like an Ethiopian rhinoceros."

We laugh: as often with jokes about physical deformity. See 1.3.67n.

77 *Campanian malady*: a mysterious phrase, but perhaps alluding to the sexual rapacity of the Oscan inhabitants of Campania (so Porph.; see 68n.). Other possibilities are a reference to Campanian hatred of and resistance to Rome (Pseudacro) or, what seems least likely, to some actual disfiguring disease endemic in the region (Pseudacro).

78 *hoedown like a Cyclops*: evidently pantomiming the writhing of the Cyclops Polyphemus either after he had lost his one eye (Hom. *Od.* 9) or, earlier in life, when he was tormented by desire for the nymph Galatea (Theocritus, *Idyll* 6). See *Ep.* 2.2.125, (a poet compared to a dancer) "who / now trips 'the satyr,' now 'the rustic Cyclops.'"

79 *mask or high-heeled boot*: because he is already frightening to look at and, unlike Sarmentus, tall. H.'s word for mask, *larva*, literally "evil ghost," suggests some kind of farce (66–67n.), but his phrase for the boots, *tragicis . . . coturnis*, "tragic buskins," points, as the epithet shows, to Greek tragedy.

82 *shackles to the Lar*: a distortion of a free-born Roman youth's assumption of adult status, when he would dedicate his child's protective amulet (*bulla*) to the patron god of his home (2.3.248–49n.). The "shackles" anticipate 84, as such things were reserved for slaves who had tried to run away (*fugitivi*); see 1.1.83n., 2.5.23, and 2.7.159.

83 *clerk*: *scriba* again (44, 65nn.).

rights: to reclaim him as her property, in which case he would forfeit all status again (68n.).

85 *A pound of grain*: the daily food allotment for a slave was 3 to 4 Roman pounds (= 2–3 American pounds) of grain. Instead of running away, this "squirt" (65n.) could have sold the excess and saved up to buy his freedom; in any case, he could not have claimed starvation as a reason to flee.

86 *Such fun it was*: probably sarcastic; cf. Lucil. fr. 131 *ROL* (possibly describing a dinner party during his "journey" [1–2n.]), "we lift up our jaws [drooping with boredom?] and force a grin."

87 *Beneventum*: literally "well-come," a name given the place by the Romans when they conquered it in 268 BCE, since its original (Oscan) name suggested the Latin word *maleventum*, "ill-come."

88 *host*: at the inn or way station (56n.) where they put up.

89 *skinny thrushes*: poor fare; thrushes (*turdi*), while much prized (2.2.103,

2.5.15), were supposed to be plump; see *Epd.* 2.33, and *Ep.* 1.15.40–41, "nothing is better than a very fat thrush."

90   *Vulcan*: the god of fire = the fire itself (metonymy; see 1.2.153n.), as in Homer (*Il.* 2.426) and Ennius (*Ann.* 589), but also (parody of epic or tragedy) in comedy (e.g., Pl. *Menaechmi* 330).

92   *You'd have seen*: i.e., if you were there. This is the only hint of an addressee in the poem and recalls the occasional acknowledgments of an audience in epic (1–2n.), e.g., Hom. *Il.* 4.223–25, 429–31.

95   *Apulia*: H. and his party exit the Appian Way and follow a shorter but more difficult road (later part of the *Via Traiana*) to Brundisium that runs just west of H.'s homeland of Venusia.

96   *crawled*: see 31n.

98   *villa near Trivicum*: probably another way station (56n.). Trivicum, "three regions," is an apt name for a place near the juncture of Campania, Apulia, and Calabria.

    tears: more eye trouble (32, 37–38, 61).

102   *the girl*: evidently a serving maid. H. omits the preliminaries.

103   *dirty dreams*: Lucil. fr. 1183 *ROL* (book and context unknown, but see 1–2n.) may describe a similar incident: "I ejaculated on the bed, I imposed corruption with my pud on the coverings." The Epicurean Lucretius attempted to explain the causes of such dreams (4.1030–36).

105   *thirty-six kilometers*: translating "twenty-four miles." One Roman mile is approximately 1.5 km or 0.9 English miles.

106   *carriages*: drawn by horses, not mules (cf. 31, 58).

107   *won't fit the meter*: as with Formiae (47). H. may mean Herdoniae, a town roughly the right distance from Trivicum and about 29 Roman miles (43 km) short of Canusium. Other candidates are either out of the way (e.g., Porph.'s Equum Tuticum) or, with a common elision, would in fact "fit the meter" (e.g., Ausculum = modern Ascoli). For the conceit, see Lucil. frr. 253–53 *ROL*, "Today is the slave holiday / that you simply cannot say in hexameter verse."

109   *water . . . is sold*: most of the Apulian region is very dry except during the spring (17n.) rainy season (117). See *Epd.* 3.16, "thirsty Apulia."

112   *Canusium*: on the Aufidus River (44n.). It and the other towns mentioned in the rest of the poem were Roman municipalities, but Greek language and culture remained strong in all of them (1.10.41, 2.3.256).

113   *brave Diomedes*: an absurdly grand pedigree for so sorry a place. Diomedes, king of Tiryns and one of the mightiest Greek warriors at Troy (1.7.20), ended up after the war emigrating to Apulia, where he founded several towns but declined to ally himself with the Latins and Rutulians against his old enemy Aeneas (Virg. *A.* 1.96–98, 11.225–95).

114   *gritty*: probably from worn-out millstones.

115   *Varius*: 50–51n.

115–16   *Everyone / depressed*: the clipped style and omission of details about the next couple of stops, Rubi and Bari, suggest haste.

120   *Gnathia*: also called Egnatia or Ignatia.

124 *Jew Apella*: Apella (Apelles) is a common name for freedmen of non-Italian origin, but there may be, as Porph. notes, a play on the Greek prefix *a-*, "without," and the Latin word *pellis*, "skin" = "circumcised"; see 1.9.99. Roman and Greek authors often speak of Jews as being especially "superstitious" (e.g., Cic. *Flac.* 67); see 1.4.185n.

126 *carefree lives*: a basic tenet of Epicurean philosophy; see Lucr. 1.44–49, 2.646–51, 1093–94, 3.23–24, and especially 5.82 (repeated at 6.58), which H. here echoes almost word for word.

127 *nature*: see 1.1.52n.

129 *Brundisi*: the stopping point for H. but not, it would seem, for others in his party (34–36n.).

   lengthy: but still far shorter than Lucilius' journey and poem about it (1–2n.).

The Itinerary
(Based on Lejay, Kiessling and Heinze, and Brown)

Lines	Day	Leg	Distance in Roman miles (English miles / km)
1–4	1	Rome to Aricia (La Riccia)	16 (14.7 / 24.0)
4–16	2	Aricia to Forum Appi (Foro Appio)	27 (24.8 / 40.0)
17–28	2–3	Canal boat to Lucus Feroniae	16 (14.7 / 24.0)
29–42	3	Lucus Feroniae to Anxur (Terracina)	3 (2.8 / 4.5)
43–46	4	Anxur to Fundi (Fondi)	13 (12.0 / 19.5)
47–49	4	Fundi to Formiae (Formia)	13 (12.0 / 19.5)
50–55	5	Formiae to Sinuessa (Bagnoli)	18 (16.2 / 27.0)
56–57	5	Sinuessa to the Campanian bridge	9 (8.3 / 13.5)
58–61	6	Campanian bridge to Capua (St. Maria di Capua)	17 (15.6 / 25.5)
61–86	7	Capua to Caudium (Montesarchio)	21 (19.3 / 31.5)
87–94	8	Caudium to Beneventum (Benevento)	11 (10.1 / 16.5)
95–104	9	Beneventum to Trivicum (Trevico)	25 (23.0 / 37.5)
105–10	10	Trivicum to Herdoniae (Ordono)	24 (22.1 / 36.0)
111–16	11	Herdoniae to Canusium (Canosa)	29 (26.1 / 43.5)
116–18	12	Canusium to Rubi (Ruvo)	23 (21.2 / 34.5)
118–20	13	Rubi to Barium (Bari)	23 (21.2 /34.5)
120–28	14	Barium to Gnathia (Torre d'Agnazzo)	37 (34.0 / 55.5)
129	15	Gnathia to Brundisium (Brindi)	39 (35.9 / 58.5)

Satire 1.6 Notes

1 *Lydian*: it was commonly believed that the Etruscans, whose language was utterly different from any other spoken in ancient Italy, had migrated there from Lydia in Asia Minor. See Herodotus 1.94, Virg. *A.* 8.479–80, Tac. *Ann.* 4.55.

    Maecenas: H.'s address to him is interrupted by apostrophes (29–31, 146–52) and an imagined dialogue (46–55).

2 *Tuscany*: the Romans called the Etrurians *Etrusci*, *Tusci*, and (from the Greek) *Tyrrheni*.

3 *mother's ancestors*: the explicit reference to Maecenas' mother contrasts with H.'s silence about his own (44, 128nn.), but it also coheres with the fact that in many inscriptions from Etruria (Tuscany) people's pedigrees are indicated by the names of their mothers rather than, as in Rome and elsewhere in Italy, of their fathers.

4 *commanded mighty legions*: they were what the Etruscans called *lucumones*, "kings." Cf. *Odes* 1.1.1, "Maecenas, descended from ancestral kings," *Odes* 3.29.1, Prop. 3.9.1.

    Most men: the first of many references in the poem to "the majority view," "popular opinion," and the like. Cf. 16, 22, 36, 43, 46–58, 59, 102, 120, 130, 149.

6 *an ex-slave's son*: at Rome, a slave (*servus*) belonging to a Roman citizen received, when he or she was formally made a free person (*libertus, libertinus*), full Roman citizenship, which was then inherited by his or her legitimate children.

6–7 *Provided / a man's freeborn*: Octavian was of the same opinion (Suet. *Aug.* 74). This proviso, like Appius' action as censor (24n.), seems to reflect a moral or social prejudice, since there was very little difference in legal status between people newly freed and their freeborn (*ingenuus*) children. See 51–52n.

9 *humble Tullius*: Servius Tullius, the sixth king of Rome (ruled 579–534 BCE). His father was unknown, his mother a prisoner of war, but traditions differed as to whether she was a slave, making him a slave by birth, or merely a non-Roman, making him at first a "resident alien" (see Cic. *Rep.* 2.37, Liv. 1.39.5–6, 4.3.10, Juv. 8.259–60). Either way, it makes sense that he was credited with instituting the *census* (24n.) and the Centuriate Assembly (*Comitia Centuriata*), in which citizens were assigned both military and civil rank according to their wealth (plutocracy), not their ancestry (aristocracy).

12 *Laevinus*: possibly the Valerius mocked (?) at Lucil. fr. 1240 *ROL* (cited by Porph. here), "the brilliant opinion of Valerius." Earlier Valerii Laevini had attained the consulate, but the ancestor mentioned here is P. Valerius Poplicola, who was elected one of Rome's first consuls (509 BCE) after he had helped expel her last king, Tarquin the Proud, the successor to Servius Tullius (9n.); cf. Cic. *Flac.* 25.

16 *popular opinion*: See 4n.

20 *funeral masks*: Romans from distinguished families displayed in their homes and at funerals wax masks (*imagines*) of ancestors who had held high public office. See *Epd.* 8.11, Cic. *Cael.* 34, *Pis.* 1, etc.

22   *the mob*: 4n.

23   *upstart*: the Latin is *novus* (literally "new," sometimes translated as "new man"), a technical term for someone who was the first in his family to attain public office; cf. 50n.

   Decius: i.e., a man like P. Decius Mus, who "came out of nowhere" to serve as a military tribune (62n.) and later, as consul (340 BCE), sacrificed his life to ensure a Roman victory in a crucial battle during the last Latin revolt against Rome. See Cic. *Tusc.* 1.89, Virg. *G.* 2.169, *A.* 8.124, Liv. 8.9, Juv. 8.254–57.

24   *censor*: the two censors, elected at varying intervals for an 18-month term, determined the "Centuriate" rank (9n.) of each citizen and reviewed the membership of the senate, removing men whom they felt were disqualified for financial reasons or on moral grounds.

   Appius: probably Appius Claudius Pulcher, an opponent of Julius Caesar, who as censor in 50 BCE—the year before the outbreak of civil war—tried to "scour" (cf. Caelius in Cic. *Fam.* 8.14.4) the senate of the sons of freedmen and of supposed reprobates, including the historian Sallust (Dio 40.63.4; see 1.2.51–52n.); many of the men he antagonized in this way threw in their lot with Caesar. But it is possible that the reference is to his grandfather, also Appius Claudius Pulcher, and also a harsh censor (136 BCE), an enemy of Scipio Aemilianus and thus possibly a target of Lucilius (2.1.24n.). Least likely is their ancestor Appius Claudius Caecus (312 BCE; see 1.5.7n.), who in fact was the first to admit sons of freedmen to the senate (Liv. 9.46.10–11).

   blacklist: by putting a mark (*nota*) next to H.'s name on the senatorial roster; cf. Cic. *Clu.* 129.

26   *outgrown my breeches*: i.e., was ambitious and not content with equestrian status. Cf. 62, 78–79, 144nn.

27–29   *Vainglory . . . decked out in chains*: elevated language, but the image is disturbing, with the men resembling captives in a Roman triumphal procession; cf. 1.9.1, 58nn.

29   *Tillius*: apostrophe, as at 146–52. This may be the Tillius whose brother L. Tillius Cimber distracted Caesar with a petition to recall him from exile just as Caesar was about to be killed. Since he was not himself one of the conspirators, nearly all of whom paid with their lives, it is at least possible that he returned to Rome after all, regained a seat in the senate by holding the tribunate (31n.), and eventually attained the praetorship (150). That there is no record of his holding either office is not surprising, since during the triumviral period the magistracies were in such a state of flux that even in years when it is evident that offices were filled, the names of most of the men who held them are not known.

31   *broad, purple stripe*: a tunic or toga with a wide purple stripe on it was the badge of a Roman senator; see 35, 1.5.46, 2.7.13n.

   tribune: the office of tribune of the plebs and that of quaestor (184) were the lowest in the sequence of elected magistracies (*cursus honorum*) and brought with them entry into the senate.

32   *Resentment*: Latin *invidia* ("envy"); see 1.1.41n.

33–34 *black / laces*: senators also (31n.) got to wear a special type of shoe (*calceus senatorius*) with four black straps to be tied around the calf. See Cic. *Phil.* 13.28, Juv. 7.192.

35 *stripe*: 31n.

36 The speaker is the *vox populi*. See 4n.

37 *sick*: with a mental illness; see 2.3.124.

> *Barrus*: the word means "elephant"; cf. *Epd.* 12.1, where H. tells an ugly hag that, for purposes of sex, she is "most worthy of black elephants." But this could be a real person: a T. Batutius Barrus from the Italian town of Asculum was "the most eloquent orator outside of Rome" in the late second century BCE (Cic. *Brut.* 169), and a man with what seems to be the same name was accused in 114 BCE of seducing a Vestal Virgin (Plut. *Quaest. Rom.* 83, but the text is corrupt). Either or both could have been mentioned by their contemporary Lucilius; cf. 1.7.11n.

41–43 *Rome . . . temples*: the elements that, taken together, define the *Res Publica*. Cf. Cic. *Catil.* 4.24

44 *mom*: 3n.

46 *a person shouts*: the *vox populi* again (36n.).

46–47 *Syrus . . . Dama . . . Dionysius*: common slave names. Syrus occurs again at 2.6.56 (cf. Lucil. frr. 652–53), Dama at 2.5.27, 138, 2.7.78; both Cicero and his friend Atticus owned slaves named Dionysius. They would have been retained as surnames when these men took their masters' names on becoming freed citizens. Cf. Cic. *Att.* 4.15.1. But their sons, like H. (2.1.27n.), would be at liberty to assume new surnames.

48 *the Rock*: executions of citizens at Rome (never very common in the Republic) could be carried out publicly, with the perpetrators being thrown off the Tarpeian Rock, a spur of the Capitoline Hill (Cic. *Att.* 14.15.1, Liv. 6.20.12, Dio 48.34.5), or, during unsettled times, in the secrecy of the *Carcer* ("holding jail") at the base of the same hill (Sal. *Cat.* 55.1–2).

49 *Cadmus*: the jailor or executioner, mentioned only here. His Greek name suggests that he, too, is a slave or a freedman.

50 *Novius*: the name (also at 168) suggests an "upstart" (23n.).

51 *one row behind my row*: since senators were seated, not by ancestry, but in order of magistracies attained (former censors, then former consuls, etc.) and by seniority of tenure, this must be metaphorical (i.e., "Novius takes a back seat to me"). Some see a reference to seating arrangements in the theater, where the orchestra was reserved for senators and the lowest tier for equites (cf. *Epd.* 4.15–16), but as the speaker's "colleague" Novius must also be a senator.

51–52 *he's what / my father was*: i.e., a freed slave. The speaker's attitude is far different from that of H. himself (118–29). During the Republic it was most unusual, if not actually illegal, for ex-slaves to attain public office and thus senatorial status, but both Julius Caesar and the triumvirs included ex-slaves among the men whom they appointed to bring up the numbers of a senate depleted by civil war (Dio 43.47, 48.34; cf. *Epd.* 4).

52–53 *Messalla / or Paullus*: i.e., a member of an ancient and distinguished family such as the Valerii Messallae, still prominent at Rome (1.10.37, 117nn.), or the Aemilii Paulli (cf. *Odes* 1.12.37–8), whose surname, which had died out in the mid-second century BCE, had recently been assumed by a collateral descendent, L. Aemilius Lepidus (consul in 50), the brother of the triumvir M. Aemilius Lepidus.

54–55   *the noise . . . wagons*: cf. *Ep.* 2.2.74 (among the sounds at Rome that distract a poet from his writing), "mournful funerals wrestle with massive wagons." The wagons are probably carrying material for building or repairing temples, since all other wheeled traffic was banned from the city between dawn and the "tenth hour" (around 3:00–4:00 p.m.).

56   *funerals*: the elaborate funeral processions of distinguished men and women, which were accompanied by musicians playing military trumpets and horns, often stopped on their way out of the city at the Forum near the law courts for delivery of the funeral oration. See Cic. *De Or.* 2.225.

57   *his voice*: developed, perhaps, as an auctioneer (113–15n.).

58   *But back to me*: a colloquial transition, possibly echoing Lucil. fr. 1076 *ROL*, "now back to you"; cf. 1.7.12n.

59   *people*: 4n.

60   *on familiar terms*: the Latin term, *convictor*, implies among other things that the two often "dine together" at banquets (*convivia*). See 2.6.54, 2.7.42–43nn.

62   *their tribune*: H. was a tribune of the soldiers (*tribunus militum*), one of six general officers assigned to each Roman legion with administrative responsibilities and, in emergency circumstances, responsibility for command. The rank was important enough to entitle a man who had reached it to membership in the equestrian order, which H. somehow retained even though his service was in the army of M. Junius Brutus (1.7.22–23n.) and he had fought on the losing side at Philippi (42 BCE) in the civil war between Brutus and the other "liberators" (killers of Caesar) and Caesar's "avengers" Antony and Octavian. See *Odes* 2.7, 3.4.26, *Ep.* 1.20.23, 2.2.46–52.

65   *resentment*: 32n.

69   *ambitious self-promoters*: such as the creature who insinuates himself on H. in *Sat.* 1.9.
        luck: 1.1.3n.; see also 1.9.62.

73   *When we first met*: possibly in June of 38 BCE. From 2.6.67–72, it is evident that the dramatic date of *Sat.* 2.6 is January of 30 BCE; in the same poem, H. says "It's the seventh and soon the eight year since / Maecenas let me join his group of friends" (2.6.51–52), which suggests that this happened in February of 37 BCE. "Eight months" (81n.) before that would be June of 38 BCE, just after Octavian's disastrous first battles with Sex. Pompeius (Spring of 38 BCE; see App. *B.C.* 5.89) and just before Maecenas was sent to Athens to ask assistance from Antony (App. *B.C.* 5.92), an embassy that eventually led to the trip to Brindisium in May of 37 BCE (1.5.34–36n.).

71–72   *Virgil . . . Varius*: 1.5.50–51n.

74–75   *To face . . . saying more*: H. would not always be so tongue-tied with Maecenas (1.3.90–95).

77–78   *riding . . . on some . . . horse*: possibly a dig at H.'s equestrian status (26, 62nn.).

78   *Satureian*: from Saturum, a village in H.'s native Apulia near Tarentum (141n.). It is possible that H. is contrasting himself with Lucilius, also an equestrian (above), who may have owned an estate in the region (cf. frr. 547–48, and Cic. *Fin.* 1.7 with fr. 635 *ROL*). But there may also be a punning reference to H.'s poetic genre of *satira* or *satura*.

80   *That's your way*: Maecenas is shown as "a man of few words" at 2.6.54–58; although a guest at the banquet in *Sat.* 2.8, he does not speak.

81   *Eight months*: the Latin is literally "in the ninth month after," but Romans tended to count inclusively; that is, they included both the month (year, day) from which they began their count and the month (year, day) that they wished to designate. Thus, women gave birth "in the tenth month," the Olympic games were in "every fifth year," and H.'s birthday, December 8, was "6 days before the Ides of December [December 13]."

87   *my faults*: see 1.3.32–33, 90–95, 1.4.166–70.
         middling: 1.1.111n.

91   *in love with wealth . . . lecherous*: like H.'s targets in *Sat.* 1.1 and 1.2.
         vile: like Tillius (145–46) and Natta (172).

94   *my father*: 1.4.131–66.

95   *poor*: the Latin words *pauper* and *paupertas* often connote not actual destitution, but modest means. Cf. 2.5.13n., *Ep.* 2.2.51–52.
         with little land: after Philippi (62n.), the estate, such as it was, along with much other land in Venusia, was handed over to veterans discharged from the armies of the triumvirs (*Ep.* 2.2.50–51; cf. 5.58n., App. *B.C.* 4.1).

96   *Flavius'*: otherwise unknown.

97   *big centurions*: discharged soldiers granted membership and property in the *colonia* ("military settlement") established on land confiscated from the Venusians in punishment for their opposing Rome in the Social War (90–88 BCE); see App. *B.C.* 1.100. As a noncommissioned officer (something like a sergeant major) in charge of a century, the smallest tactical unit (80 men) in a Roman legion, a centurion, no matter how "big," would be outranked by a tribune of the soldiers (62n.).

98   *slates*: the Latin word is *tabula*, "writing tablet" (1.4.16n.), but the translation preserves the oppressive alliteration of the verse. Unlike H. (104), the boys had to lug their school supplies by themselves.

99   *eight coppers*: the text is disputed, but the more likely reading, accepted by Svarlien, would make Flavius' monthly rate for each student 8 *asses* (copper coins), not a large sum considering that, in the time of H.'s boyhood, the centurions probably earned about 3600 *asses* (= 1440 sesterces; see 2.3.346n.) a year while on active duty.

100 *to Rome*: the school H.'s father chose had been established in 63 BCE by the *grammaticus* (101n.) L. Orbilius Pupillus, a Beneventan (1.5.87n.) of humble background but great erudition who H. would later (*Ep.* 2.1.70–71) call *plagosus*, "given to beatings," because of his frequent resort to corporal punishment. See 1.10.1n., Suet. *Gramm.* 9.

101 *arts*: what Romans called *artes liberales* or *ingenuae*, the basis of "an education appropriate for a free person" (Cic. *De Or.* 1.17). After a boy learned to read and write, he would study *grammatice*, "grammar," but also Greek and Latin literature, especially poetry, history, and oratory, and then *rhetorice*, the theory and techniques of public speaking and writing but also various philosophical subjects, such as ethics, psychology, and political theory, relevant to it. If he had leisure and time, he might then immerse himself more deeply in *philosophia*, as H. intended when he went to Athens in 44 BCE (*Ep.* 2.1.41–45).

104 *Some slaves to carry school supplies*: see 98n. The slaves would also have provided protection in the often turbulent Forum of H.'s youth; cf. App. *B.C.* 4.30.

107–8 *went / with me*: this was more usually the task of a *paedagogus* (Greek for "child conductor"), a household slave assigned to keep tabs on a boy, not just during the school day but at all times.

109 *sense of decency*: cf. Cic. *Part.* 79 (addressed to his son), "a sense of decency shunning disgrace and eagerly seeking praise is the guardian of all virtues."

113–15 *auctioneer . . . broker*: agents hired on commission for the selling of property. The auctioneer (*praeco*) announced and presided over the sale; the broker (*coactor*) collected money from the buyers and conveyed it to the seller. Neither trade was highly esteemed (cf. Cic. *Verr.* 2.33, *Pis.* fr. 9 Nisbet, *Phil.* 2.64), but they were not entirely disreputable (*Ep.* 1.7.55–59) and could be more lucrative than H. lets on here (2.2.63n.). Several of Lucilius' satires featured a *praeco* named Q. Granius, who was famous for his wit, on friendly terms with eminent men of his time, and wealthy enough to wine and dine some of them (frr. 448–49, 595–622 *ROL*; see Cic. *De Or.* 2.244, 254, 281–82, *Brut.* 160, *Att.* 2.8.1).

115 *like him, a broker*: Suet. *Vita* records a tradition that H.'s father was not a *coactor* but something even lower, a *salsamentarius*, "dried-fish dealer," who "often blew his nose on his forearm" (i.e., rather than with his salty fingers). But this was a common slur (cf. *Rhet. Her.* 4.67), and it may be significant that one of H.'s models, Bion the Borysthenite, also a freedman's son, gleefully applied it to himself (Diog. Laert. 4.46), perhaps as an allusion to the "salty" character of his diatribes. See 1.10.6n.

120 *as many others do*: 4n.

124 *Nature*: 1.1.53n. But of course what H. posits is *contra naturam*; cf. Cic. *Sen.* 83, where the aged Cato (1.2.40n.) imagines time travel as something only "some god" (1.1.19n.) could make possible.

128 *my parents*: probably not "my father and my mother" (3n.) but rather "my father, his father, and his father before him," cf. 183 and, for this sense of *parentes*, *Odes* 2.20.5–6 (H. speaking), "I, the scion of poor parents."

129 *staffs and seats of power*: the *fasces* (bundles of rods) carried by attendants (*lictores*) on consuls, praetors (150), and censors (24n.), and the *sellae* ("thrones") for the same magistrates and for one of the aediles (2.3.274n.). The latter were kept by the officeholders following their terms and displayed in their houses along with their ancestor masks (20n.).

130 *The common crowd*: 4n.

132 *responsibilities*: i.e., those associated with seeking and exercising political office.

135 *morning callers . . . calls*: at Rome on business days eminent citizens were expected to conduct their friends, clients, and flatterers to attend morning "meet and greets" (*salutationes*) at their homes. These were especially important at election times (Cic. *Mur.* 70, Q. Cic. *Pet.* 34–38), but many considered them a burden; cf. *Epd.* 2.7–8 (a man who has escaped the city for country life), "avoids the Forum and the arrogant / thresholds of the more powerful citizens," Virg. *G.* 2.461–62.

136 *companions*: but H. is happy enough to be Maecenas' companion when asked (2.6.53–54); cf. 5.34n.

141 *Tarentum's*: modern Tarento, the likely destination of the negotiators, but not H., in the previous satire (1.5.34–36n.). Although technically in Calabria, the city is close to Apulia (80n.)—it is less than 60 miles from Venusia along the Appian Way (1.5.7n.)—and was one of H.'s favorite places (*Odes* 2.6.10–20, *Ep.* 1.7.45; cf. 2.4.43).

142–44 *a pack . . . withers*: apparently an echo of Lucil. fr. 101 *ROL* (cited by Porph. here, and possibly from Lucilius' "journey poem"), "The luggage was pressing with its weight on the ribs of the gelding."

142 *gelded mule*: since a mule is sterile, the castration must have been meant, as with Lucilius' horse (above; cf. fr. 507 *ROL*), to make him more docile (cf. Var. *R.* 2.7.15). Cf. 1.9.99n.

144 *the knight*: Latin *eques*, the same word used for someone of "equestrian" status; cf. 26, 62, 78–79nn.

145 *vile*: cf. 91, 172.

146 *Tillius*: 29n.

147 *Tibur*: modern Tivoli, a fashionable resort 18 miles north-northeast from Rome, not far from H.'s Sabine farm (2.6.1–3n.). It was another (141n.) of H.'s favorite places (*Odes* 1.7.12–14, 2.6.5–8, 3.4.23, 4.2.30–32, 4.3.10; *Ep.* 1.7.45, 1.8.12) and he is said to have owned a townhouse there (Suet. *Vita*).

    all five of them: an unbecomingly small number (1.3.20n.). But according to Seneca (*Ep.* 114.6), Maecenas himself, "when the civil wars were raging at their worst and the City was in state of turmoil and full of weapons, had this as his retinue in public: two eunuchs, who were nevertheless more manly than he was."

148 *chamber pot*: to avoid pit stops.

149 *people jeer*: 4n.

150 *a praetor's style*: Tillius' mode of travel seems the inverse of that of a certain Pomponius, who, when proscribed by the triumvirs in 43 BCE, escaped Rome disguised as praetor accompanied by fake *lictores* and a crowd of attendants (App. *B.C.* 4.45).

155–78 *evening . . . take it easy*: H.'s routine would probably seem eccentric, if not Bohemian, to other upper-class Romans, who rose at dawn, not midmorning (165–69; cf. 135n.), usually had a bite to eat before, not after, exercising and bathing (172–76), and began supper in the midafternoon (*Ep.* 1.7.69–71, but cf. 2.7.48, 2.8.5nn.), not after an evening stroll (158–59). See also 178n.

155 *garden greens*: 1.1.79n.

spelt: Latin *far* or *ador* (emmer wheat), a coarse and tasteless variety of wheat that by H.'s time was spurned even by rustics (2.6.116) and was used chiefly as a survivor of early times in ritual (2.3.307). See Plin. *Nat.* 18.81–84.

156   *Circus*: the Circus Maximus, site of horse races and other spectacles, was surrounded by an arcade containing passageways into the seating areas alternating with seedy stalls frequented by equally seedy characters, including, as in the Forum, fortune tellers (Cic. *Div.* 1.132, Juv. 6.582–88).

158   *fortune tellers*: the Epicurean (cf. 1.5.126–29) H. listens for amusement; a more ambitious man might seek guidance.

159   *bean noodles*: according to Pseudacro, H.'s term, *laganum* (= Greek *laganon*), denotes a kind of flat, thin ("like a membrane") wafer made of bean pods or bean flour cooked in pepper and a sauce. But some modern scholars, assuming that the leeks and chickpeas are part of the dish, translate as "minestrone." In any case, like the garden greens (155), this is all simple, modest fare; cf. 2.3.276–77n., 2.6.79–80, 110.

160   *three slave boys*: see 1.1.48, 1.3.20, 2.7.165nn.

161   *A white stone table*: 1.3.23n. The stone could be Travertine, a durable limestone quarried at Tibur (147n.), or any of a number of inexpensive materials from the area around Rome.

163   *mass produced in Campania*: sturdy but cheap tableware; cf. 2.3.217, Plin. *Nat.* 34.94.

166–67   *the statue / of Marsyas*: this stood near, and came to symbolize, the tribunal of the urban praetor, the magistrate in charge of civil litigation between Roman citizens. From images of it on coins, it appears that it showed Marsyas, a satyr (a goat–human hybrid; see the Introduction) who was flayed by Apollo (also connected with the courts; see 1.9.112n.) because he had dared to challenge the god in a musical contest, at the moment he was about to receive his punishment. H. pretends that his look and gesture of horror is in reaction to Novius (below).

168   *Novius the younger*: presumably the younger brother or son of the "new man" mentioned at 53. According to Porph., he was a usurer (1.2.15n.), but it is also possible that he was a pettifogger well known to the tribunal.

169   *till ten*: 1.5.28n. When H. breaks routine and leaves the house earlier, he pays for it (1.9.47–48).

171   *reading quietly*: as opposed to "reciting" (1.3.124–25). But even in solitude Greeks and Romans usually read aloud rather than silently; cf. 2.2.1, 2.5.94nn.

   writing something: cf. 1.4.180–81.

172   *a nice massage*: with olive oil (173n.), in preparation for or after exercise; cf. 2.1.9, 2.7.152, *Odes* 3.12.6.

   vile Natta: cf. 91, 145. The man is otherwise unknown, but he could be a member of another old and distinguished family (cf. 52–53), the Pinarii Nattae (the surname seems to be Etruscan; cf. 1, 3), perhaps even the son of L. Pinarius Natta, one of the pontifices (and thus a senator) who sanctioned the destruction of Cicero's house in 58 BCE (Cic. *Dom.* 118; cf. Cic. *Att.* 4.8a.3).

173 *lamp for oil*: cf. 2.7.45. Natta's oil is probably rancid, like that used for eating by the misers at 2.2.79 and 2.3.192 and the negligent host at 2.4.65; see Theophrastus *Characters* 9.6 (of a "squalid" man), "since he uses putrid oil in bathing he reeks," and 2.4.82n.

174 *A game of ball*: 1.5.59n.

175 *Campus Martius*: the largest open space in greater Rome, the site for military training (*Odes* 1.8.3–11) and meetings of the centuriate assembly (*Odes* 3.1.11), but also for informal recreation (2.6.62, *Ep.* 1.7.59, *Ars* 162; cf. *Ep.* 1.11.4) and socializing between young women and men (*Odes* 1.9.18–20).

177–78 *enough . . . quiet*: a hint of Epicureanism (1.1.62n.) in the ancient understanding of the philosophy.

178 *I take it easy*: presumably until late afternoon, when he sets out again on his stroll (152–58).

180 *free from . . . misery*: the Epicurean ideal; cf. 1.1.52, 1.2.96–97nn.

181 *ambition*: 26n.

184 *wasn't quaestor*: 31n. H. does not have to live up to any family tradition of senatorial rank.

Satire 1.7 Notes

1 *Persius*: known only from this poem. As a Greek (41) with a Roman name (cf. Lucil. fr. 634 [1.10.112–19n.]) he may have been a freedman and thus a citizen (6.6n.; see below) who had become a wealthy (5) businessman; many such men are known from late Republican literary sources and inscriptions.

a mutt of a man: the Latin (?) word *hybrida*, originally denoting the offspring of a wild boar and a domestic sow, was transferred to people of mixed racial or cultural background. There may be a pun on the Greek word *hybris* ("violence," "arrogance"), anticipating the description of Persius' mode of attack (9–11).

2 *proscribed*: he had been included in a list that "declared in writing" (*proscribere*) the names of men deprived of citizen rights and made forfeit of their property and, if caught in Italy, of their lives. The triumvirs, following and surpassing the example set by Sulla (1.2.82n.), began composing and making public this list in November of 43 BCE; it included Caesar's killers and other political opponents, among them Cicero. But it appears that the majority of the men on it were senators and equestrians targeted only for their wealth, which was needed to finance the civil war that was imminent. Despite the rewards offered to informers and the punishments threatened to people harboring *proscripti*, many were able to escape and even, as conditions changed, recover their status and at least some of their property (cf. 1.3.60, 1.4.58nn.).

2–3 *the pus and poison of . . . Rex*: epic parody (1.2.40n.). Lucilius (fr. 532 *ROL*) called a "virulent" enemy, "a deadly coma, a fever, decay, vomit, pus"; cf. Catul. 44.12 (a speech), "full of poison and plague."

3   *Rupilius Rex*: the scholia say he was a praetor before his proscription, while Porph. says that he had served on the Pompeian side against the Caesarians in Africa (49–46 BCE). He may be the P. Rupilius Rex mentioned by Cicero as a leader of the tax collectors (*publicani*— usually equestrians) in the Black Sea province of Bithynia in 51 BCE (*Fam.* 13.9.2). His surname (not uncommon) is the Latin word for king (44n.).

3–4   *is a tale . . . Known in every . . . barbershop*: probably hyperbole, as it is hard to see how or why so trivial an incident would be the talk of the town. But H. might be assuming the mantle of an epic poet, whose task was to make "material in the public domain his own property" (*Ars* 131). Cf. 15–16, 19–20nn. Lucilius began a satire about a notorious trial by announcing, "We will repeat a story that, although already heard, deserves to be told" (fr. 53 *ROL*). The absence in the poem of an addressee also fits an epic stance; cf. 1.5.1–2, 93nn.

4   *drugstore and barbershop*: Rome, like American towns, had its share of "drugstore cowboys" and "barbershop loafers"; cf. Pl. *Amphitryo* 1013, *Epidicus* 198.

6   *Clazomenae*: a Greek city in the province of Asia on the Gulf of Smyrna about 37 miles (60 km) west of Smyrna (modern Izmir in Turkey) itself. See 22–23n.

8–10   *animosity . . . bluster . . . arrogance . . . biting words*: the description, along with the flood simile further on (34–36), makes Persius seem quite a bit like Lucilius (*Sat.* 1.4).

11   *horsepower*: the image is of a chariot race; cf. 1.1.122–25.

        a Barrus or Sisenna: otherwise unknown, unless the former is connected with the Barrus, possibly an orator, mocked at 1.6.37 (see n.), the latter with either Cn. Cornelius Sisenna (praetor in 119 BCE), a contemporary (and possible target) of Lucilius, or L. Cornelius Sisenna (praetor in 78 BCE), a famous historian but also an orator capable of abusive language (see Cic. *Brut.* 259–60).

12   *But back to Rex*: possibly a Lucilian transition (1.6.58n.), although here somewhat misleading, since H. only really gets "back" after a fairly long (in so short a poem) parenthesis (13–22a).

14   *like heroes on the battlefield*: the comparison is of course ridiculous, but also somewhat disturbing, since if the quarrel between these two Roman citizens (1, 3nn.) is to be thought of as a war, it is a civil war (cf. 18, 22–23, 41–42nn.).

15–16   *fierce Achilles and Priam's son . . . Hector*: epic-sounding language for a reference to a famous scene from the *Iliad* (Hom. *Il.* 22.131–366). But H. "makes it his own property" (3–4n.) by implying that the two heroes fought to the death impelled only by their bravery (17) and not, as in Homer, out of desire for vengeance (Achilles) or a reluctance to incur shame (Hector).

16   *had to die*: cf. 25n.

18   *Discord*: an epic personification (= Greek Eris, as at Hom. *Il.* 11.73–74), but also a word redolent of civil war (1.4.68n.).

19–20   *Glaucus . . . Diomedes*: another famous scene, here again (cf. 15–16n.) altered by H. to fit his context. In Homer (*Il.* 6.119–236), Glaucus, the second-in-command of Troy's Lycian allies, and Diomedes (1.5.113n.) agree not to fight, not because Glaucus "yields" (22) but because they recognize that they are linked by a hereditary friendship, and although Glaucus seems all too eager to comply (cf. Homer's mocking aside at 234–36), it is Diomedes, by far the stronger man, who in a sense "proffers gifts" (21) by suggesting that they swap armor.

22–23   *when Brutus / was praetor over . . . Asia*: probably in late 43 BCE at Smyrna (6n.), a stop on the propraetor's (below) regular circuit court and also where Brutus had agreed to meet with his fellow "liberator" Cassius to prepare for the looming civil war against the triumvirs. He had taken command of the province of Asia after a whirlwind year and a half that included the killing of Caesar (March 15, 44 BCE); amnesty from the senate; a trip to Athens (late August), where many young Romans, including Horace (1.6.62n.), joined his cause; a successful war against Antony's brother in Macedonia (January to August of 43 BCE); and the recruitment of an army from troops there and in other provinces.

23   *praetor*: technically applicable only to a magistrate still in office (Brutus had been urban praetor [1.6.166–67n.] in 44 BCE). Compare *propraetor*, the more usual title for someone whose praetorian powers were extended an extra year or who was assigned command of a province "in place of a praetor" (*pro praetore*) when the sitting praetors were engaged elsewhere.

24   *had at each other*: although the context is a trial (6–7, 26), their match resembles the kind of verbal contest depicted at 1.5.65–87.

25   *as Bacchius and Bithus*: the comparison abruptly degrades Persius and Rupilius and at the same time removes some of the tension. Gladiators, however popular (the two mentioned here seem to have been favorites of Octavian [Pseudacro, citing a lost work of Suetonius]), were usually slaves or, at best, of low social status (cf. 2.3.133n., 2.6.55–56, 2.7.81–82n.), and, contrary to modern perception, their matches rarely ended in death (cf. *Ep.* 1.2.1–6). Lucilius described at least two real gladiator matches (frr. 109–17 [1.5.65, 72nn.], 172–85 *ROL*).

29   *assembly laughs*: not at his case, presumably, but both at his praise of Brutus and the staff (29–32a), which although conventional for Greeks (30–31n.), would probably seem grotesque to Republican-era Romans, and at his clever application of the celestial metaphor to Rupilius (32b–33).

30–31   *sun of Asia . . . constellation*: cf. an Athenian poem from around 307 BCE in praise of king Demetrius I of Macedon: "Just as his comrades are stars, so he is the sun" (cited by Athenaeus, *Deipnosophistae* 6.253e).

33   *the Dog Star*: Greek *Sirius*, Latin *Canis* or *Canicula*. In the Mediterranean region its heliacal rising (August 2 at the latitude of Rome) was seen as causing or at least coinciding with the most arid and unhealthy stretch ("dog days") of the year; cf. 1.8.33n., 2.5.55, *Odes* 1.17.17–18, 3.13.9–10, *Ep.* 1.10.15–16. In Homer (*Il.* 5.4–6, 22.26–32) the light gleaming from the armor first of Diomedes (*Il.* 5.4–6) as he charges into battle, then of Achilles as he rushes to attack Hector (22.26–32), is compared to its glare.

34 *like some wild winter flood*: more epic-sounding language; cf. Hom. *Il.* 5.87–90 (of Diomedes), "he raced along the plain like a river flooding / in winter, which, flowing swiftly, has swept away its banks." But the image may also be meant to suggest Lucilian excess (1.4.11n.).

35 *seldom touched by axe*: in contrast with Rupilius' "pruned" (more stylistically refined?; cf. 1.4.13–14, 1.10.94.) vineyard (37–38).

36 *salty cataract*: the epithet refers to Persius' language. *Sal* ("salt") and its adjective *salsus* ("salty") are commonly used of sharply witty speech and people; cf. 1.6.115n., 1.9.93, 1.10.6, Cic. *De Or.* 2.217.

　　Praeneste: modern Palestrina, a Latin town on a spur of the Apennine mountains 23 miles (37 km) east-southeast of Rome. The site of a terrible battle during Sulla's (1.2.82n.) civil war, much of its land was confiscated for his soldiers (cf. 1.6.97n.), but by the 50s BCE it had become a fashionable refuge from the heat of the "dog days" (33n.; cf. *Odes* 3.4.22–23, *Ep.* 1.2.2).

37 *vintage*: i.e., of the sort to be heard among laborers in a vineyard. The modern senses of "old fashioned" and "high quality" do not seem to be attested in connection with any Latin words for wine or winemaking.

40 *yells out "Cuckoo!"*: apparently this was common if a vineyard hand had not finished his pruning (cf. 35n.), which he should have started in autumn, by the time of the cuckoo's return to Italy around the vernal equinox (Plin. *Nat.* 18.249; cf. Virg. *G.* 2.403–7). But "cuckoo" (*cuculus*) can be a term of abuse for anyone who is foolish or stupid (Pl. *Asinaria* 934, *Pseudolus* 96, *Trinummus* 245).

41–42 *Greek . . . Italian*: although Romans and Italians admired and emulated Greek culture and many ethnic Greeks were citizens of Rome and other Italian cities, both sides always maintained a strong sense of their difference from each other. Cf. 1.10.27–47.

41 *drenched*: a fitting payback for so "wet" a man (34–36).

42 *vinegar*: wine gone sour and astringent (cf. 2.2.78, 2.3.181, 368, 2.8.65), and thus another (36n.) metaphor for "biting words" (10); cf. Pl. *Bacchides* 405.

42–45 *"Great gods . . . a job just made for you!"*: trial and poem end with a ridiculous yet nasty pun, the verbal equivalent, as it were, of the desperate act that concludes the ensuing satire (1.8.68–72).

44 *this Rex*: both "this man Rex" and "this King" (3n.). Roman names and especially surnames (cf. 1.3.67n.) were an easy target for word play; cf. Lucil. frr. 28–29, 46 ROL, Cic. *De Or.* 2.257–58, Cic. *Att.* 1.16.10 (a pun on the name of another Rex), Suet. *Jul.* 79.2 (when early in 44 BCE a mob saluted Caesar as king, he said), "I am Caesar, not Rex."

　　good at getting rid of kings: Brutus and the other "liberators" claimed that they killed Caesar because he planned to become the first king of Rome since Tarquin the Proud had been expelled in 510 BCE by the founders of the Republic led by Brutus' ancestor L. Junius Brutus. Another of Brutus' ancestors, C. Servilius Ahala, had in 439 BCE killed Sp. Maelius, a populist agitator also thought to be aiming at kingship. See Cic. *Phil.* 2.26 and Plut. *Life of Brutus* 9.

Satire 1.8 Notes

1–5   *I was . . . a god*: it is immediately clear that, for the only time in *Satires* 1, the speaker cannot be H., nor does H. figure explicitly in the poem (but cf. 10–11, 33, 49nn.). Moreover, the conceit of a talking object belongs, not to satire, but to epigram and related genres, including what are known as *Priapea* (*Priap.*), poems concerned with Priapus (5n.), which became popular during the third century BCE in Greece and in Rome beginning, it seems, in the time of Catullus (fr. 1). There are *Priapea* attributed to Virgil (in the *Appendix Vergiliana*), Virgil or Tibullus, Tibullus (cf. Tib. 1.4, a "Priapic" elegy), and Ovid, but most of those in Latin survive in an anonymous late first-century CE (?) collection. Many of these also feature an image of the god describing itself, its attributes, and its functions, but none, whether Greek or Latin, involve, as here, a developed narrative.

2   *a fig tree's trunk*: fig wood is easily carved but too soft to be of much practical use. The statues were also made of oak ([Virg.] *Priap.* 2.2) and of poplar (id. *Priap.* 3.3), but fig seems appropriate since in both Greek and Latin the fruit of the tree (*sukos* [1.4.77n.], *ischas, ficus*) can be a euphemism for the anus (65); see *Priap.* 41.4, 50.2, Mart. 7.71, etc.

2–4   *A carpenter . . . fashioned me*: Cf. *Priap.* 10 (Priapus speaks), "Silly girl, why are you laughing? / Praxitiles or Scopas didn't fashion me, / I was not polished by the hand of Phidias, / but a farm bailiff hewed me / and said: 'Be thou Priapus!' / Still you stare and laugh; / I guess it seems a salty [1.7.36n.] thing to you, / the pillar jutting from my loins." The three Greeks the god mentions were famous sculptors in fifth- and fourth-century BCE Athens.

5   *a god, Priapus*: in myth the oversexed and prodigiously endowed son of Dionysus (= Liber; cf. 1.3.11, 1.4.112nn.) and Aphrodite (= Venus). Statues of him in Greek and Italian gardens served as scarecrows and as a warning to intruders that, like adulterers (1.2.54), they could be punished with anal penetration. Elsewhere in H. (*Epd.* 2.21) and in Virgil (*Ecl.* 7.33–36, *G.* 4.110–11; cf. Bib. *poet.* 1.3, Tib. 1.1.17–18, [Virg.] *Priap.* 1), the emphasis is on the god's protection of gardens, but in the anonymous *Priapea* (1–5n.), his sexuality and the fate of intruders, usually described in obscene and comically hyperbolic language, are the major themes.

7   *raised right hand*: in a gesture of "do not pass." But more often the statues were armed with pruning hooks (e.g., Virg. *G.* 4.110, Tib. 1.4.8).

8   *obscenely long and red protrusion*: what the Greeks called his *ithyphallus* (erect penis). The entire statues were often painted red (Tib. 1.1.17–18, [Virg. or Tib.], *Priap.* 83.6–8, Ov. *F.* 1.415, etc.), as was customary with Roman images of gods (see Plin. *Nat.* 33.111, Plut. *Quaest. Rom.* 98).

9–10   *A reed . . . spooks the pests*: by waving or clattering in the wind; cf. Prop. 4.7.25 (a split reed used as a rattle in a funeral ritual).

11–22   *A cemetery . . . the Esquiline*: as recently as the mid-40s BCE the cemetery was regarded as "outside of the Esquiline" (Var. *L.L.* 5.25, published in 43 BCE), but the name Esquiline (*Esquiliae*), originally denoting the easternmost of the hills within Rome's sacred boundary (25n.), was increasingly (e.g., Cic. *Phil.* 9.17, also 43 BCE) extended to the area on the other (eastern) side. At some point in the early 30s BCE, this area became a fashionable address for wealthy men such as Maecenas, who built a splendid house (*Epd.* 9.3, *Odes* 3.29.9–10) as well as the garden protected by Priapus. This garden, which still bore Maecenas' name in the time of the Emperor Marcus Aurelius (died 180 CE), featured a thermal bath, a small theater, and some sort of tower from which the Emperor Nero famously watched and "fiddled while Rome burned" in 64 CE (Suet. *Nero* 38.2).

11 *A cemetery*: it contained burial plots for slaves (12–14a), presumably covered over in Maecenas' clean-up; mass graves (*puticuli*) for paupers (14b–17), which remained to be "harvested" by the witches (31, 38–39); and larger sepulchres, of distinguished men, which were left intact (52). In 8 BCE, two more sepulchres would be added, those of Maecenas and, right next to it, of H. himself (Suet. *Vita*). Also at the spot, or nearby, was a place for execution of common criminals—including sorcerers (Tac. *Ann.* 2.32)—and slaves (46–47n.).

13 *Their fellow slaves*: from the same household (1.1.49, 2.7.116–17n.). Cf. *CIL* 6.396, a dedication of a grave plot "for the household of A. Allienus [praetor in 49 BCE] and the household of [his wife] Polla Minucia, in front 25 feet, 16 feet back." See 1.1.48n.

15 *a common grave*: possibly an echo either of Lucr. 5.258–59 (of the earth), "it is evident / that the same mother of us all is also our common grave," or of Catul. 68.89, "Troy the unspeakable, the common grave of Asia and Europe."

19 *in front . . . back*: the language is nearly identical to that found on Latin inscriptions (13n.). A Roman foot was only slightly smaller than the American measure, which means that the cemetery would have covered roughly 21 acres.

20–21 *this grave monument / does not descend to heirs*: more inscription language, meaning that the grave site cannot be sold. But while appropriate for the sepulchres (11n.), it is somewhat ludicrous for the burial plots of slaves, who could not have legal heirs, and for a mass grave, which could not be said to belong to any individual.

25 *embankment*: part of the wall supposedly built by King Servius Tullius (1.6.9n.) both as a fortification and as a sacred boundary (*pomerium*) within which burials were generally forbidden.

26 *thieves*: 5n.

27 *wildlife*: especially wolves (cf. 60), which thrive at the edges of urban spaces. At *Epd.* 5.99–100, a boy tortured by Canidia and her coven predicts as he dies that their "bones will be carried off unburied by wolves / and birds of the Esquiline."

hags: they are witches, old and ugly, which explains their resort to magic (29n.). It is possible that the garden really was a haunt of such creatures. There is evidence (curse tablets, papyrus collections of spells [see *PGM*], artifacts in or around tombs) for the practice of magic in the Roman world in all periods, and it seems to have caused particular anxiety during the triumviral era: in 33 BCE, Agrippa, while aedile (2.3.285n.), "drove from the City the astronomers and witches" (Dio 49.43.5), evidently without much effect, for in 29 BCE Maecenas himself supposedly advised Octavian to do the same thing (Dio 52.36.1–3). But magic was also a popular theme in Greek poetry from Homer on and in Latin beginning in the late Republic (e.g., Virg. *Ecl.* 8.64–109; Tib. 1.2.41–64, 1.5.11–18, 1.8.17–26; Prop. 1.1.19–24, 1.12.10, 2.1.51–54, 2.4.7–10, 16, 2.28.25–30, 3.24.10, 4.5.9–18), and although some of the mumbo jumbo described here is attested for real-life witches, much of it seems more literary than literal. See 33n.

28   *chants*: the Latin word *carmen* can be used of anything chanted or sung, and poets who write about magic (27n.) often play on the connection between their songs and magical incantations. Cf. 2.1.118n., *Epd.* 5.72, 17.4, 28, *Ep.* 2.1.138, *Ars* 403, Virg. *Ecl.* 8.67–71.

   potions: mentioned again at 2.1.72.

29   *harry human hearts*: by forcing them into erotic submission, as symbolized by the "voodoo dolls" (43–47n.).

31   *moonlit nights*: anticipating 50–52.

   bones: from the paupers' mass grave (11n.). Cf. *Epd.* 5.23 (Canidia demands from her fellow witches), "bones snatched from the mouth of a starving dog."

33   *These eyes of mine have seen*: making him an unimpeachable source. Oddly, in *Epd.* 17 (below), Canidia seems to imply that H. himself was (also?) a witness (*Epd.* 17. 58–59, 76–80).

   Canidia: this is her earliest manifestation in H.'s poetry. There are passing references to her at 2.1.72 and 2.8.123, but she is more important—and frighteningly powerful—in the *Epodes*, where she poisons friendships (*Epd.* 3.7–8), arouses a toxic mix of lust and anger (*Epd.* 8 and 12), unleashes a vengeful spirit on Rome by torturing to death an innocent boy in order to create a love potion (*Epd.* 5), and, despite H.'s pleas for mercy, vows to plague him (and Rome) forever (*Epd.* 17). The scholia identify her as a real person, with "Canidia" being a pseudonym for Gratidia, supposedly a witch from Naples, but this is probably an inference based on details in the various poems. Her name suggests both old age (*canities*) and the baleful Dog Star (*canis, canicula*; cf. 1.7.33n.), and it is possible, as a number of commentators have argued, that H. meant her to be a symbol of the "old" and "dogged" cycle of greed, anger, and vengeance that, even if temporarily checked by a Priapus, was inexorably driving Romans once again into civil war.

34   *black robe*: the color is appropriate to her "black arts"; cf. 40.

35   *her hair disheveled*: at *Epd.* 5.15–16, Canidia's hair is still a mess, but she has it tied up with "tiny vipers," as if in imitation of the Furies (47–48, 63n.), who were often depicted with snakes for hair (e.g., *Odes* 2.13.35–36, Catul. 64.193).

36   *Sagana*: she again assists Canidia in *Epd.* 5, along with a hag named Veia, who does the dirty work. Both names, like Canidia's (33n.), seem significant: *saga* is a Latin word for "witch," while *veia* is Oscan (1.5.69n.) for "wagon."

   older: the Latin word, *maior*, can also mean "bigger"; the pair might look like Mutt and Jeff.

   wailing: part of the ritual; cf. Virg. *A.* 4.609, "Hecate [47–48n.], invoked with wailing throughout the towns at benighted crossroads," Tib. 1.2.47 (of a witch), "now she restrains the infernal hordes with a magical screeching."

37   *pallor*: as of the dead; cf. *Odes* 1.4.13, "pale Death," Virg. *A.* 4.26, "pallid ghosts."

38–42   *digging . . . rise and speak*: This sacrifice recalls and travesties that which Homer's Ulysses (Odysseus) tells the Phaeacians he performed, on the advice of the witch-goddess Circe, when he went to the underworld to ask the ghost of Tiresias for directions home to Ithaca (Hom. *Od.* 11.23–99; see *Sat.* 1.2.5). Priapus does not say why Sagana calls on the ghosts here (cf. 57–59), but necromancy and amatory spells (29, 43nn.) are often linked in both real-life magic (e.g., *PGM* IV 1390–1495) and poetic depictions of it (*Epd.* 5.17–18, 26, 17.79–80, Virg. *Ecl.* 8.98, Tib. 1.2.45–48, 59–64, Prop. 3.6.29–30).

39–40   *their nails . . . their teeth*: in contrast to Ulysses, who says that he used his sword both to dig the ditch to hold the blood and to kill, not a black lamb (probably stolen), but a black ewe and ram furnished by Circe. At *Epd.* 5.47–48, Canidia is described as "gnawing on her unclipped thumb with her purplish black tooth"; cf. 69n.

42   *speak*: Priapus implies what is explicit in Ulysses' account (above), that with the exception of Tiresias, the dead who have received funeral rites cannot speak or recognize the living until they have drunk from the blood in the ditch.

43–47   *two dolls . . . afraid / of death*: the main ritual involves two "voodoo dolls" in a kind of puppet show. Such dolls are described in magical papyri (e.g., *PGM* IV 296–327) as well as in literature (e.g., *Epd.* 17.76, Virg. *Ecl.* 8.73–81). It appears that the big doll here, made of wool to protect it from another witch's magic (cf. Virg. *Ecl.* 8.64, Tib. 1.5.15–16, Prop. 3.6.30), represents Canidia, and the smaller one, made of wax so that it can be molded or tortured with a needle (cf. Ov. *Am.* 3.7.29–30) and then enflamed (61–62), represents the person she wishes to dominate erotically. At *Epd.* 5.73, Canidia identifies her target as a man named (or nicknamed; cf. 1.3.70–72n.) Varus; at 2.1.73, she is associated with a certain Albucius (see n.).

46–47   *like a slave afraid / of death*: as at the old execution ground (11n.).

47–48   *Hecate . . . Tisiphone*: the former is the divine patroness of witches, associated with the underworld, the moon, and crossroads, whose presence or assent is often indicated by the appearance or barking of dogs (50); the latter is one of the Furies (35, 63nn.), indicating infernal forces of discord (1.4.68n.) and vengeance.

49   *Then you'd have seen*: the first indication in the poem of an addressee or at least an audience (cf. 68).

50–51   *Moon . . . hid*: Priapus gives a somewhat "rationalized" explanation for a feat attributed often to witches, causing the moon and sometimes the stars to leave the sky (e.g., *Epd.* 5.45–46, 17.4–5, 76–77, Virg. *Ecl.* 8.69, Tib. 1.8.21–22).

52   *a massive sepulchre*: 11n.

52–56   *if I lie . . . let my head . . . crap*: a comic variation—as suitable for a statue as, in the United States, it would be for a fireplug—of formulas such as "may I drop dead if . . ." (1.9.51; cf. 1.9.64) and "damn me if . . ." (2.1.8; cf. 2.6.70). Priapus' language here sinks into vulgarity: the Latin words for "peeing" (*meiere*) and "shitting" (*cacare*) were avoided in polite speech.

54–56   *Julius, / Miss Pediatius . . that thief / Voranus*: the first could be a freed-man (cf. 1.6.47–48) of one of the many families in the Julian clan; of the others, Porph. says that the second was a Roman equestrian who wasted his patrimony and earned his way by *fellatio*, considered an effeminate act by the Romans, while the third, a freedman of Q. Lutatius Catulus (either the consul of 102 BCE, a younger contemporary of Lucilius, or his son, the consul of 78 BCE), "was the biggest thief anywhere, ever." His name fits the bill, suggesting Latin *vorare*, "devour," and *vorax*, "rapacious."

57   *But why tell everything*: introducing a *praeteritio* ("by-passing"), a figure of thought through which a speaker mentions something while pretending he is going to omit it. Priapus' use of this figure and his word here for "tell," *memorare*, have an epic feel (cf. Virg. *A.* 6.601–7, 8.483) that contrasts with the language of his self-imprecation (52–56n.).

57   *shrill and sad*: another epic touch; cf. Hom. *Il.* 23.101, *Od.* 11.43, 24.5, 9.

58–59   *answering / Sagana's words*: 38–42n.

60–61   *wolf . . . snake*: probably more protection against counter-spells (43–47n.). Cf. Plin. *Nat.* 28.157 (a wolf's muzzle hung on a door as a charm against magic), *Epd.* 17.28–29, Lucil. frr. 605–6 *ROL*, Virg. *Ecl.* 8.71, Tib. 1.8.20 (witchcraft involving snakes).

61   *the flame*: see 43–47n.

63   *the Furies*: they are like Tisiphone and her sisters. In Ennius (*Sc.* 74–75) and Virgil (*A.* 2.573), Helen (1.3.149n.) is called a "Fury"; and Cicero, *Fam.* 1.9.15, uses the term of his enemy P. Clodius Pulcher.

65   *figwood ass*: 2n.

   split out a fart: from desperate fear (cf. 1.7.42–45n.), but the ludicrous result makes it seem a gesture of contempt (cf. 1.9.99n.). Priapus' language has sunk once again (52–56, 57nn.) into vulgarity. Farting is a source of humor in ancient comedy, endlessly in Aristophanes and, it seems, other "Old" Athenians (1.4.2n.), more sparingly in Plautus (e.g., *Aul.* 304–5, *Curc.* 295, 314–15, *Men.* 925–26, *Poen.* 609–11). See also Catul. 54.3, Mart. 4.87.4, 10.15(14).10, 12.77, etc.

66–67   *boomed just like a popped / balloon*: possibly an echo of Lucr. 6.129–30 (a cloud exploding causes a terrific thunder clap), "and not surprisingly, since even a small balloon full of air / often makes a huge sound when it is popped." Cf. Suet. *Vita Lucani*, "once, when he [Lucan] had farted very loudly in a public latrine, he caused his fellow sitters to flee by reciting part of a verse by [the Emperor] Nero [fr. 5 *FLP*]: 'You would think that it was thundering beneath the earth.'"

68   *to Town*: 1.1.13n. The garden was technically outside of Rome's city limits (11–22, 25nn.).

68–72   *You should have seen . . . make you roar with laughter*: 49n.

69   *teeth fell out . . . wig flew off*: not to be retrieved or replaced; in *Epd.* 5, Canidia shows only a single tooth, and that purplish black (*Epd.* 5.47; cf. *Epd.* 8.3), while Sagana "bristles with short spiky hairs" (*Epd.* 5.27).

71   *scattered wide across the land*: signs of a battle lost, but Canidia isn't finished with H. (or Rome) yet (33n.).

Satire 1.9 Notes

1–4 *I'd turned . . . / up runs this man*: The beginning and end of the poem
may echo a satire by Lucilius (frr. 252–68 *ROL*) in which he seems to have
told how Scipio Aemilianus (2.1.24n.) was accosted by an ambitious "witty
sponge" (*scurra*; see 1.5.66n.) and rescued in some way by Apollo (112n.).
See also 4, 24, 59–60, 98, 106nn.

1 *by chance*: cf. 44, 62, 106, 1.1.3n.

   Via Sacra: the main boulevard within the city limits of Republican Rome,
running from the western spur of the Esquiline (47–48n.) into the Forum.
Along it were major temples (47) and monuments, and it was the route for tri-
umphal processions (58n., *Epd.* 7.7–8), but it was also a fashionable residential
area with upscale shops and a "place to see and be seen" (cf. *Epd.* 4.7–8).

2–3 *absorbed . . . (probably some verse)*: H. is on one of his "creative strolls"; cf.
1.4.171–81, 1.6.152–78.

4 *this man*: he is not named in the poem. The scholia call him *molestus*, "the
Pain" (cf. 1.3.94), modern commentators the "Bore," "Pest," "Careerist,"
etc. Lucilius (1–4n.) seems to have described Scipio's tormentor as "not a
large man, big-nosed and skinny" (fr. 259 *ROL*).

13 *my slave*: cf. 1.1.48n., 1.3.20, 1.6.104, 147. He may be a stenographer present
in case H. decides to write something (2–3n.).

14 *Bolanus*: otherwise unknown, but possibly a relative of a man mentioned
at Cic. *Fam.* 13.77.2–3.

17 *the neighborhood*: 1n.

23–24 *I'm off to see a man . . . He's sick at home*: Lucilius' satire (1–4n.) may also
have included a reference to such a person (fr. 261 *ROL*).

24–25 *across / the Tiber . . . the park of Caesar*: i.e., a walk of more than 1.5 miles
from where the Via Sacra ended at the Forum (1n.). The park was left to the
Roman people in Julius Caesar's will (Cic. *Phil.* 2.109, Suet. *Jul.* 83.2).

27 *My ears flopped down*: H. may be punning on his surname Flaccus, which
means "floppy"; cf. 2.1.27, *Epd.* 15.12.

30 *Viscus*: he and a brother are included in H.'s list of his ideal readers
(1.10.114), he (or the brother) may be one of the guests at Nasidienus' cata-
strophic banquet (2.8.28n.), and one or the other is mentioned in a fragment
of a poem by Cornelius Gallus (fr. 2.8 *FLP*). According to Pseudacro, both
"were excellent poets or, as some say, literary critics; their father, although he
enjoyed the generosity and friendship of Augustus, remained an equestrian
even when Augustus had made the sons senators."

   Varius: 1.5.50–51n.

31 *fast at writing poems, lots of them*: he is like Lucilius (4.9n.), not to mention
the windbag Crispinus (1.1.131n., 1.4.15–16).

32 *quite the dancer*: this might endear him to the rather decadent Maecenas
(cf. Sen. *Ep.* 120.19), but stodgier Romans would probably disapprove. Cf.
1.5.79, 2.1.36–37, 2.6.91–92, *Ep.* 1.14.25–26, Cic. *Mur.* 13, *Off.* 3.75, 93.

   Hermogenes: Hermogenes Tigellius (1.2.4n.).

34–36 *a mother . . . concerned about / your welfare*: H., about to cite an enigmatic prophecy (41–46), is himself enigmatic. This could be an expression of (mock) concern that someone so excellent might invite the envy of the gods and die prematurely (cf. 2.1.91–92n., 2.7.5–6), or a veiled threat (i.e., "you'd better stop bragging if you want your kin to see you alive again"), or a rather odd way of asking if the man had anyone waiting for him elsewhere.

37–46 *How blessed . . . long-winded men*: Svarlien follows Porph. and most modern interpreters in taking all of this as an aside spoken to H.'s otherwise unacknowledged addressee. But it may be part of the epic parody here (37, 39–40nn.); cf. Hom. *Od.* 19.467–502, where Athene (Minerva) distracts Penelope so that she doesn't notice either the old nurse of Odysseus (Ulysses) recognizing him from a scar on his leg or the ensuing conversation between nurse and hero.

37 *How blessed the dead*: because their troubles, including listening to the likes of H.'s companion, are over. The "felicitation" (H's word here for "blessed" is *felix*; cf. 1.2.82n.) seems meant to recall Hom. *Od.* 5.305–7 (imitated at Virg. *A.* 1.94–95), where Odysseus (above), his boat wrecked in a storm, cries out: "Thrice and four times blessed were the Greeks who perished / on the wide plain of Troy."

39–40 *This must be the doom . . . foretold*: H. recalls the prophecy too late for it to be of use. So, also, the Cyclops Polyphemus (1.5.79n.) at Hom. *Od.* 9.506–15, the witch-goddess Circe (1.8.38–42n.) at *Od.* 10.330–32, and Alcinous the king of Phaeacia at *Od.* 13.172–78, all in regard to their encounters with Odysseus (above).

39 *a Sabellan crone*: a soothsayer consulted by H.'s parents (cf. 1.6.128n.) or, possibly, H.'s nurse Pullia (*Odes* 3.4.10). The Sabellans (*Sabelli*), a branch of the Samnites (1.5.7n.) who were the original inhabitants of H.'s hometown of Venusia (1.5.96n.; cf. 2.1.55), were thought to be skilled in various types of magic (*Epd.* 7.77).

40 *divining urn*: Svarlien follows the MSS, but many editors change the word order to make "divining" agree with "Sabellan crone." In any case, the urn would contain "lots" (*sortes*) that the crone would shake out at random and somehow read. Cf. Cic. *Div.* 2.85–86, Tib. 1.3.11–12.

43 *crippling illness*: H. departs from his custom (1.10.27n.) by using a Greek word, *podagra* (literally "foot trap"; cf. *cheiragra*, "hand-trap," at 2.7.22, *Ep.* 1.1.31) that would become, in the first century CE, the technical term for "gout" (uric acid crystal accumulation in the joints), which in antiquity and until fairly recently was considered a result of dissolute living.

44–45 *be / the death of him*: a literal application of the hyperbole "talk someone to death"; cf. *Epd.* 4.15, Ter. *Eunuchus* 554, "you're killing me with your questioning," and *Ars* 475, where the poet eager to recite (1.4.24n.) is depicted as a "leech" that "once it has got his grip, holds on and kills by reading."

47 *Vesta's temple*: ruins of this can still be seen at the southeast end of the Forum at the base of the Palatine Hill. Cf. *Odes* 1.2.16. At *Ep.* 2.2.114, H. seems to speak of the inner parts of this temple as a place of sanctuary; perhaps he is to be imagined here as casting a longing look in its direction.

47–48 *half / the morning gone*: i.e., it's around 10 a.m. (1.5.28n.), when H. normally would be just getting out of bed (1.6.129). He may have broken his routine to attend a *salutatio* (1.6.135n.) at Maecenas' Esquiline mansion (1.5.11–22n.), which would explain his presence on the Via Sacra, the best way to reach the Forum from there (1n.).

49 *to court*: the Tribunal of the urban praetor (1.6.166–67n.). In the late Republic, this was set up near, and sometimes referred to as, the Puteal (cf. 2.6.44, *Ep.* 1.19.8), a covered wellhead not far from Vesta's temple (47n.).

    The case was lost: as well as a sum of money the man had posted as a bond (*uadimonium*) against his appearance.

50–51 *a little / support*: no doubt moral support (cf. 111–12n.) but H. pretends to think that the man is asking for legal help.

51 *May I drop dead if . . .*: cf. 1.8.52–56n. and 65.

54 *you know where*: see 23–24.

58 *conquered . . . I followed*: H. is like the conquered enemies to be seen trailing the general's chariot in one of the triumphal processions on the Via Sacra (1n.).

59–60 *How are things . . . Maecenas / and you?*: the man returns to where he left off (33) and finally gets to the point: he is seeking entry to Maecenas' circle. It appears that in Lucilius' satire (1–4n.), the man who accosted Scipio was likewise looking for advancement (frr. 264–65). The question here indicates that the dramatic date of this poem cannot be earlier than February or so of 37 BCE (1.6.73n.).

60–61 *very few . . . His judgment's excellent*: if the man is still speaking, this seems meant as a compliment both to Maecenas for sensibly limiting his circle and to H. for gaining access. But if H. himself is the speaker (so Porph. and a few modern editors), the first clause is a warning to the man (cf. 78–79), the second a jibe either made in an aside (37–46n.) or not perceived as such by its target.

61–62 *No one . . . to better use*: the man probably alludes to Maecenas' status with Octavian, in which case what is meant as praise seems more like an insult, since it implies that Maecenas is motivated by ambition (65n.). If, as with 60–61, the words are assigned to H. (so most editors before the nineteenth century), the remark is a further jibe: Maecenas' better use of his good luck (1n.) lies in avoiding people like H.'s companion.

64 *and damn me*: 51n.

65 *clear the field of competition*: the man assumes, as he does of Maecenas (61–62n.), that H. is ambitious to advance himself even further in his friend's graces. But cf. 1.4.26, 1.6.26nn. He seems to imagine that the scene around Maecenas is something like that described at 1.4.101–14.

68 *that sort of meanness*: generated by greed and envy (1.1.41) as well as by ambition (65n.).

76 *Your force of character*: ironic, of course.

77–79 *by storm . . . the forays*: the military imagery (cf. 58) may be meant to build up the man into a kind of Achilles in anticipation of the end of the poem (112n.). Cf. 2.5.100–1n.

84 *To mortals . . . without great toil*: a variation on a familiar thought (e.g.,

Hesiod, *Works and Days* 289, "the gods placed sweat in the path of excellence," Sophocles, *Electra* 945, "without toil, nothing is gained"), inflated here with the epic-sounding word "mortals" (1.6.43n.). H. would subvert the maxim at *Odes* 1.3.37–38, "for mortals, nothing is arduous: / in our stupidity, we seek the sky itself"; cf. Virg. G. 2.145–46.

85   *Fuscus Aristius*: the inversion of name and surname fits H.'s dactylic hexameter, but it may also suggest agitation; cf. Lucil. fr. 254 (possibly from the satire cited at 1–4n.), "Cornelius Publius our friend," Catul. 10.30, "it's Cinna Gaius." Aristius Fuscus, another of H.'s ideal readers (1.10.114), is the addressee of *Odes* 1.22 and *Ep.* 1.10. According to Porph., he was a schoolteacher (*grammaticus*; cf. 6.101n.) and a writer of comedies.

87   *we stopped*: the man might not have been spotted (106–7) if they had continued on.

88   *He asked . . .*: typical small talk; cf. 2.4.1n.

89–91   *pulling . . . pinched . . . rolled . . . nodded*: reduced to silent gestures, H. seems even more powerless than the desperate Persius (1.7.42–45) and Priapus (1.8.65–67).

93   *the smartass*: translating *male salsus*, "wickedly salty"; cf. 1.6.114n.

96   *important news*: but at 2.6.54–58, 64–74, H. insists that he is never entrusted with this sort of thing. Cf. 1.5.34–36n.

98   *the thirtieth Sabbath*: the Romans were aware of the importance to Jews of the Sabbath (e.g., Tib. 1.3.18, Suet. *Aug.* 76.2), but it is possible that Aristius has invented this special one in "fun" (93), since it does not appear to correspond to any day mentioned in ancient Jewish calendars.

99   *fart at*: metaphorically (1.8.65n.), but cf. Josephus, *The Jewish War* 2.224, who describes how in 53 CE a Roman soldier caused a riot in Jerusalem by mooning and farting at a crowd of Jews gathered around the Temple to celebrate Passover.

   gelded: a reference to circumcision; cf. Pers. 5.184, Mart. 7.30.5, Tac. *Hist.* 5.5.2.

100   *not superstitious*: as the Jews were thought to be (1.5.124n.; cf. 1.4.185n.).

103   *so dark a day*: H. term for "dark" here is *niger*, but he probably alludes to the fact that on Roman calendars unlucky days were marked in "black" (*ater*) letters, and may also play on Aristius' surname Fuscus, which also means "dark-colored."

106   *good luck*: 1n.

   opponent: in the legal case (48–52).

108   *stand as witness*: if a defendant failed to appear, it was up to the plaintiff himself ("self-help"; cf. 1.2.56n.) to "haul / the fellow off to court" (110). But he was required to furnish a witness to testify that the act of "hauling" was justified and also, possibly, that the defendant had not come of his own accord and thus should forfeit his bond (49n.) as well as whatever he stood to lose in the case.

108–9   *"Yes," / I say*: H. suddenly has no trouble "standing before the bench" or "knowing . . . the law" (cf. 51–52).

109   *touch my ear*: to ensure that H. would remember what he saw. Cf. Pl. *Persa*

747–48, Virg. *Ecl.* 6.3–4 (Apollo [112n.] touches a poet's ear to remind him what to sing), Plin. *Nat.* 11.251, "The site of memory is in the lowest part of the ear, which we touch when we call on people to stand as witnesses."

111 *people charging in*: either folks offering moral support (50–51n.) to each side in the dispute or the man's enemies hoping to see him get his comeuppance.

112 *That's how Apollo rescued me*: a version of Hom. *Il.* 20.443, "but him Apollo snatched away," which describes the god's removal of Hector from his first encounter with Achilles after the latter returns to battle, conflated, it seems, with *Il.* 20.450, "but Phoebus Apollo rescued you," in which Achilles taunts Hector for this. According to Porph., the first line was quoted in Greek (cf. 1.10.27–47) by Lucilius, possibly in connection with Scipio and the *scurra* (1–4n.). In H. at least, Apollo is an appropriate savior both as a god of poets (e.g., *Odes* 1.31, Virg. *Ecl.* 6.3–4 [109n.], Call. *Aet.* fr. 1.21–38 [1.10.43–47n.]) and as the enemy of Marsyas, the symbol of the hated law courts (1.6.166–67n.). But he was unable to rescue Hector from Achilles in their next encounter (*Il.* 22; cf. 1.5.15–16n.), and H. may have chosen to allude to this Homeric context to suggest that his own escape would prove only temporary (cf. 2.6.26–76).

Satire 1.10 Notes

[Some of H.'s MSS begin *Sat.* 1.10 with eight lines (labeled 1.10.1*–8*) mocking the poet and *grammaticus* (1.6.101n.) P. Valerius Cato (3n.) for defending Lucilius' poetry yet, in effect, admitting its faults, by trying to correct "the badly made verses" (1.10.2*–3*). Since the lines are not acknowledged by the scholia, contain some style features uncharacteristic of H., and, without emendation, cannot be readily linked to the rest of the poem, most editors believe that they are an interpolation added to it after H.'s time, possibly by someone who found the real opening too abrupt (1n.).]

1 *Yes, I said*: in *Sat.* 1.4, although H. doesn't repeat the exact words here. The abrupt beginning suggests that the audience has happened in on a conversation already going on for a while. H. does not identify the person he is addressing, but it emerges that the man is an admirer and defender of Lucilius (3n.), a Roman or at least a native Latin speaker (39–40), and a contemporary (93, "our own age") with literary aspirations of his own (35, 99–103). H. allows him to speak (27–28, 31–33) but also turns away from him with apostrophes to other contemporary poets and critics (54–55, 115–18, 123) and to the slave who is making a fair copy of Book 1 of the *Satires* (125n.).

2 *on flat, ungainly feet*: a pun on "feet" (*pedes*) both in the literal sense and as metrical feet; cf. 58n., *Ars* 80 (of the iamb), "this foot the slippers [of comedy] and the grand high-heel boot [of tragedy; see 1.5.80n.] enwrapped," Ov. *Am.* 3.1.9–10. The image is picked up again at 12–13.

3 *nuts about Lucilius*: in the late Republic, Lucilius remained popular for his wit and style not only among poets and critics such as P. Valerius Cato (c. 90–30 BCE), an equestrian from Cisalpine Gaul who feuded with M. Furius Bibaculus (48n.) and may be the man attacked (25–26n.) in Catul. 56, but also, possibly for his *libertas* (1.3.75n., 1.4.5; cf. 8, 25–26) among more important folk such as Cicero (e.g., *De Or.* 1.72, *Fam.* 9.15.2) and C. Trebonius (64n.).

6   *verbal salt*: 1.7.36n.

8   *Laberius' mimes*: cf. 106, 2.1n. D. Laberius (c. 106–43 BCE), a Roman equestrian, was considered one of the foremost writers of Latin mimes, but was also famous for his "freedom of speech" (*libertas*; cf. 3n.), which earned him the enmity of Julius Caesar (fr. 88–124 *CLF*).

12–13   *speed . . . tangle up*: cf. 1–2.

15–16   *orator . . . poet . . . urbane wit*: parts that a writer of satires plays within the genre; cf. the orators in *Sat.* 1.7 and Lucilius' representations of deliberative (frr. 5–46 *ROL*) and forensic oratory (frr. 53–93 *ROL*). It is harder to pinpoint where either H. or Lucilius consciously plays the poet, but in light of the unanswered question of whether "satire is or isn't poetry" (1.4.73), it may be significant that H. here distinguishes the poet from the "urbane wit," the part he attributes in this poem to Lucilius (87) and that he himself assumes most often in his own satire.

16   *urbane*: 1.4.113n.

19   *A good joke*: cf. 1.1.25–28.

24   *Hermogenes*: i.e., Tigellius Hermogenes (1.2.4n.); cf. 111, 123.

25   *Johnny-one-note*: possibly the Demetrius (otherwise unknown) mentioned at 109 and 123.

25–26   *apes Catullus / and Calvus*: C. Valerius Catullus (c. 84–54 BCE), most of whose works survive, and C. Licinius Calvus (82–47 BCE), a politician and orator as well as a poet, most of whose works don't survive. They wrote in a variety of forms and genres, but although their aesthetic sensibility was closer to that of Callimachus (1.4.11n.; cf. 48n. below), in a number of poems and fragments (see 3, 48, 2.4, 5.47nn.) they exhibit something of Lucilius' penchant for coarse language and free-spoken (3n.) invective; cf. 3, 48, 1.2.4, 1.5.47nn., Catul. 29, 57, 93 , Licin. (Calvus) fr. 17 (attacks on Julius Caesar), Suet. *Jul.* 73. It seems likely that H.'s criticism of their "ape" is directed not at his admiration for their poetry in general, but at his obsessive emulation of only the Lucilian element.

27   *mixing Greek and Latin*: Lucilius does this to a degree not paralleled in surviving classical Latin texts; only Varro's *Menippea* and Cicero's letters come close. In all of his works H. by and large allows only Greek words that had come into Latin long before his time, such as *poeta* (= Greek *poietes*).

30   *Pitholeon of Rhodes*: not otherwise known, unless "Pitholeon" is a metrically expedient alias (cf. 1.5.2n.) for Pitholaus, a famous wit (cf. Macr. *Sat.* 2.2.13) who, like Catullus, Calvus (25–26n.), and M. Furius Bibaculus (48n.), wrote invectives against Julius Caesar (Suet. *Jul.* 75.4).

33   *Falernian's . . . Chian*: a dry wine from Formiae in Italy (1.5.42n.) and a sweet one from the Greek island of Chios (cf. 2.8.22, 64, *Epd.* 9.34, *Odes* 3.19.5). The two are also mentioned together at 2.3.179–80.

36 *Petillius*: 1.4.118n.

37 *Corvinus*: M. Valerius Messalla (cf. 113) Corvinus (64 BCE–8 CE), orator (*Ars* 372, Seneca *Controversiae* 2.12.8, Quint. 10.1.113, Tac. *Dial.* 18.2), poet, historian, patron of poets, including the elegist Albius Tibullus (see below), and addressee of *Odes* 3.21. A member of a distinguished family (1.6.52–53), he, like H. (1.6.62, 1.7.22–23nn.), fought on the losing side at Philippi, but afterwards held commands under both Mark Antony and Octavian. In 31 BCE, when civil war was imminent, he would replace the outlawed Antony as consul, and later in the year he would command part of Octavian's fleet at the battle of Actium.

> *Pedius Publicola*: possibly a son of Q. Pedius, a nephew of Julius Caesar whom Octavian chose to be his colleague as replacement consul in 43 BCE.

39 *Father Latinus*: "your Latin-speaking father," or, more poetically, as the name of the mythical founder of the Latin people.

41 *Canusian*: 1.5.112n.

42–47 *Although Italian . . . Hellenic legions*: H. parodies scenes in which poets describe the sources of their inspiration. In the ancient world the best known of these was Hesiod's encounter with the Muses (*Theogony* 1–34), but here H. seems to have in mind Ennius' visitation from the ghost of Homer (*Ann.* 2–11; see 44–45n.) as well as Virg. *Ecl.* 6.2–5 (spoken by the bucolic character Tityrus), "When I was trying to sing kings and battles, Cynthius [Apollo] / pulled on my ear [1.9.109n.] and admonished me: 'Tityrus, a shepherd ought to feed / a fat flock but intone a slender song.'" This in turn is based on *Aitia* fr. 1.21–24, a passage in Callimachus' most detailed exposition of his "aesthetics" (25–26n.). See also 2.6.17–19n.

44 *appeared Quirinus*: probably an echo of Enn. *Ann.* 3, "the poet Homer seemed to be present." Quirinus is another name for Rome's founder Romulus, usually employed when he is spoken of as a god (*Odes* 1.2.46, 3.3.15; at *Epd.* 16.13, "the bones of Quirinus," it is used ironically).

44–45 *when midnight had passed / and dreams are true*: the implication is that H. was asleep and dreaming, as was Ennius (*Ann.* 2; cf. *Ep.* 2.1.52), but not "Tityrus" in *Ecl.* 6 or Callimachus in *Aitia* fr. 1 (42–47n.). The latter did describe a dream encounter with the Muses, but this was in a different poem (*Aitia* fr. 2).

44 *midnight had passed*: but the Hellenistic poet Moschus (1.2.1–5) and Ovid (*Ep.* 19.195–96) say that the time for "true dreams" is just before dawn.

46 *logs to a forest*: like the proverbial coals to Newcastle; cf. Ov. *Am.* 2.10.13–14, "why are you adding leaves to trees, stars to a full sky, / bottled water to the deep sea?"

48 *turgid*: cf. *Ars* 27 (a misguided poet), "aims for grandeur, but instead grows turgid." The word occurs in Latin criticism of poor oratory (e.g., *Rhet. Her.* 4.15), but H. may allude here to "Callimachean aesthetics" (25–26n.).

> *Alpine poet*: Pseudacro and most modern commentators identify him as the Furius mentioned at 2.5.55 = M. Furius Bibaculus (c. 85 BCE–?), a native of Cremona in Cisalpine Gaul who wrote an epic about Julius Caesar's wars in Gaul across the Alps and along the Rhine (frr. 7–16 *FLP*), but also short

poems abusing, among others, P. Valerius Cato (frr. 1–2; see 3n.), H.'s teacher Orbilius (fr. 3; see 1.6.100n.), and Octavian (Tac. *Ann.* 4.34). He seems likely to be the Furius abused in turn by Catullus (poems 11, 16, 23, and 26).

48–49 *cuts / Memnon's throat*: the poet is described as doing what he writes about, a common figure in Latin poetry. This probably occurred in a simile (cf. *Bell. Hisp.* 25.4) comparing the death of a Gallic or German chieftain to that of Memnon, a son of the dawn goddess Eos (Aurora) slain by Achilles at Troy (cf. Hom. *Od.* 4.186–88, 11.522, Ov. *Met.* 576–622).

50 *my sport*: 1.4.180–81n.

51–52 *Let others . . . audition songs*: before continuing his critique of Lucilius, H. indicates where his kind of verse ("lines like these") stands in relation to the work of his contemporaries in dramatic poetry and epic and bucolic.

52 *Tarpa*: Sp. Maecius Tarpa, an astute critic of dramatic poetry (*Ars* 387), who in 55 BCE, when the Theater of Pompey opened, chose the plays (including one by Accius [70n.]) to be performed in it (Cic. *Fam.* 7.1.1) and was apparently still doing this 20 or so years and two civil wars later.

54–55 *Fundanius . . . you're best*: a vivid apostrophe (1n.). Fundanius, a guest at and reporter of the disastrous banquet in *Sat.* 2.8, may be the C. Fundanius who in 45 BCE deserted the Pompeian side to join Julius Caesar just before his decisive victory at Munda in Spain (*Bell. Hisp.* 11.3).

55 *librettos*: many Greek and Latin comedies featured singing with musical accompaniment.

56–57 *courtesan . . . Davus . . . Chremes*: stock figures in New Comedy (6.2n.). Characters called "Davus" are always slaves (cf. 2.5.125, *Ars* 237), often free-spoken (like H.'s slave of that name on the occasion of *Sat.* 2.1) and clever, while those named "Chremes" (from Greek *chrema*, "possession") tend to be rich but stupid (cf. *Epd.* 1.33).

58 *Pollio*: C. Asinius Pollio (76 BCE–4 CE), one of H.'s ideal readers (116) and, later, the addressee of *Odes* 2.1, in which H. again mentions his tragedies (9–12). A "new man" (1.6.23n.) from Cisalpine Gaul, he achieved prominence as a forensic orator in Rome (*Odes* 2.1.13–14) and as an officer on Julius Caesar's staff during the civil war against the Pompeians (49–45 BCE). After Caesar's death, he sided with Antony, but as consul in 40 BCE, he helped arrange the Treaty of Brundisium reconciling, for a time, Antony and Octavian (1.5.34–36n.). In the years after that, he led a successful campaign against a Macedonian tribe, established a public library in Rome, and did his best to remain neutral during the next round of civil war, although he wrote about it and the two preceding it in his *Histories* (not yet published in 25 BCE, the date of *Odes* 2.1), now lost but a major source for later accounts. As young man he was a friend of Catullus and other poets active in the early 50s BCE (see Catul. 12, Cinna, frr. 1–5 *FLP*), and he is mentioned twice in Virgil (*Ecl.* 3.86–88, 4.11–12), but the story that he was Virgil's early patron is almost certainly an ancient invention.

kings: from Greek myth, such as Agamemnon (1.1.109n.).

trimeters: verses containing six iambic feet (a short syllable followed by long) paired in three units called *metra* (Greek for "measures"). The meter seems to have originated in and received its name "iambic" from the early Greek genre *Iambus*, a form of blame poetry that H. would imitate in his *Epodes*, then later became the principal measure for the non-sung portions of Greek and, eventually, Roman drama (cf. *Ars* 79–82); it was also one of the meters used in satire until Lucilius began writing in dactylic hexameters.

59 *Varius*: 1.5.50–51n. He, too, is one of H.'s ideal readers (112).

60 *Our native muses*: H. uses an old Italian name for the Muses (a Greek term, but long ago brought into Latin [cf. 27n.]), *Camenae*, that Virgil himself uses at *Ecl.* 3.59, where it adds a "Latin" feel to what is in other respects a very "Greek" poem.

61 *the countryside*: the setting of Virgil's *Eclogues*, which, although long in the composing, were probably published as a collection around 35 BCE.

63 *Varro Atacinus*: P. Terentius Varro of Atax (82 BCE–?), a region of Transalpine Gaul near Narbo (Narbonne), a Latin colony founded in 118 BCE. This is the only reference to his trying to write satire, but fragments survive of his epic about one of Caesar's Gallic Wars and his versions of Hellenistic Greek poems, and he is said to have written love poetry (Prop. 2.34.85–86, Ov. *Am.* 1.15.21–22, *Trist.* 2.439–40, etc.).

    and others: including a certain L. Abuccius mentioned by (M.) Varro, *R.* 3.2.17, and C. Trebonius (3n.), one of the conspirators against Julius Caesar (1.4.131n.); see his letter to Cicero, *Fam.* 12.16.3.

66 *the founder's*: Lucilius was widely considered the inventor of satire as a distinct genre.

67–68 *I said . . . edit out*: at 1.4.11–12.

69 *Homer's . . . critics*: possibly alluding to Lucil. frr. 408–10, "Nobody who finds fault with Homer / finds fault with him always or with his poems as a whole; / he finds fault with a single verse, a word, an idea, or a passage." Cf. H.'s own famous, "I am annoyed whenever the goodly Homer falls asleep" (*Ars* 359).

70 *dour Accius*: L. Accius (170–c. 86 BCE), "dour," because he was famous as a tragic poet (see Cic. *De Or.* 3.27), although he also wrote historical dramas, epic, and linguistic and literary criticism. His name occurs only once in Lucilius' fragments (844 *ROL*, from bk 36), where he seems to be mocked for erecting a ridiculously large statue of himself in the Temple of the Camenae (60n.) at Rome (cf. Plin. *Nat.* 34.19), but according to Porph., there were attacks "especially in book 3" and references to him in books 9 and 10. H. himself "twits" Accius and Ennius (below) at *Ep.* 2.1.50–56 and *Ars* 258–62.

71 *Ennius*: 1.4.70n. In fr. 413 *ROL*, Lucilius makes fun of a verse from Ennius' *Scipio* (fr. 33 *FLP*), in fr. 885, of two verses from the tragedy *Thyestes* (Enn. *sc.* 367–68 *ROL*).

76 *or what he wrote about*: i.e., the subject matter of satire may not allow for "finely made" poetry or even poetry at all (cf. 1.4.72–73).

79 *six-foot lines*: 1.4.7n.

80 *two hundred verses*: cf. 1.4.9, 16–17.

82 *Tuscan Cassius*: otherwise unknown. The scholia identify him as C. Cassius of Parma (cf. *Ep.* 1.4.3), a poet better known as one of Julius Caesar's killers, but he was probably still alive when H. was writing and, in any case, Parma, in Cisalpine Gaul, is nowhere near Tuscany (= Etruria; cf. 1.6.2n.).

83 *roaring rivers*: 1.4.11n. At *Odes* 4.2.5–8 the same image is used, in a positive way, of the Greek poet Pindar.

86–87 *amusing . . . urbane*: 15–16n.

90–91 *without a Greek / model*: either very early Latin verse of any sort, which still had its admirers in H.'s time (*Ep.* 2.1.86–89), or some kind of preliterate satire such as that described at Liv. 7.2.4–10. It seems less likely that H. means the *Satura* of Ennius (Intro. 3), since this drew on Greek models for its meters (58n.), if for nothing else.

99 *the flat end of your stylus*: the equivalent of a pencil's eraser (1.4.16n.).

101 *Less is more . . . readership*: cf. 1.4.23–24, 85–91.

103 *taught in run-down schools*: cf. 124n. This was a fate H. feared (*Ep.* 1.20.17–18) but suffered and continues to suffer anyway.

104 *the mime Arbuscula*: 1.2.1n. Arbuscula ("little tree") was a famous performer of Cicero's time (Cic. *Att.* 4.15.6, from 54 BCE).

106 *the knights*: members of H.'s own (and Lucilius') order (1.6.26, 80nn.).

107 *that bug*: cf. Antiphanes (first century CE), *A.P.* 11.322.6 (of literary critics), "you are bedbugs biting in secret."

   Pantilius: otherwise unknown. The name is real but may suggest the Greek phrase *pan tillein*, "picking at everything."

108 *tortured*: 1.2.27n.

109–11 *Demetrius . . . Hermogenes*: 24, 25nn.

109–10 *behind / my back*: 1.3.35n.

110 *Fannius*: 1.4.22n.

112–19 *Plotius . . . learned friends*: possibly a "correction" of Lucilius, who described his ideal readers as "neither the most ignorant nor the most learned men" (frr. 632–35 *ROL*).

112–13 *Plotius, Varius, . . . Virgil*: companions from the journey to Brindisium (1.5.50–51n.); see 59, 62 above.

113 *Valgius*: C. Valgius Rufus, dates of birth and death unknown, possibly from Padua or thereabouts (cf. frr. 3–4 *FLP*), addressee of *Odes* 2.9 (c. 25 BCE), and replacement consul in 12 BCE. He was a prolific writer of both prose and poetry; the latter included epigrams, love elegy (see *Odes* 2.9.9), and, possibly, bucolic (frr. 3–4 *FLP*) and epic (see [Tib.] 4.1.179–80).

   Octavius: possibly a certain Octavius Musa, whom the none-too-reliable (58n.) scholia on Virgil's *Eclogues* 8 and 9 connect with the land confiscations (1.6.95n.) in the area of Cremona and Mantua (cf. *Ecl.* 9.27). He may be the same as the historian Octavius whose purported death from drinking too much is facetiously lamented in [Virgil?], *Catal.* 11, and/or the M. Octavius who would command a squadron in Octavian's fleet at Actium in 31 BCE (Plut. *Life of Antony* 65.1). In any case, this cannot be Octavian himself, since by the time of *Satires* 1 he was known only by his adopted name of Caesar (1.3.5, 9nn.).

114 *Fuscus . . . the Viscus brothers*: 1.9.30, 85nn.

115 *It's not to curry favor*: H. continue to insists that he is not motivated by ambition (1.4.26n.).

116 *you, Pollio, and you, Messalla*: see 1, 37, 58nn.

117 *your brother*: his older half-brother, L. Gellius Poplicola. At first a supporter of Brutus and Cassius, he plotted against them and, although pardoned for this, deserted them to join Antony before Philippi. But he would remain loyal to Antony, who made him consul in 36 BCE, until the bitter end. He may be the Gellius attacked so memorably by Catullus (poems 74, 80, 88–91, 116).

Bibulus: L. Calpurnius Bibulus, another Antonian. He was a stepson of Brutus and possibly a fellow student of H. at Athens in 43 BCE (1.6.62, 1.7.22–23nn.); after Philippi, he joined Antony, whom he served as a fleet commander, as an envoy to Octavian in 36 BCE, and as governor of Syria from 34 BCE until his death in early 32 BCE (App. *B.C.* 4.38, 5.132). Since he is spoken of here as still living, *Satires* 1 must have been completed before that date.

Servius: a first name, but in the Republic used only by members of the Sulpician clan. This man is probably Ser. Sulpicius, the husband of Messalla's (37n.) sister, the father of the Sulpicia who is the subject and author of poems preserved in the Tibullan Corpus ([Tib.] 3.8–18; Servius is mentioned at 3.16.4), and himself the author of "naughty verses" (Ov. *Tr.* 2.441–42).

118 *Furnius*: C. Furnius, a renowned orator (Cic. *Fam.* 10.26.2, Tac. *Dial.* 21.1, Plut. *Life of Antony* 58.11) and yet another "diehard" Antonian, who endured the siege of Perugia (1.3.147n.) in 41–40 BCE with Antony's brother L. Antonius and, as Antony's governor in Asia in 36–35 BCE, contributed to the final defeat of Sex. Pompeius (1.1.5, 1.4.22, 1.5.34–36, 1.6.73nn.). But after the civil war he would be pardoned by Octavian, be made an honorary consul in 29 BCE, and serve as governor of northwest Spain in 22 BCE.

119 *purposely*: the adverb could simply reassure the other "learned friends" (or, for that matter, any of H.'s readers who fancies her- or himself eligible) that H. has not forgotten them. But it could also hint at discretion, as if certain names might cause offense.

123 *Demetrius, Tigellius*: 1, 24, 25nn.

124 *school girls*: the only audience they can find is in a school (103n.). The girls could be mimes (Pseudacro; see 104n.) or the likes of the noble Sempronia whom Sallust describes as "learned in Greek and Latin literature, she played the lyre and danced more exquisitely than is necessary for a reputable woman" (*Cat.* 25.2; cf. *Odes* 3.6.21–22). But H. doesn't always object to musical training for women; see *Odes* 1.17.17–20, 2.12.17–20, 3.9.9–10, 4.11.34–35.

125 *boy*: a slave (1.9.13n.).

little book: i.e., the volume that would become known as Book 1 of the *Satires* (see the Introduction). "Little" is mock modest; with 1,034 (Latin) verses, the book is longer than each of what are likely to be the separate collections of Catullus, Virgil's *Eclogues*, and any book of the *Georgics* or *Aeneid*. But there may also be, along with a nod toward Callimachus' "big book, big evil" (1.4.11n.), a last, tacit dig at the far more prolix Lucilius.

Satire 2.1 Notes

1   *HORACE*: the indications of speaker throughout Book 2 of the *Satires* are not in the MSS of H. but are added by editors.

   Some people: such as the addressees of 1.4 (1.4.12n.) and 1.10 (1.10.1n.), as well as the likes of Pantilius and Demetrius (1.10.107–9).

   my satires: here and at 2.6.22 are the only places that H. uses the word "satire" (*satira*) of his or anyone else's works in the genre. See the Introduction.

2–5   *too violent . . . a thousand lines a day*: H.'s critics seem to have mistaken him for Lucilius (cf. 1.4.1–10, 88–128).

2   *break the law*: which is why H. (humorously) needs to consult a lawyer. For the idea of literary genres having "laws," see *Ars* 135.

5   *Trebatius*: C. Trebatius Testa, the last eminent "legal consultant" (1.1.11n.) and jurist of the Republic. A native of Velia (cf. *Ep.* 1.15) in Lucania (52n.), he was a friend of Cicero (*Fam.* 7.5–22, *Top.* 1–5) and served as a legal advisor to both Julius Caesar and Octavian, and he was consulted in regard to one of Maecenas' divorces from his wife Terentia (*Dig.* 24.1.64).

8   *Damn me*: 1.8.52–56n.

   I can't sleep: because of the urge to write. This was sometimes considered a mark of excellence in a poet (*Ep.* 2.1.112–13, Call. *Ep.* 27.4, Cinna, fr. 11.1–2 *FLP*, possibly Lucr. 5.1408–11), but H.'s insomnia is at odds with his usual habits (1.6.164–69; cf. 1.9.47–48n., *Ep.* 2.2.52–54).

9   *oil up*: with a pre-exercise massage (1.6.172n.).

10   *laps across the Tiber*: from the Campus Martius (1.6.175n.). This was a common practice (*Odes* 1.8.8, 3.7.27, 3.12.7, 4.1.40). In a letter to Trebatius, Cicero calls him "a man most zealous about swimming" (*Fam.* 7.10.2).

11   *undiluted wine*: Greeks and Romans usually mixed their wine with water before they drank, although not when a "stiff one" was wanted or required (e.g., *Epd.*, 11.13–14, *Odes* 1.7.17–18, 2.7.6–7, 3.21.11–12).

14   *victorious Caesar*: an indication that the poem and book are set after Octavian's final victory over Antony and Cleopatra in Egypt (August of 30 BCE). See 2.5.85, 2.6.48, 67, 71nn.; see also the Introduction.

15   *great rewards*: H. seems to imitate Lucil. frr. 713–14, in which the satirist advises the poet (or is himself advised), "Take up this task which may bring you praise and profit: / sound off about the battle of Popilius [a Roman defeat by the Numantians in Spain in 138 BCE] and sing the deeds of Cornelius [= Scipio (24n.), the victor in a war against the same Numantians in 133 BCE]." Octavian, by then Augustus, later "enriched [H.] with his generosity" (Suet. *Vita*), and he is said to have given large amounts of money to Virgil and Varius (1.5.50–51n.); see Pseudacro on *Ep.* 2.1.245–50, Varius, fr. 1 *TRF*.

16–17   *inspiration / fails me*: H.'s response fits the pattern of a *recusatio*, "begging off," in which a poet apologizes for not composing a type of poetry, usually epic, asked for or expected from him. It appears that Lucilius did this in a few places (15n.; cf. frr. 691, 1061–70 *ROL*), but *recusationes*, often serving as assertions of both political independence and adherence to "Callimachean aesthetics" (1.4.11n.), became especially popular at the end of the Republic (Virg. *Ecl.* 6.1–10, 9.44–55) and in the early principate (e.g., *Odes* 1.6, 2.12, 4.2; Virg. *G.* 3.1–48, Prop. 2.1, 2.10, 3.3).

18–21 *battle lines . . . gruesome wounds*: a passage reminiscent of Ennian (1.4.70n.) epic (cf. *Ann.* 267, 384). It may be meant to suggest that H. could, in fact, find the "inspiration" if he chose.

20   *Gauls and Parthians*: probably anticipating future wars. Despite Julius Caesar's "conquest," the Romans had to quell a number of revolts in Gaul between 40 and 30 BCE, and C. Carrinas, with Octavian as his commander-in-chief (but not present), would put down another in late 29 or early 28 BCE (Dio 51.21.6 wrongly includes this victory in the first part of Octavian's triple triumph). The Parthians (1.1.10n.) had remained quiet during the latest round of civil war, but after Alexandria, when Octavian stayed in the east for nearly a year, many at Rome expected him to renew hostilities (cf. 2.5.85n.; *Odes* 1.2.22, 49–52, 1.12.53–56, 1.21.13–16, 1.26.5–6, 1.29.1–5, 1.35.38–40; Virg. *G.* 2.170–72, 4.560–61).

   unhorsed: and thus beaten. The Parthians were famous for shooting arrows from horseback while in retreat ("Parthian shots"); see *Odes* 1.19.11–12, 2.13.17–18.

22   *a piece that praises*: i.e., what the Greeks and Romans called a panegyric, such as the (much later) *Panegyricum Messallae* (1.10.115n.) included in the Tibullan corpus ([Tib.] 3.7).

24   *Lucilius . . . such praise*: possibly in a lost poem, since none of the fragments mentioning Scipio (frr. 252–68 [1.9.1–4n.], 424–25, 635, 714 [16–17n.], 983–84, 1035 *ROL*) seem suited to a panegyric.

   Scipio: P. Cornelius Scipio Aemilianus Africanus (185–129 BCE), recalled throughout Rome's history as one of her greatest generals and statesmen. He was a son of L. Aemilius Paullus, the conquerer of Macedonia, but given for adoption to P. Cornelius Scipio, the son of P. Cornelius Scipio Africanus, who had defeated Hannibal and Carthage in the Second Punic War. He earned the epithet "Africanus" for himself by destroying Carthage in the Third Punic War, and was also sometimes called "Numantinus" for his victory in a war against the Numantians of north central Spain (16–17n.), during which Lucilius was a member of his staff. See 97, 104–8.

25   *the right occasion*: this was not a consideration with Maecenas (1.3.90–94), but Octavian is depicted as more remote and somewhat inhuman (29n.). Even later, when H. and he seem to have become more friendly, H. is hesitant about imposing on him (*Ep.* 1.13.1–5, *Ep.* 2.1.1–4).

27   *Flaccus*: the use of the third person can be grandiloquent (e.g., Virg. *A.* 6.510) but can also suggest modesty (cf. 2.2.72, 2.6.61, 2.7.145). Here it is probably the former, but H. may also play on the literal meaning of his surname, "floppy (eared)" (cf. 1.9.27n.), in contrast to the pricked-up ears of the "Caesar-horse" (29n.).

29   *kick and guard himself*: Caesar is imagined as recalcitrant horse. The image is striking and possibly subversive. It may anticipate a contrast with the human-ity of Scipio (104–8) and, since even the most stubborn horses are usually broken, there may be a hint that someone (the poet?) will someday get the better of Caesar. See also 122, 2.7.104, 131–32nn.

31–32   *party clown . . . Nomentanus*: Trebatius quotes from 1.8.15–16; see 62n.

33–34   *despises . . . fears*: cf. 1.4.35–40, 98–99.

36   *Milonius*: otherwise unknown, but a real name.

37   *dancing*: 1.9.32n.

sees double: as at Petr. 64, Juv. 6.305, and lots of bars in lots of towns.

38–39   *Castor . . . Pollux*: the famous Dioscuri ("sons of Zeus"), hatched from an egg laid by Leda, the queen of Sparta, who had been impregnated by Zeus in the form of a swan. They were the brothers of Clytemnestra (1.1.106n.) and Helen (1.3.149n.). H. may echo Hom. *Il.* 3.237, "horse-tamer Castor and Polydeuces skilled at boxing"; cf. *Odes* 1.12.25–27.

40–41   *thousand souls . . . thousand . . . passions*: proverbial; cf. *Ep.* 1.1.80–81, 2.2.58.

41–43   *Like Lucilius . . . in verse*: H.'s identification with Lucilius here is somewhat at odds with the way he "distances" himself in *Sat.* 1.4 and 1.10.

42   *a better man*: cf. H.'s praise of Lucilius at 1.10.5–8, 63–66, 86–92.

44–45   *his books . . . friends*: Porph. cites a dictum of Aristoxenus (a pupil of Aristotle who wrote biographies of poets) "that Sappho and Alcaeus [famous lyric poets of the sixth century BCE and H.'s chief models for the *Odes*] looked to their books in the place of friends."

45   *the sort of things you'd only share with friends*: the details of his life (below), but also his unvarnished opinions about whom and what he considered foolish or reprehensible. See 1.4.108–12.

48   *The old man's*: Lucilius was probably in his late 70s when he died in 102 BCE. But the epithet could also refer to his relatively "old-fashioned" writing; cf. 1.10.89–98.

49–50   *as publicly as . . . a votive tablet*: not the most flattering analogy, since votive tables (50n.) tended to be simplistic and crudely executed. Comparison of writing with painting is common in ancient thought; see *Ars* 361, "as painting, so poetry," *Rhet. Her.* 4.39, "a poem is a talking painting, a painting a silent poem."

50   *votive tablet*: people who escaped calamities such as shipwrecks often thanked whatever god they thought responsible by dedicating in the god's shrine a picture showing the event. See *Odes* 1.5.13–15, *Ars* 20–21, Cic. *N.D.* 3.89.

51   *Lucanian or Apulian*: H. elsewhere (*Ep.* 1.16.49) refers to himself as a "Sabellan" (54n.), which suggests that he really was of "native" stock, perhaps through his mysterious mother (1.6.44, 128nn.). Lucania (modern Basilicata) is a mountainous region southwest of Apulia (1.1.60, 1.4.70, 1.5.95, 1.6.80nn.); cf. 2.8.10, *Epd.* 1.17–18, *Ep.* 1.15.21, 2.2.177–78.

52   *as you know*: Trebatius was himself from Lucania (5n.).

53   *my Venusia*: 1.5.58, 95, 1.6.95, 97, 141nn.

54   *Sabellan*: the original Oscan-speaking inhabitants (1.9.39n.). The term includes Lucanians and Apulians as well as other peoples from the region.

56   *veterans*: not the Social War veterans of H.'s boyhood (1.6.97n.), but Romans and Latins who were given land allotments in return for serving as a garrison at Venusia after it was taken in 291 BCE during the Third Samnite War.

59–60 *frontiers . . . war*: the Apulians and Lucanians had been allies of their "cousins" the Samnites (1.5.7n.) during Rome's wars with that people during the late fourth and early third centuries.

61 *But*: i.e., in contrast to Lucilius and to H.'s warlike "ancestors" (52n.).

    pen: cf. 1.4.16, 1.10.99nn., and, for the pen as a weapon, Cic. *Clu.* 123, *Phil.* 2.34.

62 *a living soul*: Pantolabus and Nomentanus (31–32n.) were already dead and buried when H. (or, rather, Priapus) mocked them.

64 *thugs*: Latin *latrones* (1.3.148n.). The civil war is as good as over.

65 *Jupiter, Father, King*: an Ennian (1.4.70n.) phrase (*Ann.* 203, 591; cf. *Odes* 1.12.49). For Jupiter (Jove), see 1.1.23n.

66 *Rust consume it*: cf. Tib. 1.10.49–50, "In peacetime hoe and plowshare gleam, but the sad weapons / of the hardened soldier are beset by decay."

70–73 *Cervius . . . Albucius*: otherwise unknown. The names are real (T. Albucius, praetor in 105 BCE, was a target of Lucilius in his book 2), but Cervius here (but cf. 2.6.98n.) may suggest an otherwise timid "stag" (*cervus*; cf. *Odes* 1.15.29–31) and Albucius, the plant asphodel (*albucum*), a possible ingredient in a potion.

71 *Canidia*: 1.8.33n.

73 *Turius*: the scholia identify this as L. Turius, praetor in 75 BCE, who was a judge in a rigged corruption trial; he may have become an eponym for a corrupt magistrate. It could also be the M. Turius who seems to have been one of Mark Antony's legates in Asia from 42 to 41 BCE.

78 *nature's law*: 1.1.52n. The thought here is one with which both Epicureans (e.g., Lucr. 5.1033–40) and Stoics (*HP* 57 C.3) would agree.

79 *wolf . . . bull*: The wolf, Latin *lupus*, may anticipate the reference to Lucilius' enemy with that surname (100); for the bull, see 1.4.36n.

81–83 *Scaeva's care . . . never raise . . . right hand*: Scaeva is otherwise unknown, but the surname (quite common) means "lefty," and H. seems to tease his readers with a word play (of course he wouldn't use his *right* hand) before revealing that the man's instinct is not for striking but for poisoning (86).

86 *hemlock*: in the ancient world used as a poison (cf. *Epd.* 3.3), but also as a remedy for various ailments (Plin. *Nat.* 25.151–54). The Latin word, *cicuta*, is the name of a usurer at 2.3.110, 267.

88 *dark-winged death*: H. suddenly breaks into lofty-sounding poetry; cf. Euripides, *Alcestis* 843, "black-winged Death" (trans. D. Arnson Svarlien), Virg. *A.* 2.360, 6.866, "black night flies around his head with mournful shadow."

92 *you haven't long to live*: cf. 1.9.34–36. In this case the "death" would be figurative, an exclusion from the kind of friendships with important men H. described in *Sat.* 1.3, 5, 6, 9, and 10.

93 *some great friend's door*: 1.6.135n. Trebatius may be thinking of Maecenas, who isn't mentioned in the book until 2.3.473 and whom H. in his own person names only twice (2.6.52, 2.6.62).

95–96   *stripped hypocrisy / off rotten men*: for the image, see *Ep.* 1.16.45 (a man), "rotten within, but swell-looking in his handsome hide."

96–100   *Did Laelius . . . ridicule?*: H. reassures Trebatius: if Lucilius' "great friends" did not give him a "cold reception" because of his satiric attacks, why should this happen to H.? But cf. 122n.

96   *Laelius*: C. Laelius (c. 190–128 BCE), Scipio Aemilianus' (24n.) good and great friend, a distinguished soldier, statesman, orator, and admirer of Greek culture in his own right. See 104–8.

97   *conquered Carthage*: 24n.

98   *wit*: the Latin word *ingenium* can mean this (cf. Eng. "ingenuity") but also suggests a quality that is "born within" (*ingigni*) and thus a matter of nature (78) or instinct (80).

99   *Metellus*: Q. Caecilius Metellus Macedonicus (c. 185–115 BCE), a successful commander in Macedonia, Greece, and Spain who later became the leader of a group in the senate that often opposed Scipio Aemilianus. Lucilius ridiculed a speech he made while censor (131 BCE) in which he proposed that marriage be made compulsory for Roman citizens (frr. 636–46 *ROL*; cf. Liv. *Per.* 59, Gel. 1.6.2). Pseudacro and many modern scholars interpret this as a partisan attack as designed to please Scipio, but that runs against the sense of 96–100 (above) and it appears that, despite their political differences, Scipio and Metellus remained on cordial terms (Cic. *Amic.* 77, *Off.* 1.57; cf. Val. Max. 4.1.12).

100   *buried . . . under ridicule*: the language suggests a public stoning; cf. Cic. *Verr.* 1.119, [while praetor Verres came close to being] "buried under stones in the Forum."

 Lupus: L. Cornelius Lentulus Lupus (c. 205–126 BCE) achieved great distinction, serving as consul (156 BCE), censor (147 BCE), and leader of the senate (131 BCE on), but Lucilius attacked him for his ruthlessness as a judge and for his degenerate private life in at least two satires (frr. 5–46, 793–814; cf. Pers. 1.114). Here again (99n.) modern scholars suspect partisanship, but there is no evidence of any hostility between Scipio and Lupus.

101–2   *high / and mighty*: in addition to Metellus and Lupus, Lucilius' targets included at least seven men who were or would become praetors or consuls (frr. 53–93, 232–34, 450–52, 1138–41, 1196–208 *ROL*).

102   *tribe by tribe*: i.e., no part of the Roman people was exempted. The 35 tribes (*tribus*), to which eligible Roman citizens were assigned on the basis of residence or ancestry, were the voting units in the "Tribal Assembly" (*Comitia Tributa*) and, with patrician members excluded, of the "Council of the Plebeians" (*Concilium Plebis*), the chief legislative bodies in late Republican Rome.

103   *to Virtue's bloc alone*: it would appear that H., at least, did not think Lucilius was a partisan of Scipio (99, 100nn.). See also 104–6n.

104–6   *The virtue of Scipio . . . the gentle wisdom of Laelius*: epic periphrases = "the valiant Scipio, "the wise and gentle Laelius" (1.2.40n.). The repetition of "virtue" seems to suggest that, for Lucilius, Scipio embodied that quality he befriended, but this would not necessarily make him a partisan, since

many other Romans, even among those who disagreed with Scipio, doubt-
less felt the same way.

105 *toga*: worn only in public. See 1.1.105.

107 *all three friends*: Lucilius was included in the fun. The scene seems meant to
show how little impact his satire had on his relations with these great friends
(96–100n.), but it also serves to humanize them in a way that contrasts with
H.'s description of Caesar (29n.).

107–8 *joke around . . . boiled down*: cf. Cic. *De Or.* 2.22 (the speaker is the great
orator L. Licinius Crassus [140–91 BCE]), "I've often heard from my father-
in-law [Q. Mucius Scaevola Augur], when he told how his own father-
in-law Laelius nearly always used to vacation in the country with Scipio
and that they used to behave remarkably like little boys when, as though
out of chains, they had flown out of the City. I hesitate to say this about
such men, but all the same Scaevola is still fond of telling that at Caieta and
Laurentum [two coastal towns] they were in the habit of collecting conches
and pebbles." According to Pseudacro, who may draw on a poem of Lucilius
describing this, "Scipio Africanus [24n.] is said to have been so human at
home that one time Laelius caught him running around the banquet couches
[1.3.127–28n.] with Lucilius chasing him and threatening to hit him with
a twisted up napkin."

109 *haven't got the gifts*: see 42n.

110 *in class*: like H., Lucilius was an equestrian (1.6.62, 80nn.), but was wealth-
ier and of more distinguished ancestry (see the Introduction).

111 *Envy*: 1.1.41n.

112 *lived among the powerful*: including those mentioned in *Sat.* 1.5 and listed
at 1.10.112–19. H. would echo this boast at *Ep.* 1.17.35, "finding favor with
the foremost men is not the lowest form of glory," and *Ep.* 1.20.23, where,
sending off what he intended to be his last book of verse, he instructs it to
say "that I found favor with the foremost men of the City [1.1.13n.] both in
war and at home." But cf. 122n.

113 *break her tooth*: Envy is often imagined as "biting"; cf. *Epd.* 5.47, 6.15,
Odes 4.3.14.

117 *time-honored legal code*: almost certainly that embodied in the Twelve Tables
(126n.; abbreviated as *Lex XII*), which were set up in Rome in 451 BCE to
make the letter of the law available to all citizens.

118–19 *ill verse . . . law and judgment*: Trebatius seems to allude, in properly old-
fashioned language, to what appear to be two separate laws from the Twelve
Tables (117n.). The first [*Lex XII* 8.1a *ROL* (= Cic. *Rep.* 4.20c; cf. *Tusc.* 4.4)],
which H. again cites at *Ep.* 2.1.152–54, specifies capital punishment (loss of
citizenship, if not life), "If someone should have chanted or composed a chant
that produced infamy or disgrace for another person." The second [*Lex XII*
8.1b (= Plin. *Nat.* 28.17)] survives only as a provision, "If someone should have
chanted a dire chant," without any details of the punishment. In the second,
"chant" (*carmen*) probably means "magic spell" (1.8.28n.), and this may also
have been the original meaning of the same word in the first passage, although
neither Cicero nor H. takes it that way. But there is much uncertainty about

the interpretation of these laws and even about whether there was ever any effective prohibition against libel during the Roman Republic.

122 *Caesar judges him*: the hypothetical "him" turns out to be H. himself (127). More surprising is that Caesar, from whom H. shied away (22–29), is now suddenly the judge not only of the imagined court case, but of the satirist's worth as a poet. This development puts an end to Trebatius' objections, as if the ancient traditions of Roman law were now subordinate to an authority quasi-legal at best, and H., who in Book 1 of the *Satires* had appealed to the judgment of a number of eminent men, including political opponents of Octavian (1.10.117–18nn.), now locates himself and his poetry in a Rome where only one man's opinion seems to matter.

123–24 *above / reproach*: something H. strives to be (1.3.31–2, 90–95, 193–95, 1.4.126–82, 1.6.66–94).

124 *barking at*: satirists and other blame poets are often represented as or compared to dogs; cf. *Epd.* 6.1–10, *Ars* 79, Lucil. frr. 3–4, 1000–1001 *ROL*, "Let me fly upon him with a dog's snarling mouth / and eyes."

126 *Then laughter strikes the tablets*: it is not clear what these "tablets" (*tabulae*) are. They are usually taken as writing pads (cf. 1.4.16n.) containing the charge, which will be laughed out of court. But the use of the word so close to a likely reference to the Twelve Tables (*Lex XII* 117–19nn.) suggests another, more troubling possibility; that, with Caesar's intervention, the law code itself will become a joke. Least likely is that the tablets contain the invective poetry at issue, which will be disarmed by laughter once it is entered into evidence.

Satire 2.2 Notes

1–11 *gentlemen . . . help you understand*: an abrupt beginning, as in some of the satires of Book 1, but in this case H. (cf. 154–55n.), accosts not Maecenas or another individual (cf. 1.1.1, 39, 1.2.9, 1.3.26, 1.4.12nn.), but a group of men who seem to be on their way to an early-starting banquet (cf. 1.6.155–78n.), and his "talk" is not his own, but that of another man (3, 12nn.). This sets a pattern for other satires in Book 2 (cf. 2.3.53, 2.4.15–16, 2.6.98–103, 2.7.61–62), although in those H. will be the listener rather than the speaker.

1–2 *the frugal life . . . how great that value*: a common topic in philosophy, both esoteric and popular, but also of social and political import at Rome, where many felt that the corruption of "good old" values such as frugality by "alien" (usually Greek) luxury and extravagance had been a factor in the collapse of the Republic and remained a threat even with the end of the civil wars in sight. In the past, the senate and censors had tried to curb the process with sumptuary legislation limiting, among other things, the number of guests and expenses allowed for banquets, and Octavian would give this another try. Yet the lesson of the satire is not that laws can bring back the old ways and avert further misfortune, but only that the frugal life can make such misfortune easier to endure.

3 *This talk . . . not my own*: possibly an allusion to Plato, *Symposium* 177a (but cf. 6n.), where one of the characters, about to propose a topic of conversation, declares, "To quote Euripides' play *Melanippe*, 'not mine is the tale,' but it belongs to Phaedrus [another participant] here."

Ofellus: a real surname of Oscan (1.5.69n.) origin, but it could be meant to suggest Latin *offela*, "meat cutlet," an apt name for a man so interested in food.

4 *a farmer*: the "good old" values (1–2n.) are often associated with Rome's (idealized) agrarian past and thought to have lingered longer in the countryside than in the city. Cf. 1.1.12n., *Epd.* 2.1–8 (parody), *Odes* 2.15, 3.6, *Ep.* 2.1.38–44, Virg. G. 2.458–74.

5 *any one philosophy*: the discourse is chiefly Epicurean (28, 37–39, 97nn.), but contains Socratic (31n.), Platonic (109n.), Peripatetic (73n.), and Stoic (109, 131n.) doctrines as well.

shrewd: Latin *sapiens* (1.1.38n.), but here indicating a kind of homegrown intelligence, not idealized philosophical wisdom (cf. 1.3.110n.).

6 *not symposiasts*: as, famously, in Plato's *Symposium* and in H.'s own 2.6.83–97.

7–8 *senseless lavishness / can trick the eye*: a hint of Epicurean doctrine; see 37–39n.

12–152 *Every judge . . . times of peace*: it is not clear from the text whether in this part of the poem H., in his own person, is paraphrasing Ofellus' "discourse" and only reports the farmer's exact words at 159–85, or whether, except at 153–59, Ofellus is supposed to be the speaker throughout. The shift in address at 19 from the group of gentlemen (1–11) to a single individual (but cf. 47, 56, 68nn.) could point to the second possibility, except that 153–59, where H. is definitely the speaker, is also addressed to an individual.

12 *taken bribes*: when the belly is the "judge," the bribes would be a splendid repast.

14 *hunting . . . or by a stubborn horse*: the "Roman army drills" referred to at 16. Cf. *Odes* 1.1.25–28, 3.12.8–12, 3.24.54–58 (again contrasted with Greek sports), *Ep.* 1.18.47–52 (again as a stimulus for the appetite).

15 *a Greek lifestyle*: see 1–2, 1.3.23, 1.7.41–42nn.

18 *playing ball*: 1.5.59n.

19 *you like the discus*: the speaker now addresses a single individual (12–152n.). *Discus* is a Greek word (cf. 1.10.27n.).

22 *turn up your nose*: cf. 1.2.149–50.

26 *growling stomach*: cf. 2.8.10, "angry appetite," Hom. *Od.* 7.216 (the hungry Odysseus [Ulysses] asks the Phaeacians to allow him to eat in silence), "for there is nothing more doglike than a man's cursed stomach."

28 *The greatest pleasure*: probably a reference to Epicurus, *HP* 21B4, "bread and water bring the highest pleasure when eaten by someone in great need of them."

31 *best condiment*: the speaker adapts an adage of Socrates, "hunger is the best condiment" (Xenophon, *Memorabilia* 1.3.5; cf. Cic. *Fin.* 2.90).

33 *binge eating*: the perils of overindulgence also figure at 57–60, 102–9, and 119–22.

34 *peacock's*: 1.2.150n. Q. Hortensius Hortalus (114–49 BCE), a great orator and greater gourmet, is said to have been the first to serve peacock (*pavo*) at Rome (Var. *R.* 3.6.6).

37–38 *Vanity . . . The presentation . . . the cost*: the man is duped by what Epicureans called *kenodoxia* (literally "empty opinion"), a false or misguided sense, based on appearances (43, 50) or on the latest rage (62–71), of what is truly desirable. Cf. 1.1.52n.

45 *at sea or in the Tiber*: in Republican times it was thought that the latter location held superior fish.

46 *between the bridges*: cf. Lucil. fr. 603 *ROL* (also of bass), "the Tiberine glutton-fish, caught between the two bridges," Plin. *Nat.* 9.61, 169. It is not clear what bridges are meant.

47 *Tuscan river's*: the Tiber's source is in Tuscany (6.2n.); cf. *Odes* 3.7.28, "the Tuscan riverbed," Virg. *G.* 1.499, *A.* 8.473.

  You lunatic: probably the same addressee as at 19 (12–152n.), who now suddenly and irrationally prefers a large mullet to any sort of bass.

48 *three pounds*: even a two-pound specimen was (and is) rare (Plin. *Nat.* 9.64).

49 *in individual servings*: i.e., a three-pounder is still too small to be served whole to even a moderate-sized banquet, and it would have to be cooked with other ingredients in some sort of stew or bouillabaisse.

50 *led by looks*: 37–39n.

54 *Harpy appetite*: in Greek myth, the Harpies are emaciated bird-winged and clawed females who constantly steal or foul human meals. See Virg. *A.* 3.210–62.

  proclaims: i.e., it "announces," like the penis at 1.2.87.

56 *south winds*: apostrophe, although people really did pray to the winds, who had temples in the Greek world and, from 259 BCE, at Rome; see *Epd.* 10.24, Cic. *Nat.* 3.51. The south wind (the modern sirocco), especially during the "dog days" (1.7.33n.), was considered extremely unhealthy; cf. 2.4.30, 2.6.24, *Odes* 2.14.15–16, *Odes* 3.23.5–6, *Ep.* 1.7.1–9, 1.16.15–16.

  taint their fancy feast: the speaker, in his indignation, wants the winds to act like Harpies (54n.).

58 *overindulgence cloys*: 33n.

59 *elecampine*: Latin *inula*, good for the stomach (Plin. *Nat.* 19.91), but also a savory addition to elaborate sauces and salads (2.8.68, Lucr. 2.430, [Virg.] *Mor.* 72).

61 *eggs*: as appetizers (1.3.12n.).

63 *Gallonius*: P. Gallonius, a notorious voluptuary of the late second century BCE (Cic. *Quinct.* 94, *Fin.* 2.90). Lucilius (frr. 200–210 *ROL* [= Cic. *Fin.* 2.24–25]; cf. frr. 211–12) contrasted his outrageous style of banqueting with that of the modest and moderate C. Laelius (2.1.96n.).

  auctioneer: 1.6.113–15n.

68 *a praetor*: possibly L. Plotius Plancus (so Porph.), whom Julius Caesar, before his death in 44 BCE, appointed praetor for 43 BCE after he had failed to win election to the office. He supported M. Junius Brutus and the other "liberators," and, late in 43 BCE, was proscribed (1.7.2n.) and executed by the triumvirs. Porph. quotes a squib against him (*vers. pop.* fr. 6 *FLP*), "This your redheaded prep-chef of storks, / the more elegant of the Plancus brothers, / did not carry seven votes in the elections: / the Roman people avenged the death of storks."

    taught you: the shift to second person plural (cf. 19n.) seems unmotivated, and it is possible that H. wrote *nos* ("us"), not *uos* ("you all"); the words are often confused by scribes copying MSS.

69   *roasted gull*: gull meat is almost inedible.

72   *Ofellus*: if he is the speaker (12–152n.), his referring to himself in the third person would seem to be grandiloquent (2.1.27n.), although it might also suggest rustic speech, as with Orlick in *Great Expectations* or Barkis in *David Copperfield*. See 125n., 183.

73   *living like a miser*: the opposite extreme from "depravity" (71n.), with *frugalness* the "mean." The mode of thinking is Peripatetic; cf. 1.1.111n.

74   *your nose*: back to single addressee (68n.).

75   *Avidienus*: otherwise unknown, but a real surname, although there may be a play, despite the difference in quantity (long a), on *auidus* (short a), "greedy." Cf. 1.1.41.

    nicknamed "Dog": because of his ability to eat vile food, but there may also be a reference to the "dogged" philosophy of the Cynics (1.3.189, 191nn.).

77   *cornel berries*: a kind of wild plum, food for animals (*Ep.* 1.16.8–9) or starving wretches (Virg. *A.* 3.649–50).

78   *wine . . . turned*: into vinegar. Cf. 84, 2.3.180–81, 2.8.65–66.

79   *olive oil*: cf. 1.6.173n.

82   *he himself must pour*: either for fear that a servant would dole out too much or because he is too cheap to own (1.1.48n.) or employ a servant.

84   *liberal*: sarcastic.

85   *wise man*: Latin *sapiens* again, here in a more technical sense (5n.).

87   *between a wolf and dog*: already quoted as a proverb at Pl. *Casina* 971. Here the wolf and the dog (75) may symbolize the glutton and the miser, respectively.

91   *Albucius*: possibly the man attacked by Lucilius (2.1.70–73n.).

92   *Naevius*: 1.1.107n.

96–97   *The benefits . . . extraordinary*: some of these, including health (97–106), energy in dealing with daily tasks (107–113), true enjoyment of occasional indulgence (113b–22), and self-sufficiency in the face of misfortune (148–52), are also enumerated by Epicurus, *HP* 21B4.

98–99   *the damage . . . to good digestion*: the medical writer Celsus, *Med.* 1.6.1, also warns against too varied a diet.

102–5   *roast . . . phlegm*: the speaker alludes to the ancient medical theory of humors, according to which combinations of opposites, such as dry (the roast) with wet (the stew) or air (the thrushes) with water (the oysters), can cause an unhealthy interaction of bodily fluids, here the hot humor (bile) with the cold humor (phlegm).

103   *thrushes*: 1.5.90n.

105   *strife*: the Latin word, *tumultus*, is nearly always used of civil strife (cf. 172n.). The speaker in effect reverses the common metaphor of civil strife as an illness of the "body politic" (e.g., Cic. *Cat.* 1.31, *Sul.* 53, 76, *Sest.* 43, 51, 135, *Att.* 2.20.3).

109   *nails . . . to earth*: the image recalls Plato, *Phaedo* 83d, "every pleasure and pain provides, as it were, another nail to rivet the soul to the body" (trans. G. M. A. Grube). But the idea of the soul as "a mote of heaven's breath" is usually associated with the Stoics, who may have taken it from the Pythagoreans (cf. Cic. *N.D.* 1.27, *Tusc.* 5.38, *Sen.* 78).

113   *daily tasks*: 97n.

123–30   *In bygone days . . . men were men*: the connection between this passage and those that precede and follow is not clear, and some scholars have condemned it as an interpolation. There may be a contrast between the bon vivant who squanders his "quota / of self-indulgence" (119–20) and these old-time Romans, who, rather than enjoy a rare delicacy such as wild boar (cf. 57) all at once while it was fresh, saved some for later even if that meant they or a late-arriving guest would eat spoiled meat. But the idea of any sane men preferring spoiled to fresh food is decidedly odd.

125   *I guess*: if the speaker here is Ofellus (12–152n.), this and 129–30, "I wish / I'd lived," are the only places where he uses the first person.

131   *reputation*: the argument veers from Epicurean doctrine, in which reputation plays little, if any, role, to that of the Stoics, who advocated the attainment of (a truly good) reputation through some of the same means mentioned by the speaker here (140–45). See Cic. *Off.* 2.31–32, 52–60, where the context is Roman but the teaching is that of the Stoic Panaetius of Rhodes (c. 180–105 BCE).

135   *your uncle's mad*: in a traditional Roman family, the father's brother (*patruus*) was responsible for the moral conduct of his nephews and nieces. See 2.3.137, *Odes* 3.12.2–3, Cic. *Cael.* 25, Catul. 74.
      the neighbors: cf. 1.1.90.

137   *he says*: see 1.2.137n.

138   *Trausius*: otherwise unknown, but a real name.

142   *in poverty*: cf. 1.1.119.

143   *temples stand in ruins*: beginning in the triumviral period and throughout Octavian's principate both Octavian and other eminent Romans spent large amounts of money restoring temples neglected in the chaos of the late Republic. See *Odes* 3.6.1–4.

146   *Fortune's pet*: cf. 172–73, 1.1.3n.

147   *Your enemies will laugh*: cf. the early Greek elegist Theognis, 1107–8, "Oh, I am a wretch; a joy to my enemies / and a burden to my friends I have become!" The opposite, "to be a sweet thing to friends, a bitter thing to friends, / respected by the former, dreaded by the latter" (Solon, fr. 13.5–6 *LCL*) was what most men hoped for.

151   *fears the future*: like the proverbial ants at 1.1.34–38.

152   *gathers war reserves in times of peace*: possibly proverbial; cf. Publ. Syr. 465, "In peace one ought to scout out what may be helpful in war." But Ofellus' turn of fortune was the result of a real war, not a metaphorical one (157n.).

153–59   *You'll give . . . You'd hear*: second person singular (12–152n.).

154–55   *I've known him / since boyhood*: the "I" is presumably H., which means that Ofellus lived and still lives in or near Venusia (2.1.53n.).

157   *Surveyors took his farm*: the land was confiscated and parceled out to veterans discharged after the triumvirs' victory at Philippi (42 BCE). See 1.6.95n.

158   *his sons*: he addresses them at 174–85.

160   *garden greens*: 1.1.79n.

164   *we enjoyed ourselves*: i.e., they were able to splurge sometimes (114).

165–66   *roasted kid . . . raisins*: locally grown, as opposed to the fish from Rome (cf. 44–47).

165   *chicken*: no peacock for Ofellus and his friends (35, 41).

168   *didn't follow formal rules*: as in the banquet at 2.6.86–88, but not in most Greek-style *symposia*, where there would often be a "director of drinking" (*arbiter, rex, magister bibendi*) to instruct participants when and how much to drink; cf. *Odes* 1.4.18, *Odes* 2.7.25–26, Catul. 27.3.

169   *Ceres*: they begin the drinking with a libation to the Roman goddess of agriculture. Cf. 2.8.20, Virg. *G.* 1.338–50.

171   *loosen . . . wrinkled brows*: an often mentioned effect of drinking; cf. *Epd.* 13.5, *Odes* 3.29.16, *Ep.* 1.5.20.

172   *Let Fortune storm*: 146n. The phrasing here has a lofty ring to it; cf. *Odes* 3.29.49–52, Sall. *Cat.* 10.1 (echoing Ennius?), "Fortune began to rage and turn all things into confusion."

   troubles: Latin *tumultus* again (105n.), here in a literal sense.

177–78   *No landlord really owns / his real estate*: a commonplace in popular philosophy (e.g., *Ep.* 2.2.158–82, Bion fr. 39 Kindstrand, "possessions are not given to the wealthy, but only lent"), but there may be an echo of Lucil. fr. 777 *ROL*, "since I know that nothing in life is given to a mortal as his own property." Cf. 185n.

180–81   *unbridled waste . . . ignorance / of tricky laws . . . his heir*: these are all normal, peacetime ways of losing property, as if, in a slightly optimistic note, Ofellus doesn't anticipate more *tumultus* (105n., 172).

181   *tricky laws*: cf. 2.5.47n.

181–82   *his heir / will take it all away*: when he dies, as is inevitable. Cf. *Odes* 2.14.21–28, *Ep.* 2.2.175–76, "the perpetual use [of property] is given to nobody and heir / follows another's heir just as wave follows wave."

182   *Umbrenus*: a real name, born by an ex-slave implicated in Catiline's conspiracy against the senate in 63 BCE (Cic. *Catil.* 3.14, Sall. *Cat.* 10.1). But it may be meant to suggest that the soldier-usurper (157n.) was from Umbria far to the north, with no roots in the area of Venusia (154–55n.), or that he is a kind of "shadow" (*umbra*) in the sense of being decrepit (cf. Cic. *Rab. Post.* 41) or ineffectual (cf. Pl. *Miles* 625).

183   *Ofellus used to call it his*: for the third person, see 72n.

184–85   *So live . . . head on*: the exhortation is addressed to Ofellus' sons (158, 174), but also to the audience of the poem.

185   *bravely*: cf. *Odes* 2.10.21–22, "When things are tough, show yourself spirited / and brave," Lucil. fr. 781 *ROL*, "It is certain that whatever may happen, I will endure it as bravely as if it is not happening."

Satire 2.3 Notes

1 *DAMASIPPUS*: see 1.2.1n. He has somehow found his way to H.'s country retreat and burst in on him, but the reader or listener cannot realize this or even that he is the speaker until H. replies (25–27).

3 *parchment*: in H.'s time, animal hide was used, like tablets (1.4.16n.), for works in progress, not finished scrolls, which were written on papyrus. See *Ars* 388–89.

   unstitching: probably an allusion to Hom. *Od.* 2.96–110, where one of Penelope's suitors accuses her of stalling the lot of them by unraveling at night a shroud she claimed she had to finish before she could choose a new husband. Cf. Cic. *Ac.* 2.95.

5 *sleeping late and drinking much too much*: classic symptoms of writer's block; cf. *Epd.* 14.1–8.

8 *Saturnalia*: the most popular holiday at Rome, celebrated publicly on December 17, then privately for six more days, during which the normal rules and strictures of Roman society were relaxed and inverted, with slaves acting as equals to their masters, togas (1.1.104n.) set aside, and presents exchanged amid general partying and freedom of speech and conduct. There may be a play here and at 2.7.8 between the name of the holiday (actually from the god Saturnus) and *satira* or *satura* (see the Introduction).

11 *reed pens*: rushes, usually from Egypt, split and sharpened to a point, as with a quill pen.

13 *angry . . . bards*: one of H.'s self-admitted faults is his temper (1.3.47–50).

15 *a cozy lodge*: probably the house at H.'s Sabine farm (2.6.1–3n., 2.7.165).

16–17 *Plato, Eupolis, / Menander*: inspiration for writing satire. Plato's Socratic dialogues have been seen as models for the dialogue form of most of the poems in *Satires* 2, while the Old Comedy of Eupolis and his peers was, according to H., an antecedent of Lucilian satire (1.4.1n.). It is less clear how Menander, a widely admired and imitated writer of New Comedy (1.4.2n.), fits in, but, like H. himself, he had a penchant for pithy and memorable adages.

17 *Archilochus*: the supposed inventor and most famous composer of the genre *iambus*, a kind of blame poetry that H. recreated in Rome with his *Epodes*.

20 *resent you less*: see 1.1.41n.

22 *Siren call*: another (3n.) Homeric reference, here to the birdlike creatures who tried to lure Odysseus (Ulysses) to his death with their irresistible singing (*Od.* 12.39–54, 154–200). Cf. *Ep.* 1.2.24.

25 *Damasippus*: probably the Damasippus mentioned by Cicero in connection with the purchase of statues and property at *Fam.* 7.23.2–3 (Dec. of 46 BCE), *Att.* 12.29.2, and 33.1 (both April of 45 BCE). He may have been the son of a Licinius Crassus Damasippus (praetor in 51 BCE?) who was killed fighting against Julius Caesar in 46 BCE ([Caes.] *Bell. Afr.* 96.1).

25–26 *may / all the gods*: a formula that usually begins a curse (e.g., Catul. 28.14), but H. contains himself and turns it into nothing more than a lame joke at Damasippus' expense.

26 *barber*: cf. 57n. A beard would be unusual on a Roman citizen between the time of Scipio Aemilianus (2.1.24n.), who set the fashion of being clean-shaven, and that of Hadrian (emperor 117–38 CE), who affected a Greek-style bearded look.

28 *the Stock Exchange*: rendering *Ianus Medius*, "the midmost Janus," where Janus means both "passageway" and the god to whom such places were sacred. This place, probably a crossing point in the central Forum over the covered *Cloaca Maxima* ("Great Sewer"), was frequented by businessmen, agents, moneylenders, and the like. See *Ep.* 1.1.54, Cic. *Off.* 2.87, *Phil.* 6.15.

30 *tend to other men's affairs*: usually an objectionable activity; cf. Menander (16n.), *Monostichoi* ["Single verse adages"] 448, "Tend to your own business, don't mind that of others," Hank Williams, "If you mind your own business / Then you won't be minding mine." But some Greek philosophers claimed that they had an obligation to be concerned with affairs of their fellow humans (e.g., Arrian, *Discourses of Epictetus* 3.22.77, 97).

32–34 *wily Sisyphus . . . wash his feet*: an impossibly antique "antique"; cf. 1.3.90–91. In Greek myth Sisyphus was a hero of preternatural cleverness who outfoxed a number of gods, including Zeus (Jupiter) and Hades (Dis Pater), but paid for it with an infamous punishment in the underworld (Hom. *Od.* 11.593–600, Lucr. 3.995–1002). His footbath was mentioned in a play by Aeschylus (fr. 225 *LCL*).

40 *'Mercury's man'*: the Roman god Mercurius (Mercury) was associated with all forms of commerce (note the "merc" in "commerce"; from Latin *merx*, "trade," "business"). Cf. Pl. *Amphitryo* 1–16, *Casina* 238, but also 107n.

41 *busy junctions*: places where people gossip; cf. 2.6.64–65.

44–45 *disorder . . . dysfunction*: H. unwittingly introduces what will be one of Damasippus' themes, the Stoic doctrine (see *HP* 65S–T) that moral failings are a kind of disease.

50–51 *insane . . . all the other fools*: Damasippus announces what turns out to be the main subject of Stertinius' (53n.) discourse, the Stoic paradox that all men, except the (Stoic) sage, are insane. Cf. 1.3.110n., 2.7.140, Cic. *Parad.* 27–32, *HP* 41I.

52 *Stertinius*: also mentioned at *Ep.* 1.12.20, where Pseudacro says that he "detailed Stoic philosophy in Latin in 220 volumes." His philosophy here is, in fact, mostly Stoic (above, 44–45, 50–51, 63, 70, 75, 149–51, 159, 186, 271, 317–18, 383, 385, 400, 430–49, 466–74nn.) and some modern scholars also identify him as a real person. But his name, which suggests *stertere*, "snoring," seems too good to be true.

56–57 *cultivate / a sage's beard*: see 26, 1.3.189nn.

57 *Fabricius' bridge*: the *Pons Fabricius*, still to be seen in Rome, built by L. Fabricius in 62 BCE to connect the left (north) bank of the Tiber with the Tiber Island (*Insula Tiberina*). The only temple of the healing god Aesculapius was on the island; possibly Stertinius was returning from "psychiatric" treatment there.

60 *I'd veiled my head*: a common gesture in the face of death; cf. Plato, *Phaedo* 118a (Socrates), Suet. *Jul.* 82.2 (Julius Caesar).

62 *You better not* . . . : just as in *Sat.* 2.2, where H. claimed that the discourse was not his, but that of Ofellus (2.2.12–157n.), so here Damasippus attributes most of what he says (until 449) to Stertinius. It is as if, in payback for his borrowed, modest Epicurean (2.2.25n.) diatribe, H. must now submit to an equally secondhand but monstrously oversized (*Sat.* 2.3 is by far the longest and, in this respect, most "Lucilian" (1.4.11n.) of H.'s satires) Stoic (53n.) harangue that ultimately turns into *ad hominem* invective (467–92).

Most of Stertinius' speech seems to be addressed to Damasippus (62–119, 181–93, 215–75, 326b–77 [see 326n.], 430–49), but he also speaks to a crowd (120–81) and appears to direct remarks to individuals in it other than Damasippus, including a criminally greedy man (194–214), an overly ambitious man (276–85), the long dead Agamemnon (286–326a; see n.), and a crazed lover (378–429). There are numerous interruptions of the direct address: quotations of characters' and addressees' own words (93–94, 99, 136–37, 145–51, 226–36, 244, 258–76, 348–63, 403–17, 433–35, 441–45), apostrophes (116–19, 186–93), and a kind of "self-examination" (237–50; see 237n.).

63 *undignified*: in Stoic thinking, neither poverty nor the general human problem of "insanity" (50–51n.) justified suicide (see Plut. *Moralia* 1042a).

65–66 *Why fear* . . . *insane*: Damasippus has given no indication that he fears any such thing.

70 *Chrysippus*: 1.3.179n.
    flock: a somewhat pejorative term for a philosophical "school"; cf. *Ep.* 1.4.16 (H. of himself), "me, a pig from Epicurus' flock," Cic. *Sul.* 77.

75 *mighty kings*: who, in Stoic thought, are not really kings unless they are sages (150–51, 1.3.175–77n.).

80 *wander off the path*: cf. Lucr. 2.9–10, where the poet describes the pleasure of watching, from a height of philosophical detachment, "other men / lost and wandering in search of the path of life."

84 *they've dragging tails behind*: i.e., they are more ridiculous than you are. Porph. connects the image with an activity of small boys, who "are accustomed to hang something from [the rears] of unsuspecting folks so that they drag a tail as if they were cows."

85–88 *One kind* . . . *Another kind*: the examples are not from Stoic writings, but from Socrates as recalled at Xenophon, *Memorabilia* 1.1.14 (Socrates said that), "Of types of madmen, some don't dread dreadful things, while others fear things that aren't fearful."

86–87 *rivers* . . . *block his way*: he is the opposite, not only of the next example, but of the greedy man addressed at 1.3.39–40.

89–94 *flood* . . . *cliff*: the man is not only insane, but lacks plain common sense; cf. *Ep.* 2.2.135, *Ars* 459.

96 *Fufius*: "this Fufius, from Phocaea [a Greek town in Asia Minor], was an actor of tragedies who, when he tried to portray Iliona [97n.] sleeping, so that he could jump up at the sound of her son's voice, fell asleep for real on the stage" (Porph.). Many actors at Rome, like mimes (1.2.1n.), were of foreign origin.

97   *Iliona*: the title character of a famous and popular tragedy by M. Pacuvius
(220–131 BCE), a nephew of Ennius (1.4.70n.). In the play, Polymestor, a
king in Thrace, killed his son Deiphilus thinking the boy was Polydorus the
last son of Priam, king of Troy. When his wife, Iliona, Priam's daughter,
found out about the murder from the dead boy's ghost, she persuaded the
real Polydorus to help her take vengeance on Polymestor.

98   *Twelve hundred voices*: of the audience in the theater. For the round number,
see 1.3.19n.

  Catienus: the actor playing Deiphilus' ghost (97n.). His name suggests he
was either Italian or had become a Roman citizen.

102   *Damasippus madly buys*: for the shift to the third person, see 1.2.137n.

103   *The man . . . is sane?*: sarcastic.

  this guy: i.e., Damasippus.

107   *a gift from Mercury*: here not the Roman Mercury (40n.), but the Latin
name for the Greek god Hermes, who was considered responsible for "strokes
of luck," which the Greeks called *hermeia*. See 2.6.5n.

108–19   *Write a loan agreement . . . never be repaid*: a notoriously obscure passage,
but the gist seems to be that the moneylender Nerius (108n.) Perellius (118n.)
is no more sane than someone who waives repayment of a loan (104–7),
since "whatever precaution a creditor may take, he cannot force a defaulting
debtor to pay" (Muecke).

108–11   *Write . . . Use . . . add*: addressed, in a kind of aside, to Perellius (118).

108   *Nerius*: evidently the first name (*praenomen*) of Perellius (so Pseudacro).
But some modern scholars take this as a distinct person, possibly a banker
who pays out the money for Perellius so that there will be a record of it.

110   *Cicuta*: from 267 it appears that he is a miser, which would explain why he
would be so careful of his accounting books. The name means "hemlock"
(2.1.86n.).

113   *Proteus*: in Greek myth, a sea god with much knowledge who could change
shape to avoid capture. See *Odes* 1.2.7–8, *Ep.* 1.1.90, Hom. *Od.* 4.414–24,
454–61 (imitated at Virg. *G.* 4.396–14, 440–52).

118   *Perellius*: clearly a moneylender, but otherwise unknown.

120–21   *Come and listen . . . Any one of you*: Stertinius shifts from addressing
only Damasippus to "preaching" to a imagined crowd; see 62n. The phrasing
here is reminiscent of 1.2.47–48.

120   *toga*: 1.1.104n.

121–24   *sick . . . mental illness*: 44–45n.

121–22   *vicious / ambition*: Stertinius discusses this at 237–341; cf. 1.4.26n.

122   *greed*: the principal topic at 126–236 as well as *Sat.* 1.1; cf. 1.9.68,
2.2.75nn.

123   *superstition's woes*: considered at 430–39; cf. 1.4.185, 1.5.125, 1.9.100nn.

123–24   *some other / mental illness*: these turn out to be "extravagance" (342–77)
and "being in love" (378–429).

126   *hellebore*: Latin *veratrum*, Greek *helleboros*, a common herbal treatment for
mental ailments; cf. *Ep.* 2.2.137, Plin. *Nat.* 25.47–61. A particularly effective
variety of the plant grew near two Greek towns called Anticyra (128, 250,

Ars 300). Chrysippus (70), among other philosophers, is said to have dosed himself with the stuff to keep his mind sharp (Petr. 88.4).

128 *Anticyra*: 126n.

129 *Staberius*: otherwise unknown, but a real name.

133 *one hundred pairs*: a ridiculously large number. "Staberius wants to perpetuate the memory of his wealth, either by record in his epitaph, or by requiring his heirs to spend an unforgettable amount on benefactions" (Muecke).

134 *Arrius*: Q. Arrius, who in 59 BCE honored his dead father with a memorably extravagant funeral feast (Cic. *Vat.* 30–32; cf. *Brut.* 242). His sons are mentioned at 371–77.

135 *all the grain of Africa*: hyperbole, as in "all the tea in China." Following the destruction of Carthage (146 BCE), North Africa became a major source for the grain supply of the Republic. Cf. *Odes* 1.1.9–10, 3.16.29–40.

145–47 *Everything . . . must yield to wealth*: an inversion of the norm in most philosophies, where "everything" is subordinated to moral excellence (*virtus*); cf. *Ep.* 1.1.53–59, 1.6.31–38, Cic. *Fam.* 9.14.4, Sall. *Cat.* 2.7.

149–51 *famous, brave . . . just . . . wise . . . king*: Staberius puts being wealthy on a par not only with traditional Roman virtues, but with the wisdom of the Stoic sage.

150–51 *wise . . . king*: 75n.

154 *Aristippus*: Aristippus of Cyrene in Libya (c. 435–366 BCE). He was the founder of the Cyrenaic school, which held that pleasure, especially simple, sensual pleasure (eschewed by the Epicureans) was life's supreme good. Cf. *Ep.* 1.1.18–19, 1.17.13–32, Cic. *De Or.* 3.62, *Fin.* 2.114. For the anecdote cited here, cf. Diog. Laert. 2.77 (= Bion, fr. 40A); another figured in a satire of Lucilius (fr. 835 *ROL*).

159 *Which . . . is more insane?*: In Chrysippus' view, the man who cared too much and the man who cared not at all about external goods such as wealth were both "insane" (Plut. *Moralia* 1047e–1048c).

169–70 *hasn't a clue . . . hallowed coins*: Stertinius almost seems to echo H.'s own words at 1.1.76–78.

179–80 *Chian . . . Falernian*: 1.10.33n.

181 *nasty vinegar*: 2.2.78n.
	Suppose: addressed to Damasippus. See 62n.

183–84 *moths . . . feasting*: cf. *Ep.* 1.20.12 (addressed to H.'s book of epistles), "you will silently feed lazy grubs," Lucil. fr. 1104 *ROL*, "the wool, a product of hard work, perishes: mildew and grubs shred everything."

187 *God-forsaken fool*: imitating a Greek expression, *theois echthros*, literally "an enemy to the gods"; cf. Hesiod, *Theogony* 766, Demosthenes, *On the Crown* 119, Stobaeus, *Florilegium* 2.7, "For the Stoics every fool is enemy to the gods."
	freedman: cf. 2.5.96–97.

188 *will guzzle all your wine*: cf. *Odes* 2.14.25–27, "A worthier heir will take up your Caecuban [1.5.42n.] vintages / guarded with a hundred keys and with unmixed / and splendid wine stain the pavement."

192 *oil for salad dressing*: 1.4.173n.

194   *you really think that less is more*: Stertinius begins to address a criminally greedy man (62n.) who has taken the philosophical ideal of "desiring only what is sufficient" (*Odes* 3.1.25; cf. 1.80, *Odes* 3.16.42–44, *Ep.* 1.2.46) to an "insane" extreme.

197–214   *throwing stones . . . Pylades*: "The argument seems to be that if senseless homicide [as in the case of Orestes] is recognized as madness, then so must be the killing of a mother or wife in order to inherit" (Muecke). Roman criminal law had long recognized the "insanity defense," which did not obtain an acquittal in the United States until the infamous Harry Thaw murder of his wife Evelyn Nesbit's former lover Stanford White in 1906 ("*dementia Americana*").

199   *every boy and girl*: "street urchins" (1.3.188n.).

201   *Argos*: in Homer (*Od.* 1.32–43, 298–300, 3.303–12, 4.512–49, 11.405–34, 24.95–96, 199–202) the story of the death and avenging of Agamemnon is set at Mycenae, but by the fifth century BCE it had been moved to the (at that time) far more important cities of Sparta (lyric poets) or Argos (Athenian tragedy).

202   *Orestes*: one of the most famous of Greek myths. On his return from Troy, Agamemnon (286–316), the leader of the Greek army, was murdered by his wife Clytemnestra (1.1.105–6) and her lover Aegisthus; years later, his son Orestes, who had been smuggled out of Argos (Mycenae), returned and, with the help of his sister Electra and his best friend Pylades, killed not only Aegisthus, but his mother. For this he was driven mad by the Furies (but cf. 207n.) until he was healed by Apollo. The story is best known today from Aeschylus' trilogy *Oresteia*, but parts of it were treated by other tragedians in both fifth-century Athens (Sophocles, *Electra*, Euripides, *Electra*, *Orestes*, *Iphigenia in Aulis*) and Republican Rome (e.g., Ennius [1.4.70n.], *Eumenides*, Pacuvius [97n.], *Dulorestes*, Accius [1.10.70n.], *Agamemnonidae*). Orestes' madness was also the subject of Varro's Menippean satire, *Eumenides* (frr. 117–165; cf. 287n.).

206   *gruesome Furies*: cf. 1.4.68, 1.8.47–48, 63nn. In Aeschylus, once the Furies (*Erinyes*) have been appeased by Athene (Minerva) and Apollo, they come to be called "Kindly ones" (*Eumenides*).

207   *The opposite, in fact, was true*: maybe, but not in any surviving version of the story.

210–13   *Pylades . . . Electra*: 202n.

212–13   *shouted "Fury" at / Electra*: as at Euripides, *Orestes* 264. But there Orestes does seem to be insane.

213   *black depression*: the Latin is *splendida bilis*, "glossy-black bile"; bile is one of the humors (2.2.102–5n.).

215   *Opimius*: a real name, but it suggests "wealth" (Latin *ops*) and may also be "an ironic allusion to the celebrated *vinum Opimianum*, a vintage of Falernian [1.5.42n.] dated by L. Opimius' consulate in 121 BC" (Muecke). See Plin. *Nat.* 14.55, Petr. 34.6.

216   *Veientine*: a cheap, low-quality wine; see Pers. 5.147–48, Mart. 1.103.9.

217   *Campanian-ware*: cf. 1.6.123.

233 *basmati rice*: most rice (*oriza*) available in the Roman world came from India via the Red Sea and Indian Ocean trade routes (Plin. *Nat.* 18.71).

235 *Eight* asses: 1.6.99n.

241 *Dear Stoic*: addressed by Stertinius to himself (62n.). This type of "self-examination" was called *percontatio* (Greek *eperotesis* or *hypophora*). See Cic. *De Or.* 3.203, *Or.* 137.

242 *Craterus*: possibly the same Greek doctor known to Cicero's friend Atticus (*Att.* 12.14.4).

243 *dyspepsia*: a physical illness, but this does not, despite what most people would think, rule out a mental one; cf. 44–45n.

245–46 *The problem . . . serious*: minus the attribution to Craterus, nearly the same words reoccur at *Ep.* 1.6.28, where they fit much better than here.

248–49 *sacrifice . . . Lares*: i.e., give thanks for his supposed soundness of body and mind. The boundaries of every Roman household were thought to be protected by small, friendly gods called Lares; see 1.5.83, 2.5.19, 2.6.84, *Epd.* 2.66, *Odes* 3.23.3–4.

249 *ambition*: 121–22n.

250 *Anticyra*: 126n.

254 *Servius Oppidius*: otherwise unknown, but the name Oppidius occurs on inscriptions found near H.'s home region of Apulia (1.5.44n.).

256 *Canusium*: 1.5.113n.

257 *his sons*: the motif of brothers that are "mad / in opposite extremes" (264–65) is common in myth, folktale, popular philosophy, and parable. Cf. *Ep.* 1.18.41–44, 2.2.183–89, Ter. *Adelphi*, Cic. *Sen.* 65.

258–62 *Aulus . . . Tiberius*: common Roman first names (*praenomina*). Their use here is appropriate for a father distinguishing between sons; elsewhere, the use of the first name can be a mark of intimacy (2.5.32n.; but cf. 371n. below).

259–60 *knucklebones / and nuts*: used in children's gambling games; cf. Suet. *Aug.* 83, "for relaxation he [Octavian] sometimes used to gamble with knucklebones and marked nuts in company with small boys."

266 *Nomentanus*: see 343, 1.1.107n.

267 *Cicuta*: 110n.

268 *gods . . . house and home*: the Penates, in charge of the space within the home, as the Lares (248–49n.) are of its boundaries. See 2.5.6, *Odes* 3.23.19, *Ep.* 1.7.94–95.

269 *don't add a jot*: the injunction reflects an old-time Roman attitude (cf. Cic. *De Or.* 2.225, *Parad.* 43), long out of date by the late Republic (Cic. *Verr.* 2.4.45, *Off.* 1.92, 2.87).

271 *Nature circumscribes*: the phrasing suggests Epicurean doctrine (1.1.52n.), but the Stoics (53n.) also advocated "living according to Nature," which they defined rather differently. See *HP* 58C–D, 63A–C.

273 *vainglory*: 1.6.27–29n.

275 *aedile*: there were two of them in Republican Rome (cf. 1.6.129n.), in charge of small-time criminal courts, the care of roads within the city and of temples (*aedes*); the office offered a great opportunity for courting public favor and advancement, public entertainments (*ludi*) on certain holidays, which the *aediles* often funded from their own pockets or with borrowed money.

praetor: the second highest ranking office at Rome, inferior only to the consul. Cf. 1.6.150, 166–67n., 1.7.23.

277–85 *You'd waste . . . Agrippa earns*: Stertinius abruptly addresses someone in the crowd (62n.) who he somehow recognizes (from his "preening" and "prominading?") as ambitious. The past tenses (281–82) show this cannot be a continuation of Oppidius' speech.

277–78 *You'd waste . . . beans*: i.e., even providing cheap food (cf. 1.6.160, 2.6.79–80, 2.6.110) at the *Ludi* (274n.) would be an enormous expense.

279 *the Circus*: the site for horse races and other elements in the *Ludi*; see 1.6.156n.

280 *figure cast in bronze*: i.e., is honored for his public service with a statue. Cf. Lucr. 3.78, (some men, driven by ambition,) "perish for the sake of statues and of fame."

283–84 *fox . . . masquerade as noble lion*: a proverbial expression (cf. Cic. *Off.* 1.41, Pers. 5.116–17, Mart. 10.100.3), possibly derived from an animal fable, like that of the donkey in a lion skin (Aesop, *Fab.* 366), that is no longer extant.

285 *Agrippa*: M. Vipsanius Agrippa (c. 63–12 BCE), a "new man" (1.6.23n.) who became, along with Maecenas, Octavian's most trusted associate, especially in practical and military matters (2.6.71n.). Although he had already been consul (37 BCE), he served as aedile in 33 BCE. During his term he greatly enhanced Octavian's popularity by undertaking many useful public works, and the magnificence and generosity of his *Ludi* were long remembered. See Plin. *Nat.* 36.104, 121, Suet. *Aug.* 42.1, Dio 49.43.1–4. In *Odes* 1.6, H. recuses himself (2.1.16–17n.) from singing Agrippa's praises, and he is mentioned at *Ep.* 1.6.26 and *Ep.* 1.12.1, 26, but there is no evidence that H. was on close terms with him.

286–326 *O son of Atreus . . . free from fault*: Stertinius now even more abruptly (276–85n.) engages in a conversation with Agamemnon (cf. 1.1.106, 1.2.151, 1.10.58nn.), dead since just after the end of the Trojan War! "Imagined introduction of imagined characters" (Cic. *De Or.* 3.205), which Latin rhetoricians called *conformatio* (in Greek *prosopopoia*; *Rhet. Her.* 3.66, Quint. 9.2.31–37), is not uncommon in oratory and philosophy (e.g., Cic. *Cael.* 33–34, *Fin.* 4.61, Arrian, *Discourses of Epictetus* 3.22.307), but this example is more than a little bizarre, since Stertinius seems not to bring the dead king into the present, but to project himself into the past, to the time just after Ajax's rampage (287n.; cf. 326n.).

286 *Atreus*: the father of Agamemnon and Menelaus (304, 1.3.43, 149nn.).

287 *Ajax*: most of the details emerge in the ensuing conversation, except that Ajax went mad in the first place (or was driven mad by Athene [Minerva]) because the armor of the recently slain Achilles was awarded by the Greeks not to him, but to Ulysses (Odysseus), and that, after he came to his senses and saw what he had done, he committed suicide by falling on his sword. The story is alluded to in Homer (*Od.* 11.541–67), and was the subject of tragedies at Athens by Aeschylus, Euripides, and Sophocles, whose *Ajax* survives, and at Rome by Livius Andronicus, the earliest Latin tragedian (fl. 240–204 BCE),

Ennius (1.4.70n.), Pacuvius (97n.), and Accius (1.10.70n.). Varro mentioned it in his *Eumenides* (202n.; see fr. 125 *Astbury*), and according to Suetonius, *Aug.* 85.2, Octavian "began to write a tragedy with great energy, but when his pen failed him, he tossed it away and, when his friends asked what was up with Ajax, he answered that Ajax had fallen on an eraser."

288 *Because I'm king*: cf. Sal. *Jug.* 31.26, "To do whatever you please with impunity, that is what it is to be king."

292–93 *I pray . . .. home*: echoing Hom. *Il.* 1.18–19 (the speaker is the priest Chryses, also about to make a request to Agamemnon), "May the gods who dwell on Olympus grant / to you that you sack the city of Priam and return home sucessfully."

295 *second to Achilles*: practically a formula in Homer (*Il.* 2.268–69, 17.279–80, *Od.* 11.550–51; cf. Sophocles, *Ajax* 1340–41).

298–99 *people . . . and Priam too rejoice*: another Homeric echo (*Il.* 1.255–58).

303 *a thousand sheep*: 1.3.19n.

305 *at Aulis*: the Greek expedition against Troy assembled at Aulis on the straits of Euboea, but was becalmed because of the anger of Artemis (Diana), who demanded that Agamemnon sacrifice to her his daughter Iphigenia. The myth is best known from Euripides' *Iphigenia at Aulis*, which was adapted by Ennius (1.4.70n.). It is alluded to in philosophical contexts at Cic. *Tusc.* 1.116 and at Lucr. 1.84–101, where it serves as an example of the harm inflicted by religion / superstition (cf. 430–39).

306–7 *sprinkled her head . . . before the altar*: a standard procedure in Roman (but not Greek) animal sacrifices. See *Odes* 1.4.11–12, Virg. *A.* 2.133, 4.517.

307 *spelt-meal*: 1.1.155n.

308 *shameless man*: cf. Hom. *Il.* 1.149 (Achilles to Agamemnon), "You, cloaked in shamelessness."

310 *his wife and boy*: Tecmessa, a Phrygian POW, and Eurysaces. See *Odes* 2.4.5–6.

312 *Teucer*: Ajax's half-brother, the son of Telamon, and his prize from the first sack of Troy led by Hercules, Priam's sister Hesione. See *Odes* 1.7.21–32.

317–18 *imagining things, mistaking false / for true*: some technical Stoic doctrine, according to which men know things from first perceiving "appearances" (Greek *phantasiai*) that may or may not really exist, then using reason to distinguish "false" from "true" ones. See Cic. *Ac.* 2.47–50, 88–90, *HP* 27, 30.

323 *an empty title*: i.e., of "Commander-in-chief" or "Conqueror of Troy." Cf. *Ep.* 2.2.206–7, "is your heart / free from empty ambition," Lucr. 3.998–99, (Sisyphus [32–34n.] symbolizes the futility of) "seeking power that is empty and not ever truly granted."

326 *Suppose a person . . . .*: it seems likely that Stertinius is now addressing Damasippus again (62n.), since the details in the ensuing passage (327–41) indicate a Republican Roman, not a heroic-age Greek setting (327, 330, 332, 340nn.).

327 *litter rides*: 1.2.127n.

330 *Posilla or Rufa*: common girls' nicknames, meaning "second-born" (or, possibly, "little olive") and "redhead" (cf. 1.2.35–36n.).

331   *some fine husband*: Iphigenia (305n.) was lured to Aulis on the pretext that she would marry Achilles, "the best of the Achaeans."

332–34   *judge . . . guardianship*: the "judge" would be the urban praetor (1.6.166–67n.), the procedure was as at least as old as the Twelve Tables (2.1.117n.); cf. *Ep.* 1.1.101–5, 2.2.136, Cic. *Inv.* 2.148 (= *Lex XII* 7a–c *ROL*), Sen. 22.

340   *Bellona*: an old Italian goddess of war (Latin *bellum*) who, during the Roman wars in Asia Minor (80s–60s BCE), came to be identified with eastern goddesses such as Cybele and Ma notorious for inspiring madness in their temple attendants (*fanatici*, from *fanum*, "temple," hence the sense, as in Eng., of "fanatic"; see *Ars* 454). Cf. Virg. *A.* 7.319, 8.703, Tib. 1.6.45–46.

342   *we*: Stertinius and Damasippus (326n.).

Extravagance: cf. 123–24n.

343   *Nomentanus*: a bad penny, if ever there was one (266n.).

346   *This man*: called a "young man" at 356, he is probably an unnamed, contemporary prodigal (1.2.10n.) rather than, as Pseudacro asserts, the long-dead Nomentanus (1.8.16).

a thousand talents: one talent (a Greek monetary unit sometimes used for convenience at Rome) = 24,000 Roman sesterces (*sestertii*, abbr. as *HS*); the legacy was thus *HS* 24,000,000, almost 17,000 times the yearly pay of a centurion (6.99n.). See 2.7.131n.

348   *Fishmongers*: practitioners of what Cicero (*Off.* 1.150) disapprovingly calls *artes ministrae . . . uoluptatum*, "arts that furnish sensual pleasures." There are similar lists at Pl. *Trinummus* 406–12 and Ter. *Eunuchus* 255–58.

349–52   *Tuscan Street . . . produce stalls . . . Velabrum*: the *Vicus Tusci* ("street of the Etruscan [1.6.2n.]"), southwest of the Roman Forum, and the Velabrum, a low-lying area through which the street passed, were, along with the *Via Sacra* (1.9.1n.), the places to buy luxury items; for the "produce stalls" (*Macellum*), see 1.6.154n.

353   *A pimp*: the young man evidently aims to follow the advice given at 1.2.39–44, 105–9, and 159–66; see 1.2.40n., but also 385–86.

356   *equitable*: 1.3.15n., but here ironic.

358   *Lucania*: 2.1.51n.

359   *wintry seas*: but cf. 2.2.25.

361   *a million*: sesterces (346n.).

362–63   *your wife . . . late at night*: the man takes the pimp at his word ("whatever . . . is ours, is yours").

364   *Aesopus' son*: the father, M. Clodius Aesopus (died before 45 BCE) was, along with the legendary Roscius, the greatest tragic actor at Rome in the late second and early first century BCE (see *Ep.* 2.1.82, *Rhet. Her.* 3.34, Cic. *De Or.* 1.259, 3.102, *Div.* 1.80, *Tusc.* 4.55), and, in his old age, a friend of Cicero (*Sest.* 120–23, *Fam.* 7.1.2, 4, *Q. Fr.* 1.2.14). In 47 BCE, Cicero expressed his anxiety about Aesopus' son (*Att.* 11.15.3), possibly in connection with what is described here, who is said to have inherited *HS* 20,000,000 (Macr. *Sat.* 3.14.14). The stunt with the pearl is mentioned by Valerius Maximus (9.1.2) and by Pliny the Elder (*Nat.* 9.122), following a description of Cleopatra's much more famous repetition of it (*Nat.* 9.119–21).

366 *Metella*: Caecilia Metella, the daughter of Q. Caecilius Metellus Celer (consul 60, died 59 BCE) and Clodia, the notorious mistress, then accuser of Cicero's friend M. Caelius (Cic. *Cael.*), the oldest sister of his mortal enemy P. Clodius Pulcher (no relation to the Clodii Aesopi), and, in the view of some scholars, the inspiration for Catullus' "Lesbia." Metella herself had quite a reputation (Cic. *Att.* 11.23.3, 12.52.2, 13.7.1).

370 *sewer*: 28n.

371 *Quintus Arrius*: 134n. It is not clear why his first name is added here (cf. 258–62n.); the only other instances of this in H. are at *Ars* 371, "Aulus Cascellius," and *Odes* 4.2.2 with 4.2.26, "Iullus . . . Antonius," where "Iullus" is not in any case a normal first name. Arrius' prodigal (1.2.10n.) sons are not mentioned elsewhere.

374 *nightingales*: Latin *lusciniae*. They were enormously expensive, but were usually purchased as song birds (Plin. *Nat.* 10.84), although both Aesopi (364n.) also had a taste for them (Val. Max. 9.1.2, Plin. *Nat.* 10.141–42).

376 *chalk them up*: white chalk was used to mark days on the calendar that were good or lucky, black chalk indicated the opposite. See *Odes* 1.36.10, Catul. 107.6.

378–429 This section seems best taken as addressed, not to Damasippus, but to someone who is "love crazy." See 62, 123–24nn.

378–80 *little houses . . . hobby horses*: children's pastimes. See Aristophanes, *Clouds* 879–90, Val. Max. 8.8.ext.1, Plut. *Life of Agesilaus* 70, Juv. 9.61, Suet. *Aug.* 71.4.

379 *odds and evens*: a game played by guessing if someone had an odd or an even number of nuts (259–60n.) in his hand; a winner would receive the nuts, or a cash prize (cf. Suet. *Aug.* 71.4).

383 *If logic demonstrates*: the comparison between adult craziness and children's irrationality is at least as old as Aristippus (154n.; cf. Plut. *Moralia* 469d), but it was taken up by the Stoics (53n.), e.g., at Sen. *Ep.* 115.8.

385 *love for prostitutes*: the problem is not the prostitutes (353n.), but the love. The idea of love as a kind of madness has a long literary and philosophical history (e.g., *Odes* 1.13.11, 1.25.14, 3.21.3, Lucr. 4.1068–72, Cic. *Tusc.* 4.68–76 [in Stoic doctrine]).

387 *playing in the sand*: as in a famous simile at Hom. *Il.* 15.362–64 (Apollo broke through the Greek defensive wall) "with ease, just as when some boy near the seashore, / after he makes toy castles, in his childishness / playfully scatters the sand again with his feet and hands."

388 *Polemon*: Athenian philosopher (c. 350–267 BCE), head of the Platonic Academy, and chief teacher of Zeno, the founder of Stoicism (53n.). According to a number of sources (V. Max. 6.9.ext.1, Diog. Laert. 4.16–17, Lucian, *Bis Accusatus* 16), as a young man Polemo led an extravagant and dissipated life until he stumbled into a lecture denouncing such conduct given by Xenocrates (c. 396–314 BCE), then the head of the Academy; Polemo was so impressed, he sobered up, studied with Xenocrates, and eventually succeeded him. The incident may have been referred to by Lucilius; see frr. 821–23 *ROL*.

390–91   *stockings . . . pillows*: used by those in poor health.

393   *garlands*: at Greek-style banquets (1.3.127–28n.) the participants would don garlands of branches and flowers when the serious drinking began. See *Odes* 1.7.23, 2.7.23–25, 3.14.17, etc.

395   *some sulky kid*: another "irrational" child (383n.).

399–417   *When . . . sanity*: the scene, and much of the language in it, is taken from the opening of Terence's (1.4.2n.) comedy *The Eunuch* (*Eunuchus* 46–63), which H. has managed to transform from iambic senarii (10.59n.) into dactylic hexameters.

399–400   *the woman's door / is locked*: making the man a "shut out lover" (*exclusus amator*), a familiar figure from Greek and Roman lyric, epigram, comedy, and, no doubt, real life; see 2.7.130–33, *Epd.* 11.19–22, *Odes* 1.25, 3.7, 3.10, 3.26, Cic. *Parad.* 36, Lucr. 4.1177–84, Catul. 67, Prop. 1.16, etc.

400   *the lover*: in Terence (399–416n.) he is Phaedria, his beloved is the prostitute Thais, and his "clever slave" (408) is Parmeno.

   argues with himself: a lover's indecisiveness is a symptom of his "insanity"; cf. Cic. *Tusc.* 4.75–76 (Stoic doctrine [53n.]).

411   *evils*: a stronger term than Parmeno's "faults" (*vitia*) at *Eun.* 59.

412   *Blind chance*: the "blindness" of chance (fate, luck, etc.; cf. 1.1.3n.) is proverbial (e.g., Pacuvius, tragic or comic fr. 37–41 *ROL*, Cic. *Amic.* 54, *Phil.* 13.10).

418–19   *shoot . . . seeds . . . ceiling*: a type of love divination. If a lover succeeded in hitting the ceiling with an apple seed shot from between his thumb and forefinger, it was a sign he would attain his desire (Porph.; see Poll. *Onom.* 9.128). Apple seeds were still put to similar uses in the parts of Britain as recently as the end of the nineteenth century.

418   *Picenian*: the region of Picenum, across the Apennines to the east-northeast of Rome, produced especially good apples. See 2.4.89, *Priap.* 51.7, Strabo, *Geography* 5.240, Juv. 11.74.

422   *baby talk*: such as lovers babble; cf. 1.3.60n.

424   *poke the fire*: violating a precept of the legendary sage Pythagoras (2.4.4n., 2.6.80), "Don't stir a fire with a sword" (Athenaeus, *Deipnosophistae* 10.552d, Diog. Laert. 8.8); cf. 485–86.

424–25   *Marius . . . Hellas*: otherwise unknown. The man's name is Roman or at least Italian, the woman's common among Greek freed slaves. See 1.2.58n.

427–29   *insane . . . criminal . . . related terms*: since the Latin terms are no more "related" in any ordinary sense than their English translations, Stertinius may be drawing on some Stoic paradox (cf. Cic. *De Or.* 3.66 for the obscurity of Stoic discourse). But Shackleton Bailey suggests emending *cognata*, the reading of all the MSS and of Pseudacro (Porph. does not comment here) to *inapta*, "inappropriate."

430–49   *freedman . . . Religion*: Stertinius abruptly turns back to Damasippus (62n.) and takes up his last topic (123n.), superstition, which was considered a major vice by most philosophical schools, including both Epicureans (Lucr. 3.990–93, Cic. *Fin.* 1.70) and Stoics ([53n.]; see Cic. *N.D.* 1.117, Sen. *Ep.*

47.17, 123.16), and was also a target in popular diatribe (see the Introduction; see also Bion, frr. 30, 34, Theophrastus, *Characters* 16) and satire (Lucil. frr. 524–29 *ROL*).

430–32 *freedman . . . cross-road shrines*: in Latium, where there were crossroads, there were shrines to special Lares (cf. 1.5.82n.) called *Compitales* ("of the crossroads"), who would be worshipped, especially by freedpersons and even slaves, at important times such as birthdays and weddings. This freedman's "madness" lies in his constant rather than occasional attendance on not just a local shrine, but all of them, as if he were hedging his bets.

431 *washed his hands*: as required before participation in any ritual (e.g., Pl. *Amphitryo* 1094, *Aulularia* 579).

435 *easy work for gods*: cf. Hom. *Od.* 3.231, Hesiod, *Theogony* 442–44, Archilochus, fr. 130.1 *LCL*, "for the gods, all things are easy," Cic. *Div.* 2.86, Ov. *Met.* 8.619 ("whatever the gods wish, it's done").

437–38 *certified . . . lawsuit*: the lawsuit would be based on a late Republican aedilician edict that prescribed that, in the sale of slaves (1.1.48n.), the vendor was obliged to reveal in advance any fault in the "merchandise." Cf. *Ep.* 2.2.16, Cic. *Off.* 3.71, Gel. 4.2.1, *Dig.* 21.1.1.1.

439 *Chrysippus*: cf. 70, 1.3.179n.

440 *Menenius' prolific family*: the reference is obscure. The Menenii were a distinguished plebeian clan in the early Republic, but the name, despite the difference in quantity (the first *e* is short), might evoke Greek *mainomai* (written in Latin either *maen-* or *men-* with a long *e*), "be crazy."

441 *Jupiter*: if this is Roman Jupiter, the mom is calling on the wrong god, since there is no evidence connecting him with the health of children or with anything like a "fast day" (445). It is possible that the woman means another, non-Roman "supreme deity" (cf. Caesar, *Bellum Gallicum* 6.17.2), perhaps the god of the Jews (1.4.185n.), who in Augustus' time, if not earlier, fasted on their Sabbath (Suet. *Aug.* 76.2, Strabo, 16.2.40, Petr. fr. 50.6 Mueller, Mart. 4.4.7).

444 *shivering*: in the Latin Stertinius specifies the shivering of "quartan fever," which recurs every 3 days (= 4 days in Roman reckoning; see 1.6.81n.), but was not usually lethal (cf. Cic. *N.D.* 3.24, Plin. *Nat.* 28.228).

445 *in the Tiber naked*: similar rituals are mentioned at Pers. 2.15–16 and Juv. 6.522–24.

450–92 The poem ends, as it had begun, with a dialogue, now increasingly testy, between the "cured" Damasippus and an apparently hopelessly "crazy" Horace.

450 *eighth wise man*: i.e., worthy of inclusion with the proverbial "Seven Sages," Greek thinkers and statesmen of the sixth century. BCE famous for their wisdom. Cf. Plato, *Protagoras* 343a, Call. fr. 587 *LCL*, Cic. *De Or.* 3.137, *Rep.* 1.12, *Fin.* 2.7, *Tusc.* 5.7, *Amic.* 7, *Off.* 3.16.

452 *if I'm attacked*: Damasippus' stance is reminiscent of H.'s at 2.1.61–69.

455 *hanging from his rear*: cf. 84.

456–57 *Stoic . . . at profit*: H. seems dubious about how much Damasippus has really changed.

461   *Agave*: in a frenzy inspired by the god Dionysus (Liber Pater), she tore off the head of her son Pentheus, the king of Thebes, thinking he was a lion. The story is best known from Euripides' *Bacchae*, of which there were Latin versions by Pacuvius (97n.) and Accius (203n.); cf. *Odes* 2.19.13–15, *Ep.* 1.16.73–78, Virg. *A.* 4.469–70.

466–74   *First . . . game*: according to Damasippus, H.'s "madness" lies in his disregard for *decorum*, "propriety," "what is appropriate [for each person]," an important aspect of Stoic [53n.] ethics. See *Ep.* 1.7.98, Cic. *Off.* 1.93–114.

467   *building plans*: evidently for the Sabine farm Damasippus has invaded (15n.). In the late Republic and well into the principate many people, including Maecenas (1.8.11–12n.), advertised their eminence with elaborate town houses and country villas; see 2.6.89–90, *Odes* 2.15, *Var. R.* 1.13.6–7.

   a midget: obviously an exaggeration, although by his own admission H. was "of small stature" (*Ep.* 1.20.24) and "fat" (*Ep.* 1.4.15); see Suet. *Vita*.

470   *Turbo*: according to Porph., "a gladiator [1.7.25n.] of short stature but spirited in fight." The name, "top," "whirlwind," seems appropriate for such a fighter.

473   *Maecenas*: the first mention of him in *Satires* 2; see 2.1.93n.

475–83   *One day . . . that large*: a fable on the dangers of ambition (121–22n.) attested for Aesop (84 Helm), Phaedrus (1.24), and Babrius (28), whose version is closest to that given here; cf. Petr. 74.13, Mart. 10.79.9–10.

475   *frog*: Maecenas' seal carried the image of a frog (Plin. *Nat.* 37.10).

476   *A calf*: in other versions it is an ox, but "even a calf is a 'huge monster' for the little frog" (Muecke).

   Just one survived: at Babr. 28.1–3, only one froglet is killed, while his brothers survive to tell the tale.

485–86   *more oil / To fuel the fire*: alluding to a common proverb (e.g., Cic. *Phil.* fr. 5.74). Cf. 424.

486   *Was any poet sane?*: poetic inspiration had long been associated with madness; cf. 2.5.102, 2.7.163, *Odes* 2.19.5–8, 3.4.5–6, *Ars* 295–303, 455–56 (1.3.188n.), Plato, *Ion* 533e, *Phaedrus* 245a, Cic. *De Or.* 2.194, *Div.* 1.80.

488   *terrific temper*: see 1.3.47–50n.

491   *Lovesick for girls and boys*: Damasippus may be turning H.'s own words against him: *Epd.* 11.3–4, "Love, which seeks me out above all men / to be inflamed with soft boys and girls." Cf. 1.3.151n.

492   *royal . . . common*: even though in Stoic doctrine, all types of madness are equally bad, Damasippus "outranks" H. because, as a sage, he is also a "king" (75n.).

Satire 2.4 Notes

1 *HORACE:* 2.1.1n.

  Where . . . Where to?: the first line evokes the beginning (227a) of Plato's famous dialogue *Phaedrus* (also a model for Cic. *De Or.*), where Socrates asks, "Whence and whither, dear Phaedrus?" This and other elements in the opening lines (1–16) of the satire create "expectations of a philosophical discourse," (Muecke) which, despite H.'s (ironic) final comments (113–23), are hardly fulfilled.

  Catius: the scholia and many modern scholars identify this as T. Catius, an Epicurean philosopher and writer mentioned by Cicero (*Fam.* 15.16.1; cf. *Fam.* 15.19.1–2, Quint. 10.1.124), but he died in 46 or 45 BCE, long before the time of the *Satires*. Another possibility is C. Catius Vestinus, a tribune of the soldiers (1.6.62n.) under Mark Antony just before the formation of the triumvirate (Cic. *Fam.* 10.23.5); others are that the name is a pseudonym for C. Matius, a noted gourmet friendly with Cicero and Trebatius (2.1.5n.; see Cic. *Fam.* 6.12.2, 7.15.2, 9.15.2, 11.27, 11.28), or his son, a food writer in the early principate (Col. 12.4.2, 6, Plin. *Nat.* 12.13, 15.49, Tac. *Ann.* 12.68), or that it is meant to suggest the Latin words *catinus* ("serving platter") or *catillus* ("plate").

4 *Pythagoras*: the famous Greek sage (late sixth century BCE?; cf. Cic. *Rep.* 2.28–30), born on the island of Samos but a long-time resident of Croton on the "heel" of Italy. He was thought to have come up with, among other things, a theory of transmigration of human souls (*metempsychosis*) that led his followers to abstain from eating animals and even beans (2.6.80n.), since these might be "reincarnations" of ancestors. Cf. *Epd.* 15.21, *Ep.* 2.1.50–52.

5 *Anytus*: the Athenian who accused Socrates of impiety, leading to his execution (399 BCE). A periphrasis is necessary since the name "Socrates" cannot fit into dactylic verse (1.5.2n.), but it also sounds learned and a bit mysterious.

  Plato: 2.3.16n.

9–10 *A gift . . . training it?*: cf. *Rhet. Her.* 3.28, "There are two sorts of memory, one natural, the other the product of art." That art was of great interest to the ancients; see Cic. *De Or.* 2.350–60, Quint. 11.2.1–51.

13 *intricate*: rendering Latin *tenuis*, which when used in connection with style can be a kind of code word for "Callimachean aesthetics" (1.4.11n.; cf. *Odes* 1.6.9, 2.16.38, Virg. *Ecl.* 1.2, 6.8). But when used of subject matter it can have, beside the positive sense Catius no doubt intends here, a pejorative meaning of "inconsequential" (e.g., Cic. *Inv.* 1.35, *Man.* 54), which is how his audience might be tempted to take it.

14 *From Rome or elsewhere?*: an echo of Plato, *Protagoras* 309c, where a friend of Socrates asks concerning Protagoras, "Is he a citizen or a stranger?"

15 *I'll sing*: as if he were "chanting" a prophecy or oracle; cf. 1.9.41.

16 *His name . . . unsaid*: like a certain "wise man" mentioned at Plato, *Phaedrus* 235c–d. It is not clear if H. means his readers to think there really was a "teacher," or implies that Catius has invented him to impart authority to what are actually his own precepts. See 17, 60nn.

17   *eggs*: beginning where Roman meals usually began (1.3.11n.).

    remember: the discourse is addressed to a single, unnamed listener (Catius himself at its original performance? See 16n.), except when the speaker indulges in polemic (31–32, 44–64, 70–73).

17–19   *oblong . . . male yolks*: so also Plin. *Nat.* 10.145, citing this passage. Ancient scientists were interested in the problem of distinguishing male-producing from female-producing eggs (e.g., Aristotle, *History of Animals* 6.2.2), but not, as here, simply for reasons of taste.

20–22   *sweeter . . . washed-out*: similar advice at Plin. *Nat.* 19.138.

23   *unexpectedly drop by*: cf. 2.2.161–68.

24   *drown . . . in wine*: both to marinate the flesh and prevent the loss of blood.

26–27   *mushrooms . . . trust*: at *Nat.* 22.92–99, Pliny discusses the dangers of wild mushrooms, but, according to W. H. S. Jones, the editor of the Loeb edition, "nearly everything [he] says about toadstools and poisonous fungi is false, and his advice would lead to fatal results if followed" (note on 22.99).

28–38   The discourse suddenly shifts from the taste of food to its affect on health.

28   *black mulberries*: thought to cool the body (Plin. *Nat.* 23.135), and also used as a laxative (Cels. 2.29.11).

30   *summer heat*: cf. 1.7.33, 2.2.56nn.

31   *Aufidius*: evidently an earlier and, in the speaker's view (17n.), inferior investigator of gastronomy. The name suggests Apulia (1.5.44n.).

    honey: often mixed with wine, especially old wine, to make a healthy drink called *mulsum* (Virg. *G.* 4.101–2, Plin. *Nat.* 22.113).

32   *Falernian*: 1.5.42n.

35–38   *For constipation . . . wine from Cos*: Cato the Censor (1.2.40n.) includes mussels and Coan wine in his recipe for "purging the bowel" (*On Agriculture* 158).

37   *sorrel*: Latin *lapithus*, elsewhere a symbol of rustic simplicity (*Epd.* 2.57, Lucil. fr. 2003 *ROL*).

38   *Cos*: the people of Cos, a Greek island in the eastern Aegean, mixed their wine with sea water, but any wine treated this way could also be called "Coan wine" (Plin. *Nat.* 14.78–79). See 2.8.15.

39–60   The speaker (16n.) returns (cf. 28–38n.) to his main focus, the taste of food. The lines about shellfish (39–43) may be meant to evoke a passage from Ennius' (4.70n.) *Hedyphagetica* (fr. 1–11 *ROL*), a poem about "good things to eat" (the meaning of its Greek title) which some scholars link with Ennius' *Satura* (see the Introduction).

39   *A waxing moon . . . shellfish*: a common belief; see Lucil. frr. 1212–13 *ROL*, "The moon nourishes oysters and fattens sea urchins; to mussels guts / she adds liver," Cic. *Div.* 2.33, Plin. *Nat.* 2.221. See also 2.8.44n.

41   *Lucrine . . . Baiae's best*: both Baiae, a resort town in Campania (5.57), and the Lacus Lucrinus, a lagoon nearby, were famous for shellfish (e.g., *Epd.* 2.49, Var. *Men.* 501 Astbury, Plin. *Nat.* 9.168).

42   *sea urchins*: already mentioned as a delicacy at Pl. *Rudens* 297 and Enn. *Hedyphagetica* fr. 11 (39–60n.); cf. 2.8.69.

    Misenum: a promontory and town also (41n.) in Campania.

43   *Posh Tarentum*: there may be a word play, since it was thought that Tarentum (6.141n.) got its name from *terenus*, an Oscan (1.5.69n.) word meaning "soft" or "luxurious." See Macr. *Sat.* 3.18.13.

44   *Let no one rashly claim*: see 17n. The speaker (16n.) may have someone like Aufidius (31n.) in mind, or is setting up a straw man, as often in (true) philosophical argumentation.

44–45   *the art / of dining*: a suitable title for the discourse. Ancient philosophers, scientists, and rhetoricians devoted considerable effort to defining and systematizing the various "arts" (Greek *technai*) relevant to human life. H.'s own *Ars Poetica* is an example, as is, with parodic intent, Ovid's *Ars Amatoria*.

47   *trawls . . . shops*: cf. *Ep.* 1.6.56–61, where gluttons are imagined fishing and hunting with full equipment in the city food markets (2.3.348–52). See 56n.

50   *upon his elbow*: at Greek-style banquets (1.3.23, 127–28nn.) a diner reclining on a couch would lean on his left elbow while taking food with his right hand.

51–52   *boar / from Umbria*: for wild boar, see 2.2.57, 124–29, 2.3.58, 2.8.10; for that from Umbria, the region northeast of Rome, see Statius, *Silvae* 4.6.10.

53   *Laurentian*: from the Laurentian Marsh on the coast just south of Rome's port Ostia. See Virg. *A.* 10.708–18, Mart. 9.48.5–6, 10.45.3–4.

55   *vine-fed deer*: but vines were a normal food for roe deer (*capreae*); see Virg. *G.* 2.374.

56   *epicure*: bringing out the play in the Latin word *sapiens* between the meanings "sage" (1.3.110n.) and "(food) taster" (cf. Eng. "sapid").

56–57   *hare . . . forelegs*: as at Nasidienus' banquet (2.8.117–18).

56   *will choose*: again (47n.), as if he were actually hunting the hare; cf. 2.138–39, 2.2.14, *Epd.* 2.35, *Ep.* 1.15.22.

58–60   The speaker (16, 60nn.) claims to be a "discoverer" (Latin *inuentor*, Greek *heuretes*) of true knowledge, as if he were a philosopher such as Epicurus (see Lucr. 1.66–77, Cic. *Tusc.* 1.48) or other benefactor of humanity (Plin. *Nat.* 7.191–215). But cf. 2.8.120–24, where Nasidienus' pseudophilosophical babble about the "provenance and properties" of his dishes finally drives his guests from his banquet.

60   *my palate*: Catius' or that of his supposed "teacher" (16n.)? See 92–96.

61   *pastries*: see 1.1.27n.

65   *cut-rate olive oil*: 1.1.173n.

66   *Set . . . wine*: the speaker (16n.) returns to his single listener (17n.).
  Massic: a highly prized subvariety of Falernian (70n.) from Mt. Massicum near Sinuessa in Campania (5.52n.). See *Odes* 1.1.19, 2.7.21, 3.21.5.
  under cloudless skies: in defiance of the usual practice with Campanian wines, which were clarified and fumigated (67–68) by exposure to open air by day as well as by night and in all kinds of weather (Plin. *Nat.* 14.136).

69   *strain . . . through linen*: a technique mentioned in a number of sources (e.g., Plin. *Nat.* 14.138). Drinkers in a hurry often strained just before imbibing; see *Odes* 1.11.6.

70   *Falernian lees*: the lees of the stronger wine (31–32) would "fortify" the lighter one; see Col. 12.30.2.

71   *Surrentine wine*: from the excellent wine-growing region near Surrentum (modern Sorrento) on the Bay of Naples. But emperors Tiberius and Caligula derided it as "distinguished vinegar" and "noble mouthwash" (Plin. *Nat.* 14.64).

71–73   *pigeon egg . . . yolk*: this seems picayune; according to other sources (e.g., *Geoponica* 7.22), any type of egg would do, and the white or even the shell (as in campfire coffee) would be more effective than the yolk.

74   *a heavy drinker*: maybe he overdid it on the Massic and Surrentine.

75   *African snails and grilled prawns*: expensive delicacies (2.8.58, Cic. *N.D.* 2.123, Var. *R.* 3.14.4, Plin. *Nat.* 30.44–46) that might seem wasted under the circumstances.

75–76   *Lettuce . . . an acidy stomach*: contradicting a common tenet that lettuce helps with digestion (2.8.13–14; see Cels. 2.24.2, Plin. *Nat.* 19.127).

78–79   *ham or sausage . . . something hot*: cheap, meaty, and greasy food is still a common treatment.

79   *fast-food joint*: an apt rendering of *popina*, a kind of take-out stand common in the city with a poor reputation among respectable Romans. See *Ep.* 1.14.21, Cic. *Pis.* 13, Mart. 1.41.9–10, Suet. *Vita* 13.3.

81   *complex sauces*: see 2.8.15, 61–68, 90–91. The Latin cookbook attributed to M. Gavius Apicius (early first century CE) contains three volumes (6, 8, 9) devoted entirely to sauces.

83–84   *fish . . . from Byzantium*: tunny fish, which were caught in great quantity, pickled, and exported from Byzantium (modern Istanbul) on the entry point to the Black Sea, where they would go to spawn (Plin. *Nat.* 9.47–53). See 2.5.60.

86   *Corycian saffron*: also mentioned at Plin. *Nat.* 21.31 and Mart. 9.38.5. Corycus, in the Roman province of Cilicia (modern southwest Turkey), was the homeland of the old gardener featured at Virg. *G.* 4.125–48.

87   *Venafran olive oil*: from Venafrum in Campania, generally considered the best Italian oil (2.8.61, *Odes* 2.6.15–16, Cato, *On Agriculture* 135.3, Var. *R.* 1.2.6).

88   *Tibur apples . . . Picenum's*: 1.6.147, 2.3.418nn.

90   *Venuculan grapes . . . in jars*: as raisins. The name seems to refer, not to a place, but a variety, and may be Etruscan. See Col. 3.2.2, Plin. *Nat.* 14.34.

91   *Alban grapes*: from the Alban hills (5.1n.). Their wine was said to be extremely sweet (Plin. *Nat.* 14.64).

92–95   *I invented . . . I / first*: 58–60n. The novelty seems to lie in combining on one plate things otherwise kept separate.

94   *fish paste*: the solids left over when fish pickled in brine was clarified to make sauce called *garum* (2.8.62n.).

95   *saltcellars*: Latin *catilli* (1n.).

96   *white pepper* and *black salt*: a reversal of the expected colors. For white pepper, see 2.8.65; for black salt, extracted from charcoaled timber, Var. *R.* 1.7.8, Plin. *Nat.* 31.83.

97–106   *It's grossly wrong . . . large-scale shame*: strong moral language for condemning what turn out to be the "crimes" of negligence and sloppiness, but cf. 2.8.73, and, for the care required in hosting a banquet, 2.8.87–96, *Ep.* 1.5.21–29, Ter. *Phormio* 338–42, Sen. *Dialogues* 10.12.5, Juv. 14.59–67.

97   *three thousand*: sesterces (*HS*); see 2.3.346, 2.7.59nn.

99   *dish*: Latin *catinus* (1n.).

100   *slaves . . . stolen licks and nibbled*: see 1.1.48n., 1.3.113–16, 2.6.85n.

104   *sawdust*: strewn on the floor of the banquet room to soak up spills; see Petr. 68.1, Juv. 14.66–67. This was still a practice in American saloons within living memory.

107   *mosaic floor*: popular in Roman houses and villas since the late second century BCE (Plin. *Nat.* 36.184–89).

108   *Tyrian*: dyed, at great expense, reddish purple with the juice of the *purpera*, a kind of mollusk. The technique was supposed to have been invented by Phoenicians (*punicus* or *puniceus* = Greek *phoinikos* is also a term for the color) from Tyre in what is now Lebanon. See. 1.6.31, 2.6.139, 2.8.18, *Epd.* 12.21.

   valences: hanging from the edges of the couches and covering their legs. See *Ep.* 1.5.22.

113   *My learned Catius*: here ironic; cf. 2.1.114.

116   *from memory*: cf. 9, 15.

121–23   *the source . . . I'll drink . . . wisdom*: almost certainly an ironic allusion to Lucr. 1.927–28 (in regard to poetic inspiration and Epicurean philosophy), "it is sweet to approach new sources and to drink from them." Here the image of drinking especially suits the topic of the discourse.

123   *human happiness*: the Latin is *vita beata* (1.1.22n.), "the promised goal of every ancient philosophical system" (Muecke), and a deep concern of H. (e.g., 1.1.23, 127, 2.2.88–89, 2.3.58, 2.6.1–6, 92–97; *Odes* 2.2, 2.6, 2.18, 3.29, 4.9; *Ep.* 1 passim).

Satire 2.5 Notes

1   *ULYSSES*: see 2.1.1n. and, for Ulysses (= Greek Odysseus), 1.5.1–2, 1.8.38–42, 1.9.37–46, 2.2.26, 2.3.22, 287nn.

   One thing more: the poem begins as if just after Tiresias has given his instructions to Ulysses in the Underworld (1.8.38–42n.), including the warning, "you shall find / Trouble in your house, arrogant men / Devouring your wealth and courting your wife" (Hom. *Od.* 11.115–18, Lombardo trans.).
   Tiresias: the most famous and reliable seer in Greek myth. Outside of the *Odyssey*, he is best known for his roles in Sophocles' *Oedipus Rex* and Euripides' *Bacchae*, but he figured in many other poems and plays and was often depicted in art.

2   *stratagems . . . wiles*: in Homer, Ulysses is often referred to as "the man of various wiles" (e.g., *Od.* 3.163, 7.168, 8.19–20, 22.115); cf. *Odes* 1.6.7, "duplicitous Ulysses."

4   *our . . . hero*: for the third person, see 1.2.137n.

5   *Ithaca*: Ulysses' homeland, a small, rocky island off the northwest coast of mainland Greece. See *Ep.* 1.6.63, 1.7.41.

6   *Penates*: the mention of these Latin gods (2.3.268n.), unknown in the Greek
world, anticipates the mostly Roman context of Tiresias' advice. See 19, 27,
37, 44, 47, 55–57, 61–63, 68–69, 77–79, 85–86, 97, 109, 125, 137, 149nn.

11–12   *lineage and character,* / *minus cash*: cf. 1.1.65–66n., *Ep.* 1.1.53–55, 1.6.37–
38, Alcaeus, fr. 360.3–4 *LCL*, "possessions are the man, the poor / man is
neither noble nor honored."

12   *seaweed*: a proverbial symbol of worthlessness; cf. *Odes* 3.7.10, Virg. *Ecl.*
7.42, "more worthless than seaweed on the shore."

13   *poverty*: the reference to a "well-run farm" (18) shows that Tiresias inter-
prets Ulysses' "destitution" (8) as something more like "modest circum-
stances"; see 1.6.95n.

15   *thrush*: 1.5.90n.

17   *an old man's house*: Tiresias is about to instruct Ulysses in the "art" of legacy
hunting (*captatio*). His advice combines uncomfortable realities of society
in the 30s BCE, when civil war and proscription (1.7.2n.) had made many
people absurdly wealthy but also bereft of natural heirs; distortions of tradi-
tional Roman concepts of the duties pertaining to friendship (*amicitia*); and
depictions of the spongers and cadgers (*parasitoi*; see 1.2.128n.) that regularly
attend richer folks in Greek and Roman comedy.

19   *Lar*: another Latin divinity out of place in the heroic world (6n.). See
2.3.248–49n.

21–22   *perjury . . . fratricide*: all too common in the era of civil war.

21   *his lack of breeding*: in most peoples' thinking, this would include H. himself
(1.6.21–62).

23   *a runaway slave*: "passing" as a free or freed man. See 1.1.48, 83nn.

25   *the traffic side*: just as, until recently, gentlemen walked on the curb side
while escorting ladies. But in Rome to do this for another man was a mark
of inferior status; see *Ep.* 1.6.51, Ov. *F.* 5.68, Juv. 3.131.

26   *shield the flank*: Ulysses, veteran of the Trojan War, uses military language.
Cf. Cic. *Phil.* 13.4, Virg. *A.* 10.314.

27   *Dama*: a slave name (1.6.47–48n.) in H.'s Rome.

28   *vied with better men*: as was expected of a Homeric hero; see Hom. *Il.*
6.207–8.

30   *Buck up, brave heart*: echoing the words of Odysseus (Ulysses) at Hom. *Od.*
20.18, "endure, my heart; at some point you endured even worse." Cf. *Odes*
1.7.30, 3.24.42–43.

33–35   *Hunt . . . the bait*: this seems to be the first example of metaphors of
hunting and fishing (cf. 60, 2.4.47n.) in connection with *captatio* (17n.);
cf. *Ep.* 1.1.78–79 (60n.). But they would become common even in prose
accounts of the practice (e.g., Sen. *Dialogues* 4.20.3, Pliny, *Epistles* 9.30,
Lucian, *Timon* 22).

36   *this craft*: Tiresias, like Catius (2.4.44–45n.), considers his teaching an "art"
or "system"; cf. 1.6.101n., Sen. *Dialogues* 6.38.4.

37   *lawsuits*: serving as an advocate (1.11n.) or even "standing up" for someone
(1.9.49–52) was an important means of demonstrating "friendship" (17n.),
whether genuine or assumed; see Cic. *De Or.* 1.199–200, *Off.* 2.65–68.

Since the first required eloquence, it would be a fitting "craft" for Ulysses (cf. Hom. *Il.* 2.246–64, 3.200–24).

38   *richer . . . no kids*: the perfect target; cf. Petr. 116.7–9, Plin. *Nat.* 14.5 (due to increase in humans of avarice), "lack of children began to rank as the highest influence and power, legacy-hunting as the most fertile source for riches."

45   *first name*: as a mark of intimacy (2.3.258–62n.); cf. 2.6.46n.

45–46   *your virtue . . . friend*: twisting an ideal of friendship described at Aristotle, *Nichomachean Ethics* 8.3.6–7, and Cic. *Amic.* 27–28.

47   *double-headed law*: Roman civil law could be notoriously ambiguous and subject to manipulation; see 2.2.181n., Cic. *Inv.* 1.20–22, 2.116–43, *De Or.* 2.234–45.

51   *rip out my eyes*: a proverbial expression of devotion. Cf. Pl. *Menaechmi* 152, *Pseudolus* 510, Catul. 14.1, "If I didn't love you more than my own eyes."

55–57   *the Dog Star . . . snow*: at Rome trials were conducted out of doors, but Tiresias' inflated way of describing weather extremes suggests the kind of "epic" hardships Ulysses, one of whose epithets is "much suffering" (*polutlas*; see Hom. *Od.* 1.4–5, 5.171, 6.1, etc.), is used to enduring.

55   *the Dog Star*: 1.7.33n.

55–56   *makes . . . statues crack*: with its heat. Cf. Virg. *G.* 2.353 ("when the heat-bearing Dog cracks the fields until they gape with thirst"), Tib. 1.7.21.

56   *speechless statues*: such as that of Marsyas (1.6.166–67n.). For the phrase, cf. *Ep.* 2.2.83, "more quietly than a statue."

   Furius: probably M. Furius Bibaculus (1.6.48n.). According to the scholia, H. has substituted the poet's name for that of Jupiter in the original verse (cf. Quint. 8.16.17, Bibaculus, fr. 15 *FLP*).

59   *patient*: another hint of *polutlas* (55–57n.).

60   *tuna*: cf. 33–35n., and, for this prized fish, 2.4.83–84n.

   fishponds: cf. *Ep.* 1.1.78–79 (some fortune hunters), "hunt widows with cakes and fruit / and round up old men to stash in game preserves."

61–70   Tiresias, as befits a seer, becomes somewhat oblique, but he seems to be advising Ulysses to avoid exposure as an arrant legacy hunter by cultivating men with heirs as well as the more obvious, childless "marks" (cf. 38, 42–43).

61–63   *sickly son . . . acknowledged . . . reared*: among the Romans a new-born child would be placed on the ground in front of its father, who could acknowledge it and consent to its rearing by lifting it from the ground; if he left it where it lay, as was often the case with ailing or deformed babies, it would be removed for exposure to the elements or wild beasts.

67   *second to the son*: among the heirs listed in the will.

68–69   *dispatch the boy / to Orcus*: an epic-sounding phrase; cf. *Odes* 1.28.10–11, "send down to Orcus," Virg. *A.* 2.398, Hom. *Il.* 1.3–4, "hurled to Hades many strong souls / of heroes." Orcus, originally a Latin or Italian death spirit, came to be identified with Greek Hades, the name both of the ruler of the dead and his kingdom. See *Odes* 2.3.24, 2.18.30, 34, etc.

71   *offers you his will to read*: to elicit gratitude but also to keep the "hunter" on his best behavior, since a will could easily be changed.

73   *sneak a sidelong glance*: to avoid the fate of Nasica (77–79n.).

74 *the second line*: the first would give the name of the person whose will it was.

77–79 Tiresias, as Ulysses' baffled response shows, lapses into even deeper "oracular" obscurity (cf. 61–70n.). The point of the anecdote seems to be "look before you leap," but this is likely to be lost on Ulysses, since even when Tiresias elaborates (85–95), he speaks in riddling language of time and place (Horace's Rome; see 6n.) as remote from the Greek hero as the scenes on his shield are from Aeneas (Virg. *A.* 8.730).

77 *a clerk*: Latin *scriba*, H.'s own profession (1.5.44, 84, 2.6.47nn.).

78 *trick the raven*: possibly a reference to a belief that foxes play dead in order to trap and eat scavenger birds (so Muecke); see Oppian, *Haleutica* 2.105–9. Porph. cites the fable of the fox tricking the crow into dropping a piece of cheese (Phaedr. 1.13), but this seems less suited to the context.

79 *Coranus . . . Nasica*: both well-attested Roman surnames, the latter borne by a branch of the distinguished Cornelii Scipiones. But the men are otherwise unknown, and of course their names would be utterly unfamiliar to Ulysses.

80 *raving mad*: the "inspiration" of Apollo (83n.) is sometimes shown inducing a frenzy (Latin *furor*) in his prophets; see Cic. *Div.* 1.66, and the Sibyl at Virg. *A.* 6.77–101. But this is not attested elsewhere in connection with Tiresias.

81–82 *What I say . . . will come to be or not*: more oracular ambiguity. Tiresias could mean either "whatever I say will be, will be, whatever I say won't be, won't be," or, more humorously, "whatever I say either will happen or it won't." Odysseus' Tiresias speaks with more assurance: "I say to you things that are infallible" (Hom. *Od.* 11.137).

83 *Apollo's gift*: cf. Hom. *Il.* 1.72 (of the seer Calchas), "his skill at divination, which Phoebus Apollo granted him." But in most accounts Tiresias received his gift either from Athene (Minerva), as in Call. *H.* 5.57–136, or from Zeus (Jupiter), as in Ov. *Met.* 3.316–38.

85–89 *The day when Parthia will quail . . . Nasica . . . will give*: Tiresias' simple prediction, of "the pattern 'When A. happens, then B. will happen'" (Muecke), is reminiscent more of Virgil's fourth *Eclogue* (3.147n.) than of Tiresias' prophecy in Homer, which is hedged with conditions (e.g., *Od.* 11.110–13, "If you should allow them [the Sun's cattle] to be unharmed and remain mindful of your return home, / you may reach Ithaca despite suffering many ills; / but if you harm them, I predict destruction / for your ship and your comrades.").

85 *Parthia will quail*: another indication (see 2.1.14n.) that *Satires* 2 is set after Octavian's defeat of Antony and Cleopatra in 30 BCE; prior to that, the Parthians had been Antony's concern (1.5, 2.1.20nn.). See the Introduction.

86 *a youth, high-born Aeneas' heir*: a riddling but not obscure reference to Octavian, who was still only 33 at the end of the civil war (cf. Virg. *Ecl.* 1.42) and claimed descent from Aeneas and his mother Venus (1.3.153n.).

89 *the fine Coranus*: the epithet is ironic here; cf. 2.3.331.

90 *tall and stately*: a desirable trait (cf. Catul. 86.1, Var. *Men.* 432 Astbury, Ov. *Am.* 3.3.8), but also an attribute of the women of Ulysses' heroic age (e.g., Hom. *Od.* 6.107, 150–52, Ov. *Am.* 2.4.33).

94 *reads in silence*: unusual (6.171n.), here possibly to conceal the contents from others present (cf. Suet. *Aug.* 39), or in a "stunned silence."

96–97 *scheming dame / or freedman*: cf. 2.3.187. Ulysses could help them by presenting a more "respectable front" for anyone concerned about the old man.

97 *senile fool*: a common object of mockery; cf. *Epd.* 5.57, *Ars* 169–76, Cic. *Sen.* 36, Catul. 17, 67.19–28, Juv. 10.232–39.

100–101 *strategy . . . besiege*: military imagery, as at 1.9.76–79, here especially appropriate for the "man . . . who sacked the sacred city of Troy" (Hom. *Od.* 1.1–2); one of Odysseus' repeated epithets is "city sacker" (*ptoliporthos*; e.g., *Od.* 8.3, 9.504, 530, 24.119).

102 *nuts and writes . . . verse*: cf. 2.3.486n.

103 *into prostitutes*: as in *Sat.* 1.2.

105 *Penelope*: Ulysses' proverbially faithful wife; cf. *Odes* 3.10.11, "Penelope, unyielding to her wooers," Prop. 2.9.3–8, 3.12.38, 3.13.24, Ov. *Am.* 3.4.3–4.

109 *the food beat Venus*: cf. *Ep.* 1.2.27–28 (most humans are) "born to consume food, / [like] Penelope's suitors." At one point in the *Odyssey* Penelope, to the delight of the disguised Odysseus, extorts gifts from the suitors by rebuking them for their parsimony (Hom. *Od.* 18.275–303).

Venus: metonymy, here for sex; cf. 1.2.153, 1.5.91nn.

112–13 *like / a hound . . . bone*: proverbial; cf. Theocritus, *Idyll* 10.11, Lucian, *Adversus Indoctum*. 25.

115 *Thebes*: Tiresias' home town.

on in years: a humorous substitution by the dead man for the expected "when I was a boy" (or the like) of most reminiscences. Cf. 2.2.155.

118 *corpse . . . upon his naked shoulder*: at Petr. 141, a man in his will requires that his heirs eat his corpse.

richly oiled: so that it would slip off.

121–22 *Don't hold back / too much or overplay*: i.e., aim for a "happy mean" (1.1.111n.).

123 *difficult and peevish sort*: as often with old men, both in plays (*Ars* 173) and in real life "old men are peevish and irritable and difficult" (Cic. *Sen.* 65).

124 *chatterbox*: like H. himself on occasion (1.3.90–94). In Homer, Odysseus is certainly given to conversation and storytelling.

125 *the comic role of Davus*: 1.10.56–57n. At 2.7.2, before launching a tirade against his master, H.'s own Davus says that "fear chokes slaves." Cf. *Ep.* 1.16.66, "he who lives in a state of fear, in my opinion will never really be a free man."

126 *head bent down*: a gesture of submission; cf. Theognis 565–66, "a slave's head is never straight, / but always bent, and he holds his neck on a slant."

129–30 *push a way / through for him*: usually a task for a slave or subservient lover (e.g., Tib. 1.5.63–64).

132 *puffing up*: the image is of inflating a game ball (cf. 1.5.59n.) made from an animal bladder; cf. Petr. 42, "we strut about puffed up [like] balls."

134 *lifts his hands to heaven*: as if praying to avert the "envy of the gods" (1.9.34–36n.).

136   *servitude*: cf. 125–26, 129–30.

   wide awake: as opposed to dreaming; cf. *Odes* 3.27.37–41.

137   *a quarter share*: an indication that Ulysses is the primary heir, who in accordance with a law of 40 BCE (the *Lex Falcidia*), was guaranteed at this amount regardless of competing claims. But it turns out there is at least one other heir (146–49).

138   *Dama*: 27n.

139–40   *Where . . . such constancy and courage*: echoing the language of serious dirges such as that which H. would compose for his and Virgil's friend Quintilius (*Odes* 1.14).

141   *a tear or two*: the "final duty for the dead" (Catul. 101.3), but here in the spirit of Publ. Syr. 19, "under the mask of an heir his weeping is laughter."

143   *the monument*: 1.8.11n.

146–49   *fellow heir . . . next to nothing*: i.e., if another of the heirs seems likely to die, the *captator* should worm his way into that man's will by offering him some part of the inheritance he may have wanted for himself.

149   *next to nothing*: to avoid legal complications, gifts at Rome were often given in the form of a fictitious sale (*mancipitio*).

   Proserpina: Greek Persephone, the queen of the dead. See *Epd.* 17.2, *Odes* 1.28.19–20, *Odes* 2.13.21. In Homer, Odysseus says that Circe told him it was Persephone who allowed Tiresias even when dead to retain "his mind and mental powers" (Hom. *Od.* 10.494–95).

150   *Go live. Farewell*: a standard formula of saying goodbye (e.g., *Ep.* 1.6.67, Pl. *Miles* 1340), but with special point addressed by a dead man to a man about to return to the world of the living. In Homer, there is no leave-taking, and Odysseus' curiosity keeps him among the dead for a considerable time until fear of Persephone sending a monster after him drives him back to his ship (Hom. *Od.* 11.150–640).

Satire 2.6 Notes

1–3   *a farmstead . . . a bit of woodland*: the location of the estate is not given, except that it is in the hills (20) in the countryside (77) away from Rome (25, 29, 42, 45, 47, 64). But it is almost certainly the "Sabine farm" where he threatens to send his slave Davus (2.7.172; cf. 2.3.15) and which he describes or mentions in a number of other poems (*Odes* 1.17, 1.22.9–12, 2.18.11–14, 3.1.47–48, 3.4.21–22, 3.18, 3.29.13–24; *Ep.* 1.14, 1.7.44–45, 1.16.1–6, 1.18.104–6). Beginning with the scholiasts (on *Epd.* 1.31–32 and *Odes* 2.18.12–14), commentators have assumed that it was given to H. by Maecenas, but H. nowhere says this explicitly, nor is there any reference to such a gift in the Suetonian *Vita*.

5   *Mercury*: the bringer of financial success (2.3.40), and, as Greek Hermes, of good luck (2.3.107n.). Hermes was also associated with agricultural prosperity (Hom. *Il.* 14.490–91, Hesiod, *Theogony* 444–47, *Homeric Hymn*

4.567–71). In the *Odes*, H. would claim a special connection with the god (*Odes* 2.7.13–14, 2.17.29–30; cf. *Odes* 1.2.43, 1.10, 1.24.18, 1.30.8, 3.11.1–8). Except for this prayer to Mercury (5–19), another to the god Janus (26–30), and an apostrophe to the countryside itself (76–82), there is no indication in the poem of an addressee, and it seems best regarded as a soliloquy, the only one among H.'s "conversations" (see the Introduction); see 2.7.1n.

6 *make my blessings last*: a common request (e.g., *Odes* 1.31.17–20, Ter. *Eunuchus* 1048–49, Suet. *Aug.* 58.2), hedging against the whims of Fortune (12, 1.1.3, 2.2.172nn.).

7–16 In the protasis ("if clause") of this part of the prayer, H. attempts to distance himself from various character types he has ridiculed in previous satires, especially 1.1.1.

12 *lucky*: 6n.

13–14 *like the man . . . plowed the field*: the treasure wasn't enough for him. Porph. cites a fable about a field hand who prayed to Hercules for wealth; Hercules took him to Mercury (5n.), who granted the request but, when the man continued to toil in the same field, concluded that nothing could make such a person happy (cf. 1.22–24). But such a fable is not attested elsewhere, and it might have been invented by Porph. or an earlier commentator to explain the reference to Hercules (15n.).

14–15 *bought the land . . . he'd worked for wages*: he is a kind of opposite to the contented Ofellus, who ended up a field hand on the property he had once owned (2.3.157–58).

15 *Hercules*: possibly a reference to his role in the fable (13–15n.). But except at Pers. 2.10–11, "O Hercules, / if only a jar of silver would crunch under the right side of my hoe," which may be based on this passage, there seems to be no other evidence for Hercules as a revealer of buried treasure. More often he was honored with a share of wealth already obtained, apparently in the hope that he would protect the rest of it (Naevius, *com.* 29–31 *ROL*, Pl. *Bacchides* 665, *Mostellaria.* 984, *Stichus* 80–81, *Truculentus* 562, Cic. *N.D.* 3.88).

17 *Maia*: Mercury (Hermes) was the son of Jupiter (Zeus) and Maia, a daughter of the Titan (or son of a Titan) Atlas, who was thought to hold up the sky. See *Odes* 1.2.43, 1.10.1, 1.34.11, Hesiod, *Theogony* 938–39).

17–19 *fatten / my flocks . . . but not / my head*: playing on the word for "fat" (*pinguis*) in the sense "fatheaded," "dense" (1.3.83n.; cf. Cic. *Fat.* 7, *Amic.* 19). But there may also be an allusion to Virg. *Ecl.* 6.4–5 and to Callimachean aesthetics (1.6.42–47n.), with the implication that H. wishes his poetry also to remain "slender."

22 *satire's Muse on foot*: the phrase incorporates at least three paradoxes: 1) the idea of "satire" (a term H. avoids; see 2.1.1n.), which H. has insisted is not really poetry (1.4.41–73), having a Muse such as presides over epic (1.5.65–67n.; cf. 29n. below) and other more elevated genres (1.10.60n.; cf. *Odes* 1.26, 1.32.9–10, 2.1.9–10, 37–38, 2.12.13–14, etc.); 2) the image of a Muse, often depicted as dancing (*Odes* 2.10.18–20, Hesiod, *Theogony* 1–8), soaring (*Odes* 3.4.1, 21–24), or riding in a chariot (Pindar *Olympian Ode* 9.80–81, *Pythian Ode* 10.65, etc.), moving simply "on foot" (below); and 3) the thought that satire, so intimately connected with the urban scene (see the Introduction), could "celebrate" a "pastoral citadel."

on foot: Latin *pedester* (the root of "pedestrian"), in its literal sense often contrasted with "on horseback" or "in a chariot" (above). Here, as at *Odes* 2.12.9 (of a historical work by Maecenas) and *Ars* 95 (of a "comic"-sounding passage in a tragedy), H. seems to be imitating Greek use of *pezos* (also literally "on foot") of prose and humble genres of poetry (e.g., Call. *Aet.* fr. 112.9).

23 *burdensome ambitions*: 1.4.26n.

24 *sirocco . . . autumnal heat*: 2.2.56. At 32–33 and 56–57 the season is winter; at 62–63 it would appear to be spring.

26–29 *Father . . . my song*: the address to Janus (5n.) is both a prayer with traditional elements such as the offer of an alternative name for the god (cf. *Odes* 3.21.5–6, *Saec.* 13–16, Catul. 34.31–34) and a call for poetic inspiration (29n.), with Janus "pinch hitting" for a Muse (22n.).

26 *Father*: all male Roman gods, not just Jupiter (2.1.65), were addressed as *Pater*; cf. *Epd.* 2.21, *Odes* 1.18.6, 3.3.13, *Ep.* 2.1.5, Lucil. frr. 24–27 *ROL*.

Janus: the god associated with war and peace (1.4.68–69n.) and the "Stock Exchange" (2.3.28n.), but also with beginnings of every sort, whether of the year, the day, or a prayer or sacrifice (*Ep.* 1.16.59, Cic. *N.D.* 2.67). Cf. Ov. *F.* 1.63–298.

29 *Begin with me my song*: Muses and other sources of poetic inspirations are often invoked as the "beginners" of songs; cf. *Ep.* 1.1.1, Hesiod, *Theogony* 1, 34, 48, Theognis 1–4, Virg. *Ecl.* 8.11.

29–75 *At Rome . . . wastes my day*: H.'s routine in the city is changed beyond recognition from what he described at 1.6.130–78.

32–33 *The north wind . . . winter's short . . . days*: see 24n. The north wind (Latin *Aquilo*, Greek *Boreas*) is often mentioned as a bringer of harsh storms and cold (e.g., 2.8.56, *Epd.* 10.7, *Epd.* 13.3).

35–36 *wrestle . . . the slow*: despite his supposed importance (41–56), H. has no one to "shield his flank" (2.5.25–26). There also may be a hint of "the comic 'running slave,' who must push through crowds in the street in order to deliver news" (Muecke), as at Pl. *Mercator* 115–19.

40 *Maecenas*: the source of H.'s prestige, if not his wealth (1–3n., but cf. 47n.). Apparently no one in the crowd recognizes him for his poetry; cf. 1.4.28–40, 85–116, 1.10.100–25, but also, from around 15 BCE, *Odes* 4.3.21–24 (to the lyric Muse Melpomene), "It is your work, / the fact that I am pointed out by the fingers of passersby / as the master of the Roman lyre."

41 *How sweet this sounds to me*: but, if H. is to be believed (cf. 73–74), for him this is now (cf. 29–75n.) the only "sweet" thing about city life.

42 *the doleful Esquiline*: the site of Maecenas' mansion (1.8.11–22n.; cf. 1.9.47–48n.), infested now not with witches but with favor-seekers.

44 *Roscius*: otherwise unknown.

45 *bright and early*: literally "at the second hour," which in winter would be around 6 a.m., cf. 1.5.28n., 1.6.169.

the Puteal: the *Puteal Libonis*, "Well of Libo," possibly built in 80 BCE by

the urban praetor L. Scribonius Libo close to the tribunal where he would
preside (1.6.166–67n.). It was frequented by thirsty lawyers and, it seems,
moneylenders eager to "help" the losers of lawsuits (*Ep.* 1.19.8, Cic. *Sest.* 18,
Ov. *Rem.* 561–62, Pers. 4.49).

47 *the Records Office*: the *Aerarium* ("treasury") in the Temple of Saturn on
the slope of the Capitoline Hill, where state monies and public records were
kept. It was the headquarters of H.'s guild of *scribae* ("government clerks";
cf. 1.5.44, 2.5.77nn.), *equites* (1.6.26n.) who, in terms of public distinction,
ranked just below senators. Since there is no reason to think that H. attained
this position with anyone's assistance, the reference here to his duties may
be meant as a reminder that, even if he was regarded as a kind of factotum
for Maecenas (48–49; cf. 40n.), he nonetheless had a status independent of
his supposed patron.

48 *Maecenas signs these papers*: this is often taken as further evidence that the
poem is set sometime between Actium (September of 31 BCE; see 2.1.14n.)
and Octavian's permanent return to Italy (mid-29 BCE), as during this
time Maecenas was in charge of affairs at Rome (Dio 51.3.5) and had been
entrusted with a copy of Octavian's distinctive seal ring bearing the image
of a sphynx (Plin. *Nat.* 37.10).

51–75 H. attempts to play down his supposed influence with Maecenas ("You
can do it, if you want" [50]) and defuse the envy it arouses (60n.) by depict-
ing himself not as a respected member of an elite group (contrast 1.6.64–86,
1.9.59–71, 1.10.112–22) or even a reliable dependent, such as he describes in
Ep. 1.18, but as little more than a sidekick.

51 *seventh year and soon the eighth*: 1.6.73n.

54 *on carriage trips*: cf. 1.5.107, 1.6.135–39.

55–56 *Thracian / bantam . . . Syrus*: gladiators (1.7.25n.). "Thracian" refers to
the man's style of equipment (small shield, grieves, hooked sword), not his
ethnicity (cf. *Ep.* 1.18.36). "Bantam" translates the Latin name, or possibly,
affectionate nickname (cf. Pl. *Asinaria* 666) *Gallina* ("hen"), while the name
of his opponent is a common slave name (1.6.47–48n.).

56–57 *this morning / cold really bites*: 24n. The image, common in English
("there's a nip in the air"), is less so in Latin; cf. *Ep.* 1.8.5, "the heat has
bitten my olive tree."

58 *leaky ears*: cf. Ter. *Eunuchus* 105 (the slave Parmeno claims that, if told the
truth, he conceals it, but if told lies), "I am full of leaks and here and there I
pour out." A trusty friend or client was supposed to "keep hidden what has
been entrusted to you even if tortured by wine or by anger" (*Ep.* 1.18.38;
cf. *Odes* 1.27.17–18).

60 *jealousy*: 1.1.41n.

61 *our man*: H., "with assumed humility, speaks of himself in the third person"
(Muecke). See 2.1.27n.

62 *the games*: chariot races and theatrical performances (2.3.274n.). H.'s sit-
ting with Maecenas at the latter is an indication of their shared status as
equestrians (1.6.51n.).

playing ball: 1.5.59n.

63   *the Campus*: 1.6.175n.

"*the son of Fortune*": i.e., H. is the (unworthy) beneficiary of "dumb luck" (1.3n.). But cf. 1.6.69–70, where H. denies that this is the case. For the phrase, cf. Sophocles, *Oedipus Rex* 1080, Petr. 44, Plin. *Nat.* 7.43.

64–65   *A rumor . . . like a chill*: a variation on the idea of fear chilling the blood or heart; cf. Virg. *A.* 1.92, 2.120, 3.29, 259, etc.

64   *the Rostra*: a platform for public speaking located, after 42 BCE, on the northwest side of the Forum, so called because it was ornamented with "beaks" (*rostra*) of ships captured in naval victories.

67   *Dacians*: a group of tribes north and south of the Danube in what are now Romania and Serbia who beginning in the mid-first century BCE posed a constant threat to the Roman province of Macedonia. During the civil war, they allied themselves with Antony, and an expedition would be sent against them sometime in either late 30 or early 29 BCE (Dio 51.22–25; see 48n.). H. would again mention them as enemies at *Odes* 1.35.9 (29 BCE), 2.20.17 (25 BCE), 3.6.13–14, and 3.8.18 (23 BCE).

68   *the gods*: flattering or envious hyberbole. Cf. Ter. *Adelphi* 535, Cic. *Red. Sen.* 8, Lucr. 5.8, Virg. *Ecl.* 1.6.

70   *God damn me*: 1.8.52–56n.

71   *the vets*: from Octavian's army and those who defected from Antony's after Actium (48n.). In winter 31–30 BCE, a large number who had been discharged and sent back to Italy without the usual donatives and land allotments (1.6.95n.) formed a kind of "Bonus Army"; to avert a crisis, first Agrippa (1.3.285n.), then Octavian himself, had to return to Italy and pacify them with cash and land seized from Italian communities that had sided with his enemies (Dio 51.2–4).

77   *you again, my country home*: 5n.

78   *The ancient authors*: cf. 2.3.16–18, *Ep.* 1.2.1–2 (while on vacation at Praeneste [7.36n.] H. has reread Homer).

nap: a siesta (5.60n.), even more pleasant for its country setting. Cf. *Epd.* 2.27–28, *Odes* 1.1.21–22, 2.26.13–16, 3.1.21–24, *Ep.* 1.14.35, 1.17.6–7, 2.2.77–78, Virg. *G.* 2.470–71 (in the countryside, as opposed to the city), "soft sleep under a tree / is not absent."

79–81   *beans . . . bacon fat . . . cabbage*: cheap but plentiful fare (1.6.159n.).

80   *Pythagoras' next of kin*: a joking reference to the tradition that Pythagoras and his followers abstained from beans, possibly for fear of eating the souls (made of "wind") of ancestors (2.4.4n.), but ancient sources offer other explanations as well (e.g., Cic. *Div.* 1.62 (the "wind" from beans would disturb the "tranquility of the soul").

84   *my Lar*: 2.3.248–49n.

85   *saucy servants*: the Latin term here for "servants" is *vernae*, "house boys (or girls)" (see 141, 1.2.151), which denotes slaves bred in the household. They were considered more useful (141, *Ep.* 2.2.6) and tended to be treated more leniently than slaves obtained from elsewhere; cf. *Epd.* 2.65–66, *Odes* 2.17.14–16.

86 *aren't those drinking bouts with crazy rules*: see 2.2.3, 6, 168nn. In Plato's *Symposium* (176e), the participants likewise agree that each will drink only so much as suits him.

89 *we talk*: the Latin, *sermo oritur*, "conversation arises," may allude to H.'s title for the *Satires* (see the Introduction; see also 1.4.43n.).

89–97 *Not about . . . "highest good"*: H. seems to follow the advice of Varro, who in a Menippean satire (see the Introduction) cited by Aulus Gellius (13.11= *Men.* 333–42) in outlining the "rules" for symposia, "decreed that conversations at such times ought not to be about vexing and tormenting matters, but they ought to be pleasant and engaging and combine utility with a certain allure and pleasure so that our minds might themselves become more charming and attractive. And indeed he [Varro] said that this will occur if we chat about matters relevant to the common good, the kind of things that there is no leisure to discuss in the Forum and in the press of daily concerns." Cf. *Ep.* 1.5.10–11 (during a holiday), "it will be permitted without consequence / to extend the night with benign conversation," Lucil. frr. 200–7 *ROL*, Cic. *De Or.* 1.27, *Fin.* 2.25, *Sen.* 46.

89–90 *vacation homes . . . townhouse*: 2.3.467n.

91 *Lepos, the famous mime*: 2.1n. Pseudacro says that this Lepos was "a most excellent dancer, a favorite of [Octavian] Caesar." His name means "charm" (cf. Suet. *Vespasian* 19.2—a mime named *Favor*), but there could be, as Palmer suggests, a play on *lepus*, "hare" or "rabbit."

93–94 *wealth . . . or . . . excellence*: moral excellence (*virtus*). Cf. *Ep.* 1.1.52, "Silver is less valuable than gold, gold than virtues," Plato, *Republic* 550e (Socrates speaking), "Or aren't virtue and wealth so opposed that if they were set on scales, they'd always incline in opposite directions?," Cic. *Fin.* 2.49. The Academic (1.3.388n.) philosopher Crantor (c. 335–275 BCE; cf. *Ep.* 1.2.4) wrote a work in which he ranked virtue the highest and wealth the lowest of possible goods.

94 *what makes us happy*: cf. 127, 1.1.22, 2.4.123n.

95 *friendships*: another topic of importance to philosophers (e.g., Plato, *Phaedrus*, Aristotle, *Nichomachean Ethics* books 8–9, Cic. *Amic.*), but also to H. not only in this poem (41, 51–58, 68), but in other satires (1.3, 1.5, 1.6, 1.9, 1.10), not to mention the rest of his works (e.g., *Epd.* 1, *Odes* 1.3, 1.20, 1.24, 2.6, 2.12, 2.17, 3.8, 3.29).

95–96 *self-concern / or moral sense*: "the question contrasts the opposed theories of Epicureans and Stoics" (Muecke). The former emphasized self-interest or "utility" (1.3.177n.; cf. Epicurus, *HP* 22F, Lucr. 5.1019–27, Cic. *Fin.* 1.66–70), the latter a shared "virtue" (Cic. *Amic.* 20, *HP* 67P]).

97 *"the good" or "highest good"*: philosophical language; see 1.1.84n.

98 *Cervius*: not otherwise known. The name is a real one, but here may be meant to suggest that the man is very old (so Palmer), as the stag (*cervus*) was proverbial not only for its timidity (2.1.70–73n.) but for its supposed longevity (Cic. *Tusc.* 3.69, Plin. *Nat.* 8.119, Juv. 14.251).

100 *but never pointlessly*: he is somewhat, but not too much like Lucilius (1.1.18n.).

101–3   *someone . . . wealth*: "someone" like the characters in *Sat.* 1.1.

103   *Arellius*: another real name, but here possibly hinting at Latin *area*, the "threshing floor," where the man's agricultural wealth would be in evidence (1.1.46n.).

104   *The story goes*: indicating that the fable, however altered here, is traditional. There are versions attributed to Aesop (number 297) and to two writers later than H., Octavian's freedman C. Julius Phaedrus (*Fabulae Novae* 9) and the Greek poet Babrius (108 *LCL*). In Cervius' telling, it is linked to themes of *Sat.* 2.6 in its contrast between the humble but secure independence of the country and the luxurious but uneasy dependency of the city. But unlike the country mouse, H. cannot simply hide in a "forest den" (151), since his obligations to friends, not to mention his desire to write satire (22n.), bind him, at least at this stage of his life (the situation will be different in *Epistles* 1), to the urban scene he longs to escape.

108–9   *less tight / when guests arrived*: like Ofellus (2.2.159–66).

110–12   *chickpeas . . . bacon*: luxuries for a country mouse, but humble fare for city slickers, whether murine or human (cf. 81, 1.6.160, 2.2.166, 2.3.277, Plin. *Nat.* 18.149). The verbs "laid away" and "dragged out" indicate that this mouse relies on his own frugality and labor; cf. 136n.

116   *reclining*: in Greek banquet style (1.3.127–28n.); see 139, 143.

   chaff . . . spelt and darnel: the leavings of the threshing floor (103n.), a frequent haunt of mice (Virg. *G.* 1.181–82). Darnel (*lolium*), a type of rye grass, is a weed whose seeds are difficult to separate from those even of a coarse wheat such as spelt (6.155n.); see Virg. *Ecl.* 5.34–35, *G.* 1.154, Plin. *Nat.* 18.153.

120   *steep, wooded ridge*: possibly that above the "shaded valley" in which H.'s farm lay (*Odes* 1.17.17, *Ep.* 1.16.5–6), making the country mouse his neighbor.

124–28   *we're creatures . . . life is short*: the city mouse evokes, in suitably elevated language, themes from the kind of Greek banquet poetry (e.g., Alcaeus, fr. 38, Mimnermus, fr. 2 *LCL*) that H. would make his own in the *Odes* (*Odes* 1.4, 1.9, 1.11, 2.3, etc.).

125   *However great or small*: cf. *Odes* 1.4.13–14, "Pale death bangs with impartial foot on the huts of poor men / and the mansions of kings," *Odes* 1.28.15–16, 2.3.21–24, 2.18.31–40, *Ep.* 2.2.175–79.

127   *the good life*: the word for "good" here is *beatus* (74n.).

131   *creep*: a reminder that the travelers are mice, not epic heroes (below); see 1.5.30n.

132–33   *Night . . . the heavens*: epic-sounding language; cf. 1.5.10–11n., Enn. *Ann.* 33, 348, Virg. *A.* 5.835–36, "And now damp Night had almost touched the mid / turning point of the heaven."

134   *a mansion*: like that of Maecenas on the Esquiline (1.8.11–22n.).

135   *ivory couches*: indicating great wealth; cf. *Odes* 1.31.6, 2.18.1, *Ep.* 2.2.180.

136   *left from some great feast*: unlike his rustic friend (110–12), the city mouse lives on meals prepared by and for others. In this respect he resembles the professional "tablemates" (*parasitoi*; cf. 1.2.128n.) of Greek and Roman comedy (*Ep.* 2.1.173), who are themselves compared to (real) mice (Pl. *Captivi* 77).

139–43   *reclining . . . lay back*: 116n.

139   *on a purple fleece*: as opposed to "chaff" (116). The purple dye is yet another mark of wealth (2.4.108n.).

141   *a home-bred slave*: 85n.

142   *samples each . . . dish*: probably the ensure that it is properly cooked rather than, as with the "pre-tasters" (*praegustatores*) later employed by emperors, to guard against poisoning.

145–50   *all at once . . . tore through the house*: the frantic ending of the banquet recalls that of the adulterous assignation at 1.2.167–76.

149   *big Molossian hounds*: a breed originally from Molossis in Epirus (northwest of Greece), prized as guard and hunting dogs (*Epd*. 6.5, Var. *R*. 2.9.5, Lucr. 5.1063, Virg. *G*. 3.405).

150–52   The country mouse's parting words echo those in other versions of the fable (104n.), but they also suggest Epicurean doctrine (e.g., *HP* 22C, D, Lucr. 2.20–36) as well as what H. presents as his own view both here (16, 23, 76–82) and in *Sat*. 1.6.

152   *vetch is comfort food*: appropriate for a real mouse, since in the Roman world "bitter vetch" (Latin *ervum*), unlike the items at the country feast (110–16), let alone the dishes in the mansion, was food only for animals (cf. Cato, *On Agriculture* 27, Virg. *Ecl*. 3.100).

Satire 2.7 Notes

1   *DAVUS*: 2.1.1n.

You've had my ear for quite some time: Davus seems to have been eavesdropping, not only on the preceding monologue (2.6.5n.), but also on H.'s readings to himself (1.4.23–24, 180–81, 1.6.170–71) or to close friends (1.4.88–91) mentioned in other satires of which he will show some knowledge.

2   *fear chokes slaves*: Davus will allude often to slave punishments (40, 60, 65, 82, 91–92, 108, 118, 126, 146); cf. 27, 111, 1.2.27, 151, 1.3.113, 118, 1.5.83, 1.8.46–47, 2.3.198, 437–38, 2.5.125–26nn.

3   *Davus*: a common slave name (1.10.56–57n.). It becomes evident that this Davus is not "house-bred" (63n.) and that he is on the staff of H.'s townhouse (cf. 1.6.160), not his estate (165n.), but has considerable leeway to move about the city (62, 64–73, 135–9).

4   *friend*: some of "December's license" (6n.), since slaves and masters would not normally refer to each other as "friends."

4–5   *good . . . survive*: 1.9.34–6, 2.1.91–2nn.

6   *December's license*: furnished by the holiday of Saturnalia (2.3.8n.).

7–25   *Some people . . . slack*: Davus begins his discourse by aping, in miniature, the relaxed tone and style of the opening sequence of poems in *Satires* 1 (*Sat*. 1.1–4; cf. Ofellus' speech in *Sat*. 2.2), calling attention, without fuss or preamble, to a moral issue, illustrating it with specific but humorous examples, then restating it in a more pointed manner. Davus' contrast between the extremes of perseverance (even if in vice) and moral inconsistency suggests Peripatetic doctrine (1.1.111, 2.2.73nn.; see Aristotle, *Nichomachean Ethics* 7.2), but he doesn't offer any kind of happy mean, and, as he proceeds, the philosophy (such as it is) seems more Stoic than anything else (58, 62, 65, 66, 80, , 94, , 101, , 116, 117, 121, 123, 128, 133–34, 156–61nn.).

11   *Priscus*: otherwise unknown. The surname, fairly common, means "old-fashioned"; cf. 29n.

   three rings: in H.'s time a member of the equestrian or senatorial orders was entitled to wear a large ring advertising his status (cf. 80, Ov. *Am.* 3.8.15, Plin. *Nat.* 33.29), but sporting more than one was considered excessive (Plin. *Nat.* 33.24–25, Isidore, *Etymologiae* 19.32.4).

12   *inconsistent*: the Latin word is *inaequabilis* (1.3.15n.).

12–13   *toga . . . broad to narrow stripe*: 1.1.105, 1.6.31nn.

17   *Rome . . . Athens*: the action-packed "big city" is contrasted with the quiet "university town," as Athens had become by H.'s time. So, too, at *Ep.* 2.2.81–84, Prop. 3.21.

   Don Juan: translating *moechus* (1.2.48n.); cf. 101.

18   *Vertumni*: Vertumnus (or Vortumnus), originally, it seems, an Etruscan god, was associated by Romans with change and transformation; some derived the name from *vertere*, "turn" (as in "convert," "divert," etc.). He had a temple on the Aventine hill (cf. 1.3.19n.) as well as a small shrine with a statue on the "Tuscan Street" (2.3.349–52n.; cf. *Ep.* 1.20.1); see Prop. 4.2, Ov. *F.* 6.409–10. The plural, attested only here, may refer to the different sites of worship or (jokingly) to the various forms the god could assume, or, since he is shown influencing a person's character at birth, it may echo or parody the plurality of the "Birth Goddesses" (*Parcae* or *Fata*), the deities traditionally attributed with that function.

19   *Volanerius*: otherwise unknown. The name is real, but may be meant to suggest here "flying" (*volare*) or "rolling" (*volvi*) dice.

   party clown: the Latin is *scurra* (1.5.65n.).

20   *gout*: 1.9.43n.

21   *paid someone by the day*: evidently to avoid the cost of maintaining a slave in his household.

22   *dice*: dice games were extremely popular among Romans, despite the risk of immense losses (*Ep.* 1.18.21) and several laws prohibiting them (*Odes* 3.24.58, Cic. *Phil.* 2.56). Octavian was a notorious "addict" (Suet. *Aug.* 71.1; cf. 2.3.259–60n.).

24   *the less distressed he is*: because he won't suffer any qualms of uncertainty. Cf. Aristotle, *Nichomachean Ethics* 7.2.10.

25   *now tight, now slack*: the image may be of a mule towing a boat (cf. 1.5.16n.), pulling hard, but suddenly released and sent sprawling if the boat catches up with her.

27   *whip-bait*: translating *furcifer*, a term of abuse frequent in comedy (e.g., Pl. *Amphitryo* 285, 539) for a punishment (2n.) in which a slave was tied to a wooden frame (*furca*) and either flogged or paraded about as a warning to other slaves. See 91–92n.

27–28 *You are . . . the point*: in what follows (33–166), Davus shifts from Horatian moralizing (7–25n.) to a more Lucilian (cf. 1.4.6n., 2.1.94–103) mode of direct, personal attack, accusing his master of compounding both extremes (7–25n.) represented by Priscus and Volanarius by joining hypocrisy to inconsistency (29–56, 155–61) and persevering, not just in a single vice, but in several (63–155).

29 *You praise the past*: at 1.4.145–47, 2.2.123–30, and *Epd.* 2.1–2, but in the first passage the speaker is H.'s father, in the second it's Ofellus (2.2.125n.), and in the third it's a usurer named Alfius (*Epd.* 2.67–70; see 1.2.15n.). Davus may also have in mind *Epd.* 16.3–8 (contrasting the old Romans who overcame their external foes with the current generation destroying itself in civil war), but H.'s fullest "praise of the past" is at *Odes* 3.6.32–44, composed at least two years after *Satires* 2.

31 *some god*: 1.1.19n.

33 *filth . . . foot*: proverbial; cf. Pl. *Bacchides* 384, Ter. *Phormio* 790, Catul. 17.25–26.

35–36 *In Rome . . . star*: although in *Sat.* 2.6, H. does not openly admit to it (but cf. 2.6.41), there are passages in the *Satires* that show his enjoyment of city life (1.1.13–14, 1.4.171–78, 1.6.152–178) or betray a certain restlessness (1.6.140–44, 2.3.7–8; cf. *Ep.* 1.8.11–12); see 155–61.

39 *garden greens*: 1.1.79n.

40 *in chains*: as if H. were the slave (2n.), a theme familiar from Stoic philosophy (9–27n.; see Cic. *Parad.* 33–41) to which Davus returns again and again (78, 81–82, 91–92, 94, 95–100, 105–17, 126–32, 146, 153–55, 158–59).

41 *say you're blessed*: as at 1.6.182.

42–43 *Let / Maecenas . . . to dine*: "now Davus glances at those dinners with Maecenas which H. omitted to mention in *Sat.* 2.6" (Muecke); see 1.6.60, 2.6.54nn.

43–44 *last- / minute*: Davus may imply that H. was invited only to make up the proper number of banqueters (1.4.109, 2.2.1–2nn.).

44 *evening*: Maecenas dines late (1.6.155–78n.), probably because he has been busy all the daylight hours; cf. *Ep.* 1.5.3 (H. invites a hardworking lawyer [1.1.11n.] to dine), "at the last hour of daylight," which at the dramatic date of that poem (indicated at *Ep.* 1.5.9) would be around 6:00 p.m.

45 *lantern oil*: 1.4.57n.

47–48 *Mulvius / and all the other party clowns*: scurrae (19n.) who are H.'s guests but whom he can or will not bring with him to Maecenas' banquet as Maecenas brings his "extras" to that of Nasidienus (2.8.31). The presence of such men at H.'s house seems at odds with what he says about his dining customs elsewhere (1.6.158–63, 2.6.79–88).

47 *Mulvius*: otherwise unknown, but a real Roman name. Some MSS have *Milvius*, which would mean "like a carrion bird" (from *milvus*, "kite"), an apt name for a "parasite" (1.2.128n.).

51 *my stomach's slave*: 40n.

54 *just like me, and maybe worse*: Mulvius, himself a glutton, thinks that is H.'s motivation (cf. 142–55), but also at issue here are H.'s claims of self-sufficiency and independence (*Sat.* 1.6); cf. 105–16.

55 *unprovoked scold* me: challenging H.'s insistence that, as a satirist, he doesn't attack "without good cause" (2.1.61–64; cf. 1.4.25–128).

56 *with polished language*: as at 1.3.31–33, 90–95, 1.4.129–31, 166–70.

58 *even greater fool*: Davus edges toward a Stoic viewpoint (1.3.110n.); cf. 7–25n.

59 *cost five hundred drachmas*: indicating he isn't house-bred (3, 2.6.85n.) and, since drachmas were Greek coins, that he was obtained from a Greek trader. The amount, equivalent to *HS* 2000 (2.3.346n.), was more than a centurion's yearly pay (1.6.99n.) but less than the price of a fancy serving dish (2.4.99n.) or than what H.'s supposed girlfriend demands (126n.).

60 *hit me*: 2n.

61 *your temper*: one of H.'s self-confessed "vices" (1.3.47–50n.).

62 *the doorman at Crispinus'*: an absurd source for the "doctrine" of an absurd Stoic (9–27n.) philosopher; see 1.1.131n.

63 *captivated*: 40n.

    by another's wife: of H.'s "persevering vices" (27–28n.), Davus' first target is his supposed lust for married women (63–101). In *Sat.* 1.2, H. objects to this conduct in others, and here Davus allows him to insist "I'm no adulterer" (101n.). For many readers, this shows either that Davus' charges are exaggerated, if not false, or that the "you" he addresses is someone other than H. But it's possible that the attack, coming from someone who might be in a position to know, is meant to raise doubts in the audience over what exactly they know about the "real" H., as opposed to the version of himself he has fashioned for his poetry.

64 *a prostitute*: a slave could pay for "services" from his *peculium*, "personal stash," money that he, like a minor child, was legally allowed to accumulate for his own use. See 112n.

65 *Whose sin is worse?*: a hard-line Stoic (9–27n.) would say "they're equally bad" (1.3.134–35), but Davus deals not with moral absolutes, but with practical consequences.

    crucified: the ultimate slave punishment (2, 1.2.27, 1.3.113nn.).

66 *nature*: 104, 1.1.52n., 1.2.146.

67 *who the woman is*: cf. 1.2.164–66.

68 *naked*: cf. 1.2.106–7.

    bright lamplight: not from a lamppost (45n.), as in the modern image, but from a torch or brazier in the brothel. Cf. Juv. 6.121–32.

69–70 *has mounted / and rides*: a common metaphor for a woman "on top" (94–95n.); cf. 133, 135–37nn., Ov. *Ars* 2.731–32, 3.777–78, Mart. 11.104.14, Apul. *Met.* 2.17.

71–72 *no concerns about / a damaged reputation*: this might be true for a slave, but cf. 1.2.72–80.

72–73 *richer / or better-looking guys*: a concern of H. himself at *Epd.* 15.17–24 and, especially in regard to the "richer . . . guys," of the Latin elegists (e.g., Prop. 1.8, Tib. 1.2, Ov. *Am.* 1.8).

75 *knight's ring*: 11n.

    Roman dress: the toga (1.1.104n.).

    hood: the *lacerna*, originally military issue, was a hooded cloak convenient for bad weather and anonymity (cf. Cic. *Phil.* 2.76), but considered so unbecoming of citizens that Octavian would try to ban the wearing of it in the Forum (Suet. *Aug.* 40.5).

76 *perfumed head*: like one of the guys in *Guys and Dolls*, he "smells of Vitalis and Barbasol." See *Epd.* 5.57–59, "The dogs of the Subura [the valley between the Esquiline and Viminal hills] are barking at / an old man adulterer . . . drenched with perfume," *Odes* 3.24.20, *Ep.* 1.14.32, Pl. *Casina* 239–40.

77 *a reputable juryman*: an indication of H.'s equestrian status and supposed moral character (1.4.155n.).

78 *Dama*: a slave name (1.6.47–48n.).

80 *lust and panic clash*: in Stoic (7–25n.; see Cic. *Parad.* 40, *Tusc.* 4.11–12) but also Epicurean doctrine (e.g., Lucr. 6.25), desire (including ambition [105–6n.]) and fear were paired as irrational feelings about the future. The idea appealed to H.; cf. 108, 118–20, *Odes* 2.16.15–16, *Ep.* 1.2.51–52, 1.4.11–12, 1.16.65–66, "he who will desire, will also be afraid; what's more, / he who lives in fear, in my view will never be free," *Ep.* 1.18.98–99, 2.2.155–57.

81–82 *sold yourself . . . brand, the rod, . . . sword*: 40n. In H.'s time, the only way a Roman citizen could actually become a Roman slave was to sell himself into service as a gladiator (1.7.25n.) who, when he wasn't fighting (sword), would be subject to slave punishments (brand, rod; see 2n.).

83 *some disgusting chest*: a common hiding place (Juv. 6.44, Apul. *Met.* 9.5–6) long before Falstaff's mishap in *Merry Wives of Windsor*.

84 *maid . . . confederate*: at 1.2.172 she is the adulterer's "accomplice."

86 *legal power*: 1.2.56n.

89–90 *isn't / on top*: unlike the prostitute at 69–70. The brackets enclosing the rest of 95 indicate that most editors think the words were added by someone other than H. But the idea might be that the woman doesn't trust H. to protect her if she is struck first by her husband coming up from behind.

91–92 *base / punishment*: the Latin specifies attachment to a *furca* (27n.).

92–93 *goods . . . reputation*: as in the case of Villius (1.2.82–86).

94 *mad master*: H. is "enslaved" (40n.) by his irrational lust. Cf. 130, *Ep.* 1.10.40, Cic. *Parad.* 33, "unseemliness and baseness, the wickedest of masters," *Fin.* 2.117 (a Stoic point of view; see 7–25n.), "when pleasure is master, all the highest virtues must lie useless," *Off.* 2.37, "sensual pleasures, the most alluring of mistresses."

99–100 *What beast . . . chain*: cf. *Ep.* 1.16.50–51, "the careful wolf fears the trap, the hawk / the snares he can see from above, the fish the hidden hook," and the saying recorded by Zenobius in *Paroemiographi Graeci* ("Greek proverb writers") 1.67, "Not twice will the fox be taken."

101 *'I'm no adulterer'*: Davus allows H. to protest, as H. allowed Marsaeus (1.2.67), but turns even this against his master, alleging he only avoids adultery for fear of punishment, which in Stoic thinking (7–25n.) is not a true form of virtue. Cf. *Ep.* 1.16.46–49, Cic. *Parad.* 34.

104 *nature, not reined in*: here "nature" (66n.) is the "bronco" (cf. 1.2.129n., *Odes* 4.15.10–11, *Ep.* 1.2.62–65, Var. *Men.* 177 Astbury), but further on the image is reversed, with H. being the "horse" and his passion the "charioteer" (131–32).

105–6 *scrape and bow / to circumstance and men of rank*: Davus implies that H.'s "servility" (40n.) is due to ambition (1.4.26n.).

107 *manumitted*: the word derives from Latin *manu*, literally "from the hand," but also "from the mastery," and *mittere*, "release." Roman slaves could be freed privately, by testament, or in elaborate public ceremonies; in all cases they would receive full citizenship (1.6.7n.).

108 *your fear*: 80n.

111–12 *'under-slave' . . . 'fellow-slave'*: in the Roman world a slave could, with his *peculium* (64n.), purchase another slave to assist him in his work, but this under-slave (Latin *uicarius*, "substitute") would belong legally to the first slave's master, making him a fellow-slave (*conservus*; see 1.1.49, 1.8.13) of his purchaser. Cf. Pl. *Asinaria* 433–34, Cic. *Parad.* 36–37, Paullus, *Dig.* 9.4.19, Ulpian, *Dig.* 14.3.11.8.

115 *another man*: Davus no doubt means Maecenas.

116 *puppet . . . string*: the comparison is at least as old as Plato, *Laws* 644d–645c, where the "puppeteers" are the gods; cf. Pers. 5.128–29.

117 *The sage*: i.e., the ideal Stoic "wise man" (*sapiens*); see 7–25, 1.3.110, 175–76, 2.3.50–51, 2.8.80nn.

118 *chains*: 2n.

121 *Externals*: a technical term from philosophy, including Stoicism (7–25n.), for the things that are outside of a human's control; cf. Cic. *Tusc.* 5.25, *Off.* 1.66, 3.21.

　　　roundness: following earlier Greek thought (e.g., Plato, *Timaeus* 33b), the Stoics considered the sphere to be the perfect shape, appropriate for the cosmos, its presiding divinity (Cic. *N.D.* 1.18, 2.45–49), and, metaphorically, the ideal "sage" (M. Aurelius, *Meditations* 12.3, 8.41).

123 *Fortune*: see 1.1.3n. and Cic. *Parad.* 34 (the Stoic sage [122n.]), "to whom Fortune herself, who is said to have the ultimate power, yields."

125–28 *A woman . . . calls you back*: H. is now depicted as a "shut-out lover" (*exclusus amator*); see 2.3.399–400n.

126 *five talents*: equivalent to *HS* 120,000 (2.3.346n.), a ridiculous amount of money. In Roman comedy (e.g., Pl. *Truculentus* 739) a typical gift is 5 *minae* = 1/12 of a talent = *HS* 2000, the price H. paid for Davus (59n.).

128 *yoke*: a common symbol of "enslavement" (40n.; cf. *Odes* 2.6.2, Cic. *Rep.* 2.46, *Phil.* 1.6, Prop. 3.6.2), but here also anticipating the imagery of 130–32.

130 *A master*: 94n.

131–32 *goads . . . driver*: 105n.

133–34 *paralyzed . . . painting*: Davus shifts abruptly to another fault, irrational astonishment, in this case over art (cf. 1.1.77, 1.3.128–29, 2.3.32–37). Pythagoras (2.4.4n.) is said to have warned "don't be awe-struck" (Plut. *Moralia* 44b), and this became a watch word of both Epicurean and Stoic (9–27n.) philosophy. Cf. *Odes* 3.29.11, *Ep.* 1.1.47–48, *Ep.* 1.6 passim, *Ep.* 1.10.31–32, Cic. *Parad.* 37.

134 *Pausias*: a Greek artist (fl. mid-fourth century BCE) from Sicyon, famous for his small-scale paintings of flowers and pretty boys (Plin. *Nat.*

35.123–27). Many of his paintings were brought to Rome in 56 BCE, when the Sicyonians sold them to repay public debt (Plin. *Nat.* 35.127).

136   *dashed off . . . charcoal*: as a kind of "advertising poster" (Muecke). These began to be displayed at Rome in the mid-second century BCE (Plin. *Nat.* 35.52), but gladiators were also a popular subject in mosaics and more ambitious types of painting.

137   *gladiators*: 81–82n.

>   *Rutuba and Fulvus*: otherwise unknown. Their names mean "Trouble" (cf. Var. *Men.* 488 Astbury) and "Tawny."

138   *Pacideianus*: the name of a gladiator, "the single best by far / since men came into existence" (Lucil. frr. 174–75 *ROL*), whose fight with a certain Aeserninus was described in a satire by Lucilius (frr. 172–83 *ROL*). Davus could refer to the memory of the man, as one might to "a [fighter like] Joe Louis," or the name could have been adopted by someone in H.'s time, as was common with the names of singers (1.2.4n.).

140   *Davus*: referring to himself in a "modest" third person (2.1.27n.).

142–55   Davus confesses to and accuses H. of gluttony, for which both are punished, the slave with flogging (146; see 2n.), the "enslaved" (40n.) master with illness (144–50) and disgrace (153–54).

148–9   *sours / the stomach*: Davus sounds a bit like Ofellus (2.2.31–33, 56–59, 98–109, 119–21).

149   *feet*: either stricken with gout (20, 1.9.43n.) or wobbly with drink.

152   *strigil*: a squeegee-like implement used at the baths for scraping excess oil from the skin after a massage (1.6.172n.).

153–54   *sells . . . stomach*: 1.2.10n.

155–59   *a slave . . . Like a slave . . . desert yourself*: 40n.

156–61   *your own company's . . . never leaves*: Davus returns to the fault of "inconsistency," but now attacks H. directly (cf. 7–25n.). H.'s restlessness (35–36n.) resembles that described in a famous passage of Lucretius (3.1053–70), where the poet argues that if men knew the real cause of their misery (in his view, fear of death), they would not "lead their lives as so often we see, / each one ignorant of what he wants for himself and always seeking / a change of scene, as if he could drop his burden there. . . . In this way each tries to run away from himself, yet that self, whom, as it turns out, / he cannot escape, he unhappily clings to and despises, / since although he is sick, he does not know the cause of his disease." Cf. Sen. *Ep.* 2.1 (Stoic viewpoint; see 7–25n.), "I reckon that the first symptom of a sound mind is for someone to be able to sit still and spend time with himself," *Ep.* 28.1–4, *Dialogues* 9.2.13–15.

160   *swindle care*: a striking expression; cf. Prop. 1.3.41, "I swindled sleep," Ov. *Tr.* 5.7.9.

160–61   *care . . . That dark companion*: cf. *Odes* 1.7.31, "Now smite Cares with wine," *Odes* 2.16.21–22, "Vicious Care scales bronze-clad ships / and does not leave troops of horsemen," *Odes* 3.1.40, "Care sits behind the horseman."

162   *a rock*: as if to ward off a dog (cf. Pl. *Mostellaria* 266). According to Damasippus, throwing rocks at slaves is a sign of insanity (2.3.198–99).

arrows: more "epic" than a stone, but maybe also hinting at the myths of Heracles and Athamas, who, when driven insane by Hera (Juno), shot their children with arrows (Euripides, *Hercules* 969–71, Apollodorus, *Library of Greek Myth* 1.9.2).

163   *insane or . . . writing verse*: Davus seems to be "channeling" Damasippus (2.3.485–88).

165   *the ninth drudge*: 1.3.20n. For slaves, life in the city seems to have been less harsh than in the country, where they toiled outside, often in chains, were subject to more frequent corporeal punishment, and were often poorly clothed and fed. Cf. *Ep.* 1.14, Pl. *Mostellaria* 15–19, Ter. *Phormio.* 247–50, Col. 1.8.1–19, Sen. *Dialogues* 3.29.1–2, Juv. 8.178–79.

   my Sabine farm: 2.6.1–3n.

Satire 2.8 Notes

1–6   The opening of the satire, with H. meeting a friend and asking about a banquet that had already occurred, seems meant to evoke that of Plato's *Symposium*, just as the opening of *Sat.* 2.4 evokes the *Phaedrus* (2.4.1n.). But here, too, in contrast to H.'s ideal banquet (2.6.89–97n.), the main topic of discussion (food and dining again) is hardly philosophical, and even when, following a minor disaster, the conversation turns to other subjects, it remains ludicrously banal (78–93).

   Lucilius wrote at least two satires describing banquets, one in book 5 (frr. 200–210 *ROL*; see 2.2.63n.) and one in book 20 (frr. 595–614; see 17–18n.).

1   *HORACE*: 2.1.1n. The identity of H.'s interlocutor does not become evident until 23.

   rich: the Latin is *beatus* (1.1.22n.), as if to raise right away the question of whether wealth (26) can bring (true) happiness.

2   *Nasidienus*: not mentioned elsewhere. Pseudacro infers that he is an equestrian and an Epicurean. His name is real, if rare, as is his surname Rufus (74; cf. 1.2.35–36, 1.5.60, 1.10.113, 2.3.330nn.), but together they might be meant to suggest someone with a "red nose" (Latin *nasus*; cf. 85n.), an appropriate feature for a high-living social climber, although it is the guests from outside his household circle who, scarcely able to conceal their contempt for him, resort to heavy drinking (53–56). Some have suggested that the name is a pseudonym for Q. Salvius Salvidienus Rufus, a former ally of Octavian, but he was either executed or committed suicide in 40 BCE, a decade before the dramatic date of Book 2 of the *Satires* (2.1.14n.).

3–5   *I came by . . . early afternoon*: H. would have "come by" either at the customary midafternoon time or, if he is to be believed about his own habit, in the early evening (1.6.155–78n.; cf. 2.7.48n.). The starting time of N.'s banquet would mark it as especially luxurious, since it would mean knocking off work early (cf. Cic. *Mur.* 13, *Sen.* 46, *Att.* 9.13.6, 9.16.8).

6–7   *Tell me . . . what dish first*: H. asks about the first course (*gustatio*) but with a trace of epic parody; cf. Hom. *Il.* 16.692–93, "What man first, what man last did you slay and despoil, / Patroclus?"

8   *angry appetite*: 2.2.26n.

  Lucanian boar: 2.1.51, 2.3.358, 2.4.51–53nn. This would be an unusual and extravagant appetizer, as opposed to a main course.

12   *fish paste*: made from garum (62n.); cf. 2.4.94n.

  Coan wine: 2.4.38n.

13–14   *tunic hiked / way up*: both so he could move around better and so that the guests could check out his legs and buttocks (1.2.151n.). Cf. 91.

14–15   *wiped . . . towel*: adapted from a verse in one of Lucilius' banquet satires (1–6n.), fr. 589 *ROL*, "Then he [or she] scrubbed the wide tables with a thick red towel."

14   *table*: 1.3.23n.

17   *Grave as an Attic maid with Ceres' ark*: at Athens, as at Rome (1.3.17–18), in religious processions objects sacred to the gods were carried with great ceremony by basket bearers (*kanephoroi*).

18   *dark-skinned Hydaspes*: more "eye candy" (16–17), named for an exotically remote river in India (cf. *Odes* 1.22.7–8, "the legendary Hydaspes," Virg. *G.* 4.211), either because he was from its vicinity or resembled such a person (cf. Tib. 2.3.55–56). More often dark skin was looked down on, not out of racial prejudice (4.107n.), but as a sign of rustic or servile labor (e.g., Lucr. 4.1160, Virg. *Ecl.* 2.16–18, 10.38–39).

  Caecuban: 1.5.42n.

19   *Alcon*: a common Greek name.

  sans seawater: many Greek wines were mixed, either for flavor or for preservation, with seawater (cf. 2.4.38n.), but this Chian (61, 1.10.33n.) is evidently too special for that (cf. Plin. *Nat.* 14.73, Galen, 10.833K). But there may be a word play here: the Latin phrase *maris expers* can also mean "without masculinity," indicating that Alcon is a eunuch, which would be especially pleasing to Maecenas (1.6.147n.). Cf. 66n.

20   *our host pipes up*: H.'s reaction, "Killjoy wealth!" (23), suggests that, however polite it may seem to a modern reader, N.'s offer of other wines is somehow excessive or inept. In Petronius' *Satyricon*, the absurd host Trimalchio makes a similar offer (48.1).

  Maecenas: after hearing that his supposed best buddy was present, H. at once (23–24) asks about the other guests, as if wondering why he wasn't included.

21   *Alban or Falernian*: 1.5.42, 2.4.91nn.

23   *Fundanius*: the comic poet (1.10.54–55n.); cf. 68n. The Old Comedy poet Aristophanes (1.4.1n.) is one of the speakers in Plato's *Symposium* (1–6n.).

25   *top couch*: the banquet is Greek-style (1.3.127–28n.), with nine guests, three to a couch (1.4.109n.). Two of the couches, the "top" (*summus*) and "bottom" (*imus*), face each other, with the host, flanked by his two parasites (29n.), in the center position of the bottom. The "middle" (*medius*) couch, above and between the others, is the place of honor for Maecenas and his "extras" (28).

Viscus Thurinus: possibly one of the Visci brothers (1.9.30, 1.10.114nn.), although the surname Thurinus (also part of Octavian's original name [Suet. *Aug.* 2.3, 7.1; cf. *Odes* 3.9.14]), indicating some connection with the town of Thurii on the gulf of Tarentum, may be meant to distinguish him from that duo.

26   *Varius*: 1.5.50–51n.

27   *Vibidius and Servilius Balatro*: otherwise unknown. The names are real, but *balatro*, which means "stand-up comic," could be a designation of Servilius' profession (see 1.2.2) rather than a surname.

28   *extras*: the Latin is *umbrae*, literally "shadows," a not very flattering way of referring to uninvited guests brought by an invited one. Cf. *Ep.* 1.5.28 (H. inviting a friend to a banquet), "there's room for any number of shadows." Davus (2.7.48) might be amused; H. himself (1.6.60) is puzzled that Maecenas did not bring him (cf. 20).

29   *Nomentanus*: evidently a namesake or "avatar" of the Lucilian high liver (1.1.109n.). He begins the "tutorial" (39) that N., in the manner of Ofellus (*Sat.* 1.2.2) and especially Catius (*Sat.* 1.2.4), will continue (56–67, 116–17) and serves as a cheerleader when calamity strikes (76–80).

   Porcius: a real name, as of the famous M. Porcius Cato (1.2.40n.), but here its meaning, "hog-man," suits the character, who is otherwise unknown.

36   *mysteriously unfamiliar*: Romans enjoyed dishes that tasted differently than they appeared; cf. Apicius (2.4.81n.) 4.12.4, Petr. 40.4, 69–70.

38   *turbot and flounder loin*: since fish don't really have loins, this must be cuts of these delicacies (2.140n., Plin. *Nat.* 9.72) made up to look like the parts of boar or some other beast (cf. Mart. 10.45.4), although not rabbit (118n.).

39   *honey apples*: Fundanius uses the Greek term *melimela* (from *mel*, "honey," and *mela*, "apples"), the root of the word "marmalade." Such apples ripen in the summer, earlier than other varieties (Var. *R.* 1.59.1, Plin. *Nat.* 15.51).

41   *moon is on the wane*: the Romans, like many people even today, believed that the phases of the moon needed to be taken into account for planting and harvesting. Cf. 2.4.39n., Var. *R.* 1.37.1–3, Virg. *G.* 2.276–98, Plin. *Nat.* 15.59.

44   *perish unavenged*: an epic-sounding phrase, possibly from Ennius (1.4.70n.), as shown by its recurrence in Virgil (*A.* 2.670, 4.659) and Ovid (*Met.* 9.131). At *Odes* 1.18.7–16 and *Odes* 1.27.1–8, H. warns against the violence that can erupt at banquets.

45   *He calls for larger cups*: Vibidius is out of line: at a Greek-style banquet, it would be the part of the host, not of a guest—an uninvited one, at that (28n.)—to decide on the amount of wine to be drunk.

   caterer: a demeaning reference to N., which "suggests that the guests see him only in this light" (Muecke).

48   *drinker's nasty tongue*: cf. 1.4.108–12.

49   *blunt the palate's edge*: thus wasting the "caterer's" effort.

50–51   *tipped whole / wine jugs*: cf. Lucil. fr. 132 *ROL* (from his "journey poem" [1.5.1–2n.]), "The bottom of a jar of wine is turned upside down, and so is our opinion." But a possible echo of Virg. *A.* 9.165, "they tip bronze drinking vessels," may indicate an Ennian source (44n.) for all these passages.

51 *Allifae-ware wine cups*: presumably large ones. Allifae was a town in Samnium near the border with Campania, not far from Capua (1.5.58). It is not clear whether its products were expensive to replace if broken, or if the men have gotten hold of the equivalents of fruit jars.

52–53 *except for those who had / the lowest couch*: i.e., N. and his familiars (25n.).

54–55 *A moray eel . . . round it*: this seems meant as the main dish, but the ease with which another is prepared suggests that N. had several in the works.

54 *moray eel*: a highly prized delicacy at Rome beginning in the late Republic. The best were caught in the sea off Sicily, but they were also bred in artificial fishponds for eating, as pets and, in a notorious incident, as a means of executing slaves (Plin. *Nat.* 9.77, 169, 171–72).

56–67 N. now takes over from Nomentanus (29n.).

58 *sauce . . . Venafrum's oil*: 2.4.81, 88nn.

59 *first pressing*: this produces the highest grade (Col. 12.52.11).

   garum: a Greek word for the liquid separated from fish paste (2.4.94n.). It was as commonly used in Roman cooking as similar fish sauces are today in Asian cuisine. This is the first mention of *garum* made from Spanish mackerel, but by the mid-first century CE this was the most prized variety, fetching *HS* 1,000 (half the price of H.'s slave Davus [2.7.63; cf. 2.3.346n.]) for about 6 pints (Plin. *Nat.* 31.94).

60 *a five-year-old Italian wine*: many ancient Italian wines improved with age. The Romans took pains to keep track of vintages, often by painting the name of a year's consul on the storage jar. Cf. *Epd.* 13.6, *Odes* 1.9.7, 1.19.15, 1.20.3, 3.8.11–12, 3.14.18–20, 3.12.1, *Ep.* 1.5.4.

61 *Chian*: 19n.

62 *white pepper*: 2.4.96n.

   vinegar: 2.2.78n.

63 *Methymnean grapes*: from the town of Methymne on the Greek island of Lesbos, which was famous for its grapes and wines (*Epd.* 9.34, *Odes* 1.17.21).

64 *arugula*: Latin *eruca*, a pungent herb thought to be an aphrodisiac ([Virg.] *Mor.* 84, *Priap.* 47.7 [1.1–5n.], Plin. *Nat.* 19.154).

65 *elecampine*: 2.2.59n.

66 *Curtillus*: an otherwise unknown "gastronomer." The name suggests Latin *curtus*, "curtailed" or even "castrated" (19n.).

   unwashed sea urchins: 2.4.42n. They are "unwashed" to preserve their own brine, as with clams and oysters on the half-shell.

68 *the heavy tapestries*: wall hangings or canopies over the table, a mark of luxury (*Odes* 3.29.15, Virg. *A.* 1.697). But the word *aulea* is also used for theater "curtains" (*Ep.* 2.1.89, *Ars* 154), which were lowered to stage level at the start of a performance, raised high at its end. Here Fundanius, a playwright, after all (23n.), may be hinting that this is when the real "show" (99) began.

70 *Black dust*: N.'s housekeeping also doesn't measure up; cf. 2.4.106–9. But the phrase may be meant to suggest the "dark dust" of Homeric and Ennian battlefields (e.g., *Il.* 11.151–52, 163, *Ann.* 264, 315, 612; cf. *Odes* 1.6.14, 1.15.19–20, 2.1.21–22) and, along with the simile (71), lend a (mock) epic feel to the calamity.

72 *the worst*: that the whole house was collapsing.

74 *Rufus*: 2n.

75 *his little boy had died*: his grief is all out of proportion; see 89–91.

76 *Nomentanus*: 29n.

77 *sagely*: the Latin is *sapiens* (1.1.38, 1.3.110, 2.2.5, 85, 2.4.56, 2.7.122nn.), used here sarcastically, of course.

78–80 *Fortuna . . . efforts*: compared to H.'s own musings on Fortuna (1.1.38n.), Nomentanus' are trite and banal. Cf. 107n.

80 *Varius*: 26n.

81 *his napkin*: furnished by the host (*Ep.* 1.5.22, Catul. 22). Varius either laughed into it or stuffed it in his mouth.

82 *Balatro*: he lives up to his surname or epithet (27n.) with a snide "consolation," although N.'s reply (94–96) shows he "is impervious to the irony" (Muecke).

  sniffing out absurdity: the Latin phrase, *suspendens omnia naso*, could also mean "turning up his nose [in scorn]"; cf. 6.5. Either way, there may be a word play on the host's name (2n.).

84 *fame*: Balatro pretends that N., like a noble Roman or an epic hero, seeks fame, rather than what is more likely for such a man, gratitude and social advancement.

84–85 *To fete / me*: but of course Balatro wasn't even invited (28n.).

88 *tunics wrong*: not properly "hiked up" (13–14n.).

  hair not right: this was still a concern in the mid-first century CE (Sen. *Ep.* 47.7, 95.24).

90–91 *crash . . . breaks a dish*: by equating it with a trivial accident (cf. 1.3.128–29), Balatro mocks N.'s excessive reaction to the fall of the tapestry (77–78).

91–92 *host . . . general . . . genius*: combining a truism (e.g., Euripides, fr. 237 *LCL*, "troubles give birth to glory," Lucr. 3.55–56) with a possible allusion to a remark by L. Aemilius Paullus, the conqueror of Macedonia (168 BCE), who followed his victory by regaling the cities of Greece with banquets. "To those marveling at his skillful attention to these, he said, 'the successful handling of a campaign and of a banquet requires the same spirit'" (Plut. *Life of Aemilius Paullus* 28.5; cf. Plut. *Moralia* 615f).

94–95 *I pray the gods . . . every wish*: N.'s almost pathetically naive response (cf. 82n.) is a more elaborate version of a common formula of thanks (e.g., Pl. *Stichus* 469, "You speak well and as a friend: the gods grant what you wish!").

97 *slippers*: which he had removed when he reclined on his couch. Cf. *Ep.* 1.13.15, Pl. *Truculentus* 363–67, 479.

105 *You, Nasidienus*: a parody of a kind of apostrophe occurring especially in epic, where the poet, instead of referring to a character in the story in the third person, addresses him directly (e.g., Hom. *Il.* 4.127, 146, 15.365, 582, 16.692–93 [8–9n.], 20.152, Catul. 64.69, Virg. *A.* 6.30–31, 8.643, 10.324–25).

107 *artistry . . . bad luck*: cf. Cato, *Dicta* ("Sayings"), "Whatever befalls unexpectedly, this a man can fix with artistry," Ter. *Adelphi* 741. *Fortuna* is no longer a goddess (78–80), but mere "bad luck" (cf. 1.1.38n., Juv. 10.365–66).

109–10 *crane . . . male / no less*: in H.'s time crane, while less fashionable than stork (2.2.68; cf. Plin. *Nat.* 10.60), was still popular, whether taken in the wild (*Epd.* 2.35) or bred in aviaries (Var. *R.* 3.2.14). The Latin word (*gruis* or *grus*) is usually feminine, suggesting that male birds were harder to come by.

111–12 *pâté de foie gras . . . figs*: the liver from force-fed domestic geese, especially white ones (Var. *R.* 3.10.2, Col. 8.14.3), was a delicacy as prized in Rome as it is in many places today (Plin. *Nat.* 10.52, Juv. 5.114, Athenaeus, *Deipnosophistae*, 9.384c). The French word for liver (Latin *iecur*) comes from the Latin epithet *ficatum*, "fig-fed" (e.g., Apicius [2.5.81n.] 7.3).

113–14 *rabbit legs . . . loins*: N. seems to have taken Catius' advice (2.4.56–57); see 38n. above.

114 *blackbirds*: hunted (*Ars* 458) and eaten (Var. *R.* 3.5.1–2) just like other songbirds (1.5.90, 2.3.274nn.).

115 *pigeons*: wild or domestic rock or wood doves, not their urban descendants. See Cato, *On Agriculture* 90, Var. *R.* 3.8.

   rumps removed: but some Romans consider the bird's rump a delicacy (Sen. *Ep.* 47.6, Mart. 3.60.7, Gel. 15.8.2).

116 *delicious treats*: as throughout, there seems to be nothing wrong with the food in and of itself.

117 *provenance and properties*: N.'s resumption of his Catius-like (cf. 2.4.58) "philosophizing" (cf. 2.4.58–60n.) is the last straw for his guests.

118–20 The banquet, Fundanius' story, the poem, the book, and the *Satires* as a whole end suddenly, with no resolution, summary, explanation, or even words spoken by H. in his own person. Whatever the significance of this, the mention of revenge (118), even in an absurd context, so soon after civil war (2.1.14n.), and of the dread Canidia (119n.), even after the silliness of the Priapus episode (*Sat.* 1.8), is unsettling and can hardly fail to arouse a certain queasiness.

119 *Canidia*: 1.8.33n. In *Epd.* 3, a poem both humorous and yet disturbingly symbolic of civil war, Maecenas nearly disrupts his friendship with H. by giving him food that makes him as sick as if "Canidia had handled the foul meal" (*Epd.* 3.7–8).

120 *Africa's snake venom*: the snakes of (North) Africa were legendary for their size, fierceness, and lethality; cf. *Odes* 3.10.18, Lucil. 9.619–734.

SUGGESTIONS FOR FURTHER READING

There have been hundreds of publications about Horace, Roman satire, and the late Roman Republic. The following list leans toward recent books in English that include extensive bibliographies, that are accessible to general readers, and that, it is hoped, will prove informative, interesting, and provocative.

Editions of and Commentaries on the *Satires*

Bailey, D. R. Shackleton, ed. *Q. Horati Flacci Opera*. Stuttgart: Teubner, 1991.

Brown, P., ed., trans., com. *Horace Satires I*. Warminster: Aris and Phillips, 1995.

Kiessling, A., and Heinze, R., eds. *Q. Horatius Flaccus Satiren*. Berlin: Weidmann, 1921.

Klingner, F., ed. *Horatius Opera*. Leipzig: Teubner, 1959.

Lejay, P., ed., com. *Oeuvres d'Horace: Satires*. Paris: Hachette, 1911.

Muecke, F., ed., trans., com. *Horace Satires II*. Warminster: Aris and Phillips, 1993.

Palmer, A., ed., com. *Horace Satires*. London: Macmillan, 1883.

Other Translations of Horace's *Satires*

Bovie, S. P. *The Satires and Epistles of Horace*. Chicago: University of Chicago Press, 1959.

Davie, J. *Horace: Satires and Epistles*. Oxford: Oxford University Press, 2011.

Fuchs, J. *Horace's Satires and Epistles*. New York: Norton, 1977.

Juster, A. M. *The Satires of Horace*. Philadelphia: University of Pennsylvania Press, 2008.

Matthews, W. *The Satires of Horace*. Keene: Ausable Press, 2002.

Rudd, N. *Horace: Satires and Epistles. Persius: Satires*. Harmondsworth: Penguin, 1973.

Translations of Horace's Other Works

Alexander, S. *The Complete Odes and Satires of Horace*. Princeton: Princeton University Press, 1999.

Carne-Ross, D. S., and Haynes. K., eds. *Horace in English*. Harmondsworth: Penguin, 1996.

Ferry, D., *The Odes of Horace*. New York: Farrar, Straus and Giroux, 1997.

————, *The Epistles of Horace*. New York: Farrar, Straus and Giroux, 2001.

McClatchy, J. D., ed. *Horace: The Odes. New Translations by Contemporary Poets*. Princeton: Princeton University Press, 2002.

Michie, J. *The Odes of Horace*. New York: The Orion Press, 1963.

West, D. *Horace: The Complete Odes and Epodes*. Oxford: Oxford University Press, 1997.

Studies of Horace, the *Satires*, and Roman Satire

Anderson, W. S. *Essays on Roman Satire*. Berkeley and Los Angeles: University of California Press, 1982.

Armstrong, D. *Horace*. New Haven: Yale University Press, 1989.

Coffey, M. *Roman Satire*. London: Methuen, 1989.

Davis, G., ed. *A Companion to Horace*. Chichester: Wiley-Blackwell, 2010.

Fantham, E. *Roman Literary Culture*. Baltimore: Johns Hopkins University Press, 1996.

Fraenkel, E. *Horace*. Oxford: Oxford University Press, 1957.

Freudenburg, K., ed. *The Cambridge Companion to Roman Satire*. Cambridge: Cambridge University Press, 2007.

————, ed. *Oxford Readings in Classical Studies. Horace: Satires and Epistles*. Oxford: Oxford University Press, 2009.

Gowers, E. *The Loaded Table*. Oxford: Oxford University Press, 1993.

Harrison, S. J., ed. *Homage to Horace*. Oxford: Oxford University Press, 1995.

————, ed. *The Cambridge Companion to Horace*. Cambridge: Cambridge University Press, 2007.

Henderson, J. *Writing Down Rome*. Oxford: Clarendon Press, 1999.

Keane, C. *Figuring Genre in Roman Satire*. Oxford: Oxford University Press, 2006.

Kenney, E. J., Clausen, W. V., eds. *The Cambridge History of Classical Literature* II 1. Cambridge: Cambridge University Press, 1982.

Oliensis, E. *Horace and the Rhetoric of Authority*. Cambridge: Cambridge University Press, 1998.

Rudd, N. *The Satires of Horace*. London: Bristol Classical Press, 1982.

————, ed., *Horace 2000*. Ann Arbor: University of Michigan Press, 1993.

Woodman, A. J., and Feeney, D. C., eds. *Traditions and Contexts in the Poems of Horace*. Cambridge: Cambridge University Press, 2002.

The Fall of the Roman Republic

Flower, H., ed., *The Cambridge Companion to the Roman Republic*. Cambridge: Cambridge University Press, 2006.

Galinsky, G. K., ed., *The Cambridge Companion to the Age of Augustus*. Cambridge: Cambridge University Press, 2005.

Osgood, J. *Caesar's Legacy*. Cambridge: Cambridge University Press, 2006.

Syme, R. *The Roman Revolution*. Oxford: Oxford University Press, 1939.

INDEX